SPSS® Interactive Graphics 9.0

For more information about SPSS® software products, please visit our WWW site at *http://www.spss.com* or contact

Marketing Department
SPSS Inc.
233 South Wacker Drive, 11th Floor
Chicago, IL 60606-6307
Tel: (312) 651-3000
Fax: (312) 651-3668

SPSS® Interactive Graphics 9.0

Printed in the United States of America.

1 2 3 4 5 6 7 8 9 0   03 02 01 00 99

ISBN 0-13-021711-5

Preface

SPSS® 9.0 is a comprehensive system for analyzing data. This manual, *SPSS Interactive Graphics 9.0,* documents **interactive charts,** an important feature in the SPSS Base:

- In the Viewer, start with a blank interactive chart, assign variables to the axes and legends, and specify which graphical elements (bars, lines, a cloud of points, etc.) you want. As soon as you choose each graphical element, it is added to the chart.
- From the Graphs menu, choose Interactive, and then choose a chart type (Bar, Line, Scatterplot, etc.). A dialog box, in which you can assign variables to the axes and legends, specify summary functions, and change appearance attributes before the chart is created, is displayed.

Once you have created a chart, you can make many modifications dynamically. For example, you can insert or delete graphical elements, change colors and textures, rotate 3-D graphs smoothly, and adjust fit lines and surfaces.

This manual is to be used along with the *SPSS Base 9.0 User's Guide,* which documents the graphical user interface of SPSS for Windows. The User's Guide contains complete information about statistical procedures and the original graphics system (which can be used for types of charts not available in interactive graphics). A companion book, the *SPSS Base 9.0 Applications Guide*, provides examples of statistical procedures and related data transformations, with advice on screening data, using appropriate procedures, and interpreting the output. Beneath the menus and dialog boxes, SPSS uses a command language that can be used to create and run production jobs. Dialog boxes can "paste" commands into a syntax window, where they can be modified and saved; a few features of the system can be accessed only via command syntax. Complete command syntax is documented in the *SPSS Base 9.0 Syntax Reference Guide,* which is included on the CD version of the software and is available for purchase separately in print. The Help system contains brief syntax diagrams in addition to full help on the graphical user interface.

SPSS Options

The SPSS family of products includes add-on enhancements to the SPSS Base system, which are available on several computer platforms. With the addition of statistical procedures to the Base, the contents of the Advanced Models option have changed. Contact your local SPSS office or sales representative about availability of the following options:

- **SPSS Regression Models**™ provides techniques for analyzing data that do not fit traditional linear statistical models. It includes procedures for probit analysis, logistic regression, weight estimation, two-stage least-squares regression, general nonlinear regression, multidimensional scaling, and reliability analysis.
- **SPSS Advanced Models**™ focuses on techniques often used in sophisticated experimental and biomedical research. It includes procedures for general linear models (GLM), variance components analysis, loglinear analysis, actuarial life tables, Kaplan-Meier survival analysis, and basic and extended Cox regression. It also includes a powerful matrix command language for customized analyses.
- **SPSS Tables**™ creates a variety of presentation-quality tabular reports, including complex stub-and-banner tables and displays of multiple response data.
- **SPSS Trends**™ performs comprehensive forecasting and time series analyses with multiple curve-fitting models, smoothing models, and methods for estimating autoregressive functions.
- **SPSS Categories**® performs and optimal scaling procedures, including correspondence analysis.
- **SPSS Conjoint**™ performs conjoint analysis.
- **SPSS Exact Tests**™ calculates exact *p* values for statistical tests when small or very unevenly distributed samples could make the usual tests inaccurate.
- **SPSS Missing Value Analysis**™ describes patterns of missing data, estimates means and other statistics, and imputes values for missing observations.

The SPSS family of products also includes applications for data entry, text analysis, classification, neural networks, and flowcharting.

Compatibility

The SPSS Base 9.0 system is designed to operate on computer systems running Windows 95, Windows 98, or Windows NT 4.0.

Serial Numbers

Your serial number is your identification number with SPSS Inc. You will need this serial number when you call SPSS Inc. for information regarding support, payment, or an upgraded system. The serial number was provided with your Base system. Before using the system, please copy this number to the registration card.

Registration Card

Don't put it off: *fill out and send us your registration card.* Until we receive your registration card, you have an unregistered system. Even if you have previously sent a card to us, please fill out and return the card enclosed in your Base system package. Registering your system entitles you to:

- Technical support services
- New product announcements and upgrade announcements

Customer Service

If you have any questions concerning your shipment or account, contact your local office, listed on page vii. Please have your serial number ready for identification when calling.

Training Seminars

SPSS Inc. provides both public and onsite training seminars for SPSS. All seminars feature hands-on workshops. SPSS seminars will be offered in major U.S. and European cities on a regular basis. For more information on these seminars, call your local office, listed on page vii.

Technical Support

The services of SPSS Technical Support are available to registered customers of SPSS. Customers may contact Technical Support for assistance in using SPSS products or for installation help for one of the supported hardware environments. To reach Technical Support, see the SPSS home page on the World Wide Web at *http://www.spss.com*, or call your local office, listed on page vii. Be prepared to identify yourself, your organization, and the serial number of your system.

Additional Publications

Individuals worldwide can order manuals directly from the SPSS World Wide Web site at *http://www.spss.com/Pubs*. For telephone orders in the United States and Canada, call SPSS Inc. at 1-800-253-2565. For telephone orders outside of North America, contact your local SPSS office, listed on page vii.

Individuals in the United States can also order these manuals by calling Prentice Hall at 1-800-947-7700. If you represent a bookstore or have a Prentice Hall account, call 1-800-382-3419. In Canada, call 1-800-567-3800.

Tell Us Your Thoughts

Your comments are important. Please send us a letter and let us know about your experiences with SPSS products. We especially like to hear about new and interesting applications using the SPSS system. Write to SPSS Inc. Marketing Department, Attn: Director of Product Planning, 233 South Wacker Drive, 11th Floor, Chicago, IL 60606-6307.

Contacting SPSS

If you would like to be on our mailing list, contact one of our offices, listed on page vii, or visit our WWW site at *http://www.spss.com*. We will send you a copy of our newsletter and let you know about SPSS Inc. activities in your area.

SPSS Inc.
Chicago, Illinois, U.S.A.
Tel: 1.312.329.2400
Fax: 1.312.329.3668
Customer Service:
1.800.521.1337
Sales:
1.800.543.2185
sales@spss.com
Training:
1.800.543.6607
Technical Support:
1.312.329.3410
support@spss.com

SPSS Federal Systems
Arlington, Virginia, U.S.A.
Tel: 1.703.527.6777
Fax: 1.703.527.6866

SPSS Argentina srl
Buenos Aires, Argentina
Tel: +541.816.4086
Fax: +541.814.5030

SPSS Asia Pacific Pte. Ltd.
Singapore, Singapore
Tel: +65.3922.738
Fax: +65.3922.739

SPSS Australasia Pty. Ltd.
Sydney, Australia
Tel: +61.2.9954.5660
Fax: +61.2.9954.5616

SPSS Belgium
Heverlee, Belgium
Tel: +32.162.389.82
Fax: +32.1620.0888

SPSS Benelux BV
Gorinchem, The Netherlands
Tel: +31.183.636711
Fax: +31.183.635839

SPSS Central and Eastern Europe
Woking, Surrey, U.K.
Tel: +44.(0)1483.719200
Fax: +44.(0)1483.719290

SPSS East Mediterranea and Africa
Herzlia, Israel
Tel: +972.9.526700
Fax: +972.9.526715

SPSS Finland Oy
Sinikalliontie, Finland
Tel: +358.9.524.801
Fax: +358.9.524.854

SPSS France SARL
Boulogne, France
Tel: +33.1.4699.9670
Fax: +33.1.4684.0180

SPSS Germany
Munich, Germany
Tel: +49.89.4890740
Fax: +49.89.4483115

SPSS Hellas SA
Athens, Greece
Tel: +30.1.7251925
Fax: +30.1.7249124

SPSS Hispanoportuguesa S.L.
Madrid, Spain
Tel: +34.91.447.3700
Fax: +34.91.448.6692

SPSS Ireland
Dublin, Ireland
Tel: +353.1.66.13788
Fax: +353.1.661.5200

SPSS Israel Ltd.
Herzlia, Israel
Tel: +972.9.526700
Fax: +972.9.526715

SPSS Italia srl
Bologna, Italy
Tel: +39.51.252573
Fax: +39.51.253285

SPSS Japan Inc.
Tokyo, Japan
Tel: +81.3.5466.5511
Fax: +81.3.5466.5621

SPSS Korea
Seoul, Korea
Tel: +82.2.552.9415
Fax: +82.2.539.0136

SPSS Latin America
Chicago, Illinois, U.S.A.
Tel: 1.312.494.3226
Fax: 1.312. 494.3227

SPSS Malaysia Sdn Bhd
Selangor, Malaysia
Tel: +603.704.5877
Fax: +603.704.5790

SPSS Mexico SA de CV
Mexico DF, Mexico
Tel: +52.5.575.3091
Fax: +52.5.575.2527

SPSS Middle East and South Asia
Dubai, UAE
Tel: +971.4.525536
Fax: +971.4.524669

SPSS Scandinavia AB
Stockholm, Sweden
Tel: +46.8.102610
Fax: +46.8.102550

SPSS Schweiz AG
Zurich, Switzerland
Tel: +41.1.201.0930
Fax: +41.1.201.0921

SPSS Singapore Pte. Ltd.
Singapore, Singapore
Tel: +65.2991238
Fax: +65.2990849

SPSS South Africa
Johannesburg, South Africa
Tel: +27.11.7067015
Fax: +27.11.7067091

SPSS Taiwan Corp.
Taipei, Republic of China
Tel: +886.2.5771100
Fax: +886.2.5701717

SPSS UK Ltd.
Woking, Surrey, U.K.
Tel: +44.1483.719200
Fax: +44.1483.719290

Contents

3 *Area Charts* *37*

4 *Bar Charts* *53*

5 *Boxplots* 71

6 *Error Bars* 85

7 *Histograms* *99*

8 *Line, Dot, and Ribbon Charts* *111*

9 *Pie Charts* 129

10 *Scatterplots* 147

11 *Fit Lines, Surfaces, and Spikes* *161*

12 *Modifying Interactive Charts* *171*

Chapter

1

Introduction to Interactive Charts

An interactive chart is dynamic. Not only can you change its cosmetic appearance, you can also change the assignment of variables having various roles in the chart. Variables can be moved between axes, between axes and legends, and between axes (or legends) and panels. Changes to interactive charts are evident in the Viewer as soon as the variables are reassigned. The interactive chart can go from 2-D to 3-D and back again as you watch. Dragging the mouse and clicking the right-mouse button are keys to easy chart manipulation.

Interactive charts can be created in the following ways:

- Starting with a chart type from the Interactive submenu of the Graphs menu
- Starting with a blank chart from the Insert menu

This chapter provides an introduction to creating interactive charts by starting from the Graphs menu. It includes facilities that are common to many types of charts. Later, each type of chart is described in a separate chapter. Another way to create a chart interactively is to start with the Insert menu, as described in Chapter 2. Modification of existing charts is described in Chapter 12.

Before you can create a chart, you need to have data in the Data Editor. You can enter the data directly into the Data Editor, open a previously saved data file, or read a spreadsheet, tab-delimited data file, or database file. A tutorial (available from the Help menu) has online examples of creating interactive charts.

The chart examples provided in the online tutorial and the examples presented in this book represent only a few of many charts possible with interactive graphics.

Interactive versus Standard Charts

In addition to the new interactive charts, SPSS also produces many other charts. Interactive charts are available only from the Interactive submenu of the Graphs menu. All other charts on the Graphs menu, as well as charts created by statistical procedures, are standard, high-resolution charts. Like interactive charts, standard charts are presentation-quality graphics that can be edited in many ways. The main difference is that standard charts lack interactive features such as the ability to change the charted variables and update the chart on the fly, change summary functions after creating a chart, or insert additional chart elements.

The interface for creating and modifying standard charts differs from the interface for interactive charts in a number of ways, including:

- Drag-and-drop variable selection is available for interactive charts only; variable selection in standard chart dialog boxes is the same as variable selection in statistical dialog boxes.
- You can toggle between display of variable names and variable labels in interactive chart dialog boxes by using a context menu that appears when you right-click a variable list. For standard chart dialog boxes, display of variable names or labels is controlled by General Options (Edit menu, Options, General tab) and doesn't take effect until the next time you open a data file.
- Variable lists in interactive chart dialog boxes have icons that identify variables as built-in, scale, or categorical, and you can change the classification of scale and categorical variables with right-mouse context menus. In standard chart dialog boxes, icons identify variables as either numeric or string (alphanumeric), and this classification is based on the variable type as defined in the Data Editor.
- Right-mouse button "What's This?" help is available for controls in standard chart dialog boxes; this feature is not available in interactive chart dialog boxes.
- Right-mouse button variable information is available in variable lists in standard chart dialog boxes. This feature is not available in interactive chart dialog boxes. (The Variables item on the Utilities menu provides similar information.)
- Interactive charts are edited in the Viewer window; standard charts are edited in a separate window.
- Interactive charts can be modified to insert additional variables, elements, summary functions, and so on. Standard chart modification features are largely limited to changing attributes of the elements that were present in the chart when it was created.

- Interactive charts can be embedded in other applications as fully interactive ActiveX objects or pasted as bitmaps. Standard charts cannot be embedded in other applications; they can be pasted as metafiles (pictures) or bitmaps.

Creating Interactive Charts from the Graphs Menu

By using the procedures listed on the Interactive submenu on the Graphs menu, you can specify variables and chart options before a chart is created. Later, the chart can be modified in the Viewer. When you choose a chart type from the Interactive submenu on the Graphs menu, the corresponding dialog box is displayed with its Assign Variables tab selected.

Figure 1-1
Assign Variables tab for bar charts

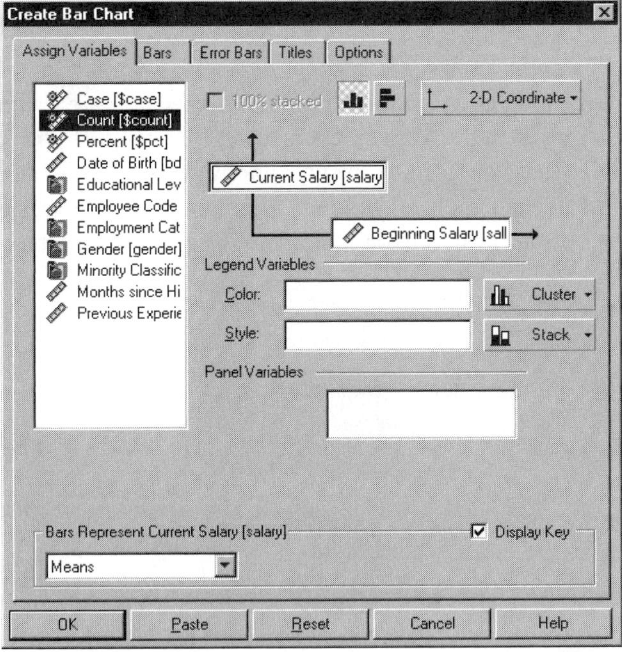

To create a chart, you need only to assign variables, but you can visit other tabs if you want to customize your chart.

Source list. Variables available for the chart type are in the source list. You can change the order in which variables are listed by right-clicking a variable and from the context menu choosing Sort By Name, Sort By File Order, or Sort By Type. You can also choose Display Variable Labels or Display Variable Names. On the context menu, these entries and data dimensions take the place of What's This? and Variable Information found in other dialog boxes in the system.

Assigning variables. Axis variables are assigned by dragging them from the source list and dropping them on the axis targets. You can also drag variables from one target to another. If a variable is dropped on a target that already has a variable assigned, the variables swap places. You can also assign multiple variables to each axis using the Ctrl-click method.

Summary functions. A scale variable that has been assigned to a dependent axis may have a summary function for many types of charts. For example, the summary function *Means* would often be appropriate for the variable *Salary*. The summary function for a scale variable can be specified by selecting from a list of summary functions near the bottom of this dialog box.

Completing the chart. As soon as a minimum number of variables are assigned, a chart can be created and displayed in the Viewer. OK is always enabled. If you click OK and the program determines that you need to specify more information, an alert box gives information on what is needed. Before clicking OK, you may want to refine the chart by selecting from the options available on the other tabs of the dialog box.

Figure 1-2
Chart in the Viewer

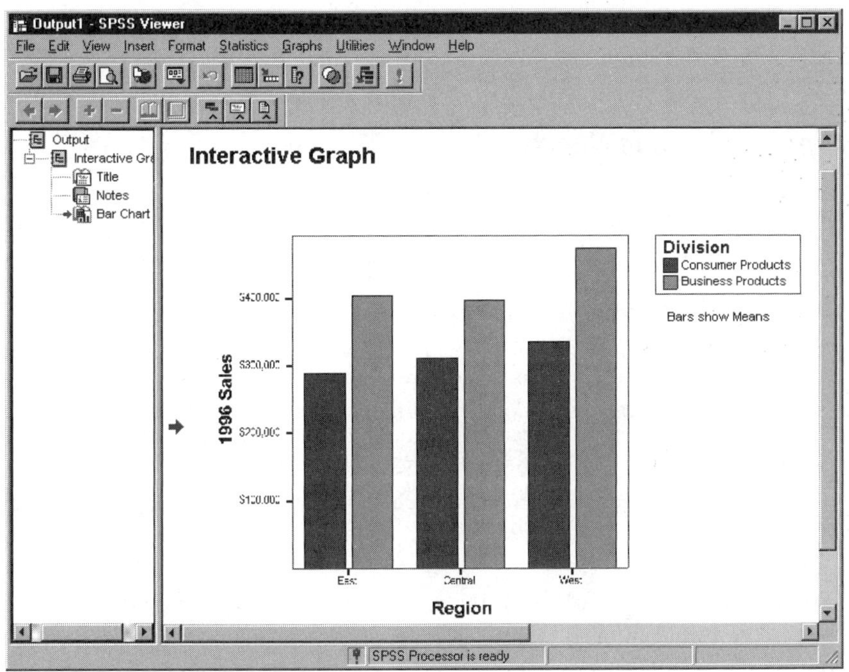

To Assign Variables in a New Interactive Chart

▶ From the menus choose:

Graphs
  Interactive

▶ Choose a chart type.

▶ Drag one or more variables to each axis target. (Use the Ctrl-click method to select and drag multiple variables).

Optionally, you can:

- Split the chart element into categories by assigning categorical variables to Color, Style, and Size, where appropriate for the chart type.
- Assign colors to the chart objects by assigning a scale variable to Color.

- Assign sizes to the chart objects by assigning a scale variable to Size.
- Split the chart into separate panels by assigning categorical variables to Panel Variables.
- Change the summary function for the dependent variable.

Data Dimension Types in Charts

In an interactive chart, the types of data dimensions are indicated by an icon for each type (scale, categorical, and scale built-ins) in the chart variable list.

Dimension	Icon	Description
Scale		Values can fall anywhere along a scale. Distance along the axis encodes values. All values are available.
Categorical		Contains a limited number of discrete values. Along an axis, categories are represented by evenly spaced ticks. Values between categories are not used.
Built-in		Produces a chart of counts or percentages, or a casewise chart.

You can define a variable as scale, ordinal, or nominal in the Define Variable dialog box in the Data Editor. A change in level of measurement in the Define Variable dialog box applies to all charts created after the change. (Changing the level in a chart creation dialog box or in an interactive chart applies only to the current chart.) In interactive charts, ordinal and nominal variables are both treated as categorical data dimensions.

Changing data dimensions in a chart. The data dimension of a variable in a variable list can be changed by right-clicking the variable and choosing Scale or Categorical from the context menu. This change applies only to the current chart.

Summary built-in dimensions. The summary built-in dimensions are *Count* and *Percent*. For example, in a bar chart, the bars could represent the number of employees (count) in each job category or the percentage of employees in each job category.

Case. The built-in dimension *Case* indicates that each case in the data file is represented on the axis.

To Change the Measurement Level of a Variable in a Chart

▶ From the menus choose:

Graphs
  Interactive

▶ Choose a chart type.

▶ On the Assign Variables tab, right-click a variable in one of the lists.

▶ Choose Scale or Categorical.

This choice affects only the current chart.

After the chart is created, you can also change the dimension in the variable list in the Assign Graph Variables dialog box.

Legend Variables

Categorical legend variables split the elements in the chart into categories. Scale legend variables apply color or size to the elements based on the value or summary value of the legend variable.

Categorical variables. If a legend variable is categorical, the colors or styles are assigned according to the discrete categories of the variable. For example, in a bar chart, if *Region* is assigned to Color, the bars for the East, Central, and West divisions are different colors. In a scatterplot, if *Year* is assigned to Style, the markers are a different shape for each year.

Figure 1-3
Scatterplot with a style legend

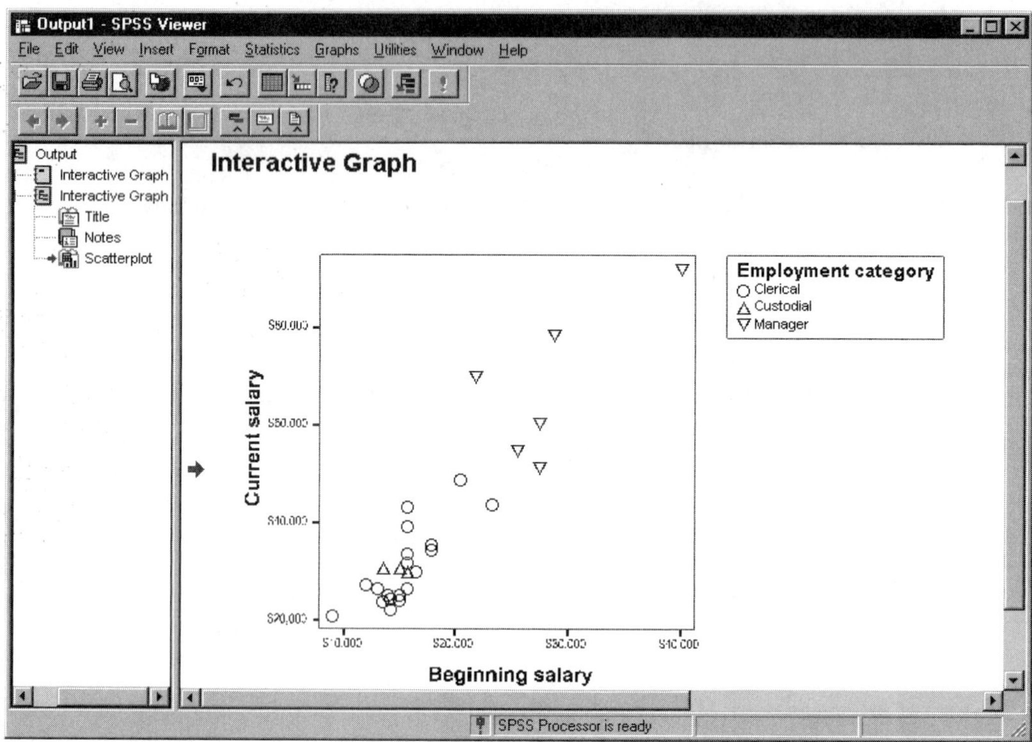

Scale variables. If a scale variable is assigned to Color in a scatterplot, symbols take colors from a continuous scale. For example, if the color variable is *Age,* each symbol is colored according to the value of the age variable for the case. A scale variable can also be assigned to Size. The symbols are sized according to the values of the scale variable.

If a scale variable is assigned to Color in a summary chart, the colors of the chart objects are based on a function of the scale variable. For example, if the color variable is *Age*, the colors of the elements vary along a gradient as the *mean age* of the group increases. In a bar chart, the color of each bar would be determined by the mean age of the cases represented in the bar.

Panel Variables

Panel variables divide the chart into small panels, each representing a different set of cases. Only categorical variables can be assigned as panel variables. For a single panel variable, each category is represented in one panel. For multiple panel variables, each combination of categories across variables is represented in a panel. For example, if one of two panel variables has three categories and the other has two, the total number of panels is six.

Figure 1-4
Panels for the categorical variable Region

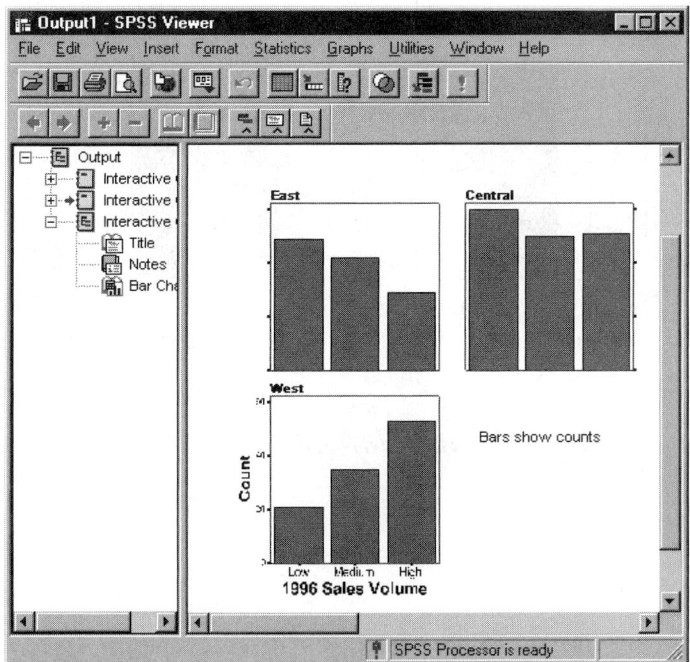

Summarizing Multiple Variables

Depending on how your data are organized, you may want to create charts that summarize and compare multiple variables. For example, if sales data for each year are recorded in a separate variable, you can create a single chart that summarizes sales data for each year in a separate bar.

Figure 1-5
Bar charts summarizing two variables

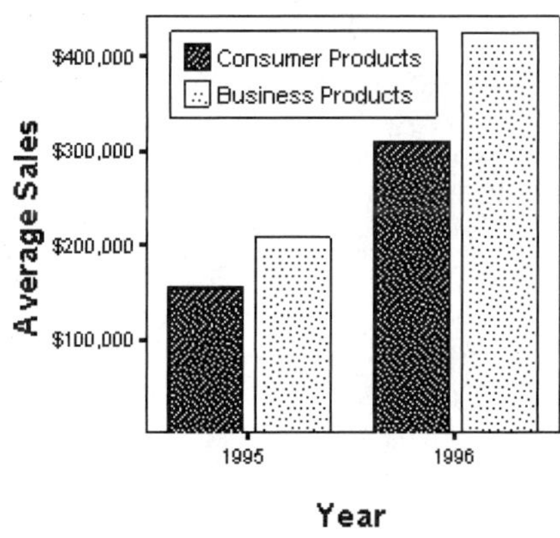

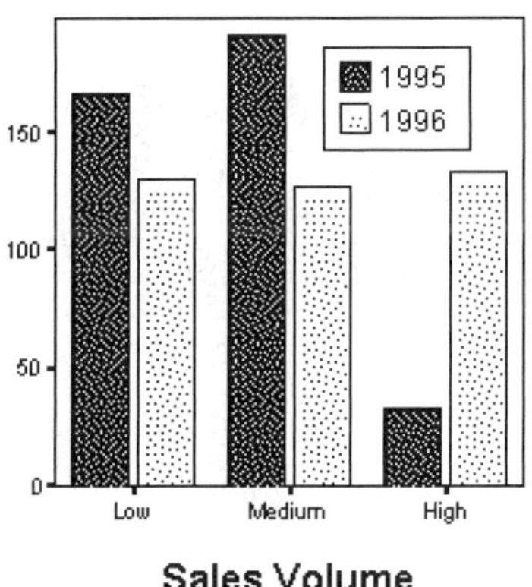

To Create a Chart Summarizing Multiple Variables

▶ From the menus choose:

Graphs
 Interactive

▶ Choose a chart type.

▶ On the Assign Variables tab, use the Ctrl-click method to select multiple variables in the source list.

▶ Drag the variables to one of the axes.

Optionally, you can specify category and value axis labels as well as modify value labels for categories in the Specify Labels dialog box.

This creates two temporary variables that are used in the procedure:

Category (or the label you specify for categories). A categorical variable in which each "category" is one of the selected variables. For categorical variables, you can use this variable as a color, style, or panel variable to identify each variable.

Value (or the label you specify for values). For scale variables, a variable that contains the summary values for each category. For categorical variables, a variable that contains the category values of each variable.

You can use these variables when you edit the chart and when you create the same type of chart again, but they are not available for any other interactive graphics procedures and you cannot save them with the data file.

Specify Labels

Figure 1-6
Specify Labels dialog box

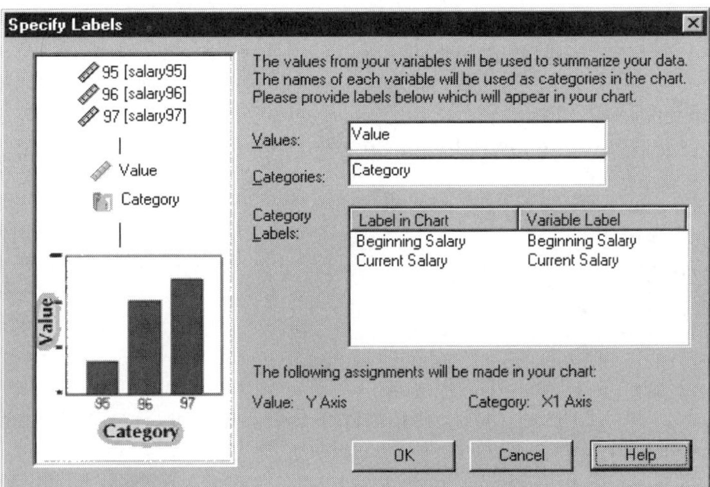

This dialog box provides options for labeling charts of multiple variables.

Values. Label for the values axis. For scale variables, the values axis represents the values of the summary function displayed in the chart. For categorical variables, the values axis represents the different categories of each variable. This label is also used to identify the temporary variable associated with the values axis.

Categories. Label for the category axis. The category axis represents the different variables displayed in the chart.

Category Labels. Labels used to identify each variable displayed in the chart. By default, the defined variable labels are used. For variables without defined variable labels, variable names are used.

To Create a Chart from a Pivot Table

- Double-click the pivot table to activate it.
- Select the rows, columns, or cells you want to display in the chart.
- Right-click anywhere in the selected area.
- Choose Create Graph from the context menu and select a chart type.

Coordinate System

Number of dimensions. Many types of charts can be 2-D or 3-D. Selecting a coordinate system from the drop-down list changes the number of axes available for assigning variables.

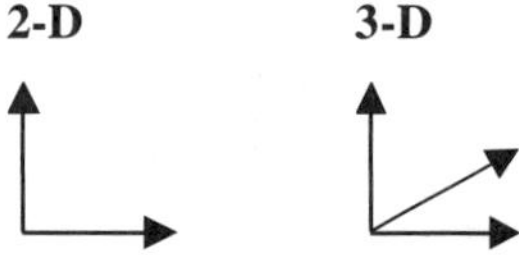

Another choice, 3-D Effect, gives depth to the graph objects in a 2-D chart.

Chart Orientation

Whenever a chart type can have either horizontal or vertical orientation, orientation icons are available on the Assign Variables tab of the chart creation dialog box. The icons vary according to chart type. The following is an example of bar chart orientation icons:

Vertical **Horizontal**

Horizontal orientation is available for 2-D charts only.

Orientation can be changed after a chart has been created by activating the chart and clicking the vertical or horizontal icon on the toolbar. This changes the location of the axis targets.

Vertical **Horizontal**

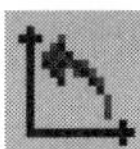

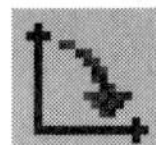

Create Chart: Titles

Text for titles, subtitles, and captions can be specified on the Titles tab of chart creation dialog boxes.

Figure 1-7
Titles tab

To specify the initial font, point size, color, alignment of titles, subtitles, and captions, use a ChartLook.

Create Chart: Options

Figure 1-8
Options tab

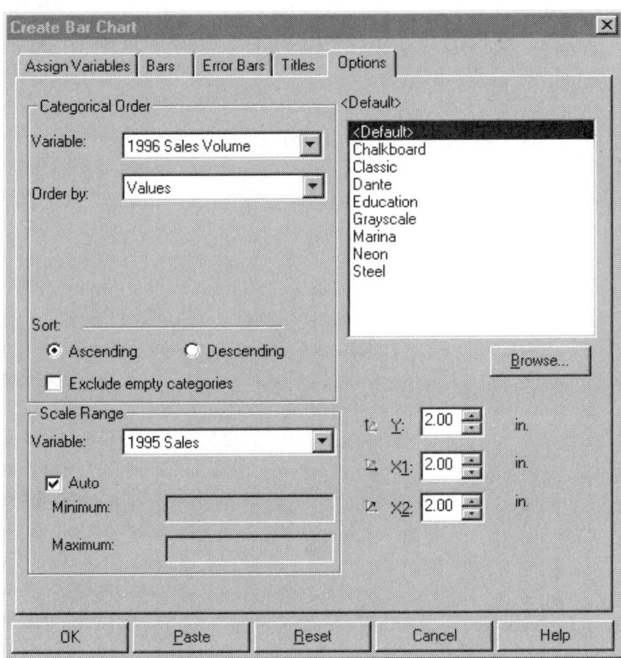

The Options tab for each type of interactive chart offers additional ways to customize your output. You can determine the order of categorical variables as well as the range for scale variables. You can also select a ChartLook and the size of the data region.

Categorical Order. Categorical variables can be ordered in several ways. You can order a variable by a property (such as values, label, occurrence, and counts), or you can order the variable by the summary function of another variable. Optionally, you can determine if the order will be ascending or descending, and you can exclude categories that have no data.

Scale Range. Minimum and maximum values can be set for all for scale variables. You can use the default values from the data set, or you can create a custom range.

ChartLook. This list contains the ChartLooks stored in the *Looks* directory (or the default directory selected from Options on the Edit menu. A ChartLook controls the initial visual properties of the chart, such as colors and symbols. To find ChartLooks that are stored in other directories, click Browse.

Size. The size of the data region is determined by the length of each axis. The units of measurement are specified in Options (Interactive tab) on the Edit menu in the Viewer. If you assign a panel variable, the *y* and *x1* lengths are used to determine the aspect ratios of the panels.

Y, *x1*, and *x2* are assigned as shown in the following diagrams:

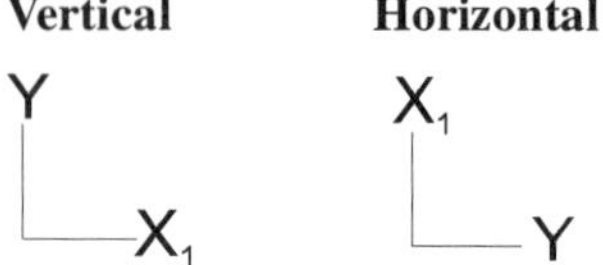

For 3-D charts, *y* is the dependent axis.

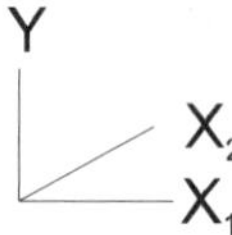

Persistence in Dialog Boxes

Selections made in a dialog box for creating a chart persist; that is, the next time the same chart creation dialog box is opened, the program *remembers* the previous selections. For example, a triangle shape selected for a previous scatterplot is still selected when you open the dialog box to create another scatterplot.

To clear all selections and reset to default values, click Reset. Clicking Reset once sets default values for all tabs in a dialog box.

Missing Values in Interactive Charts

Cases are excluded listwise for all interactive charts. That is, a case with a missing value for any variable used in the chart is excluded.

If you want the cases to be included in a chart, in the Data Editor remove any variable definitions of user-missing values. Also, assign values where there are system-missing values. You may want to save a duplicate data file before changing the missing value designations.

Summary Functions in Charts

Summary functions apply to scale variables selected for a dependent axis or a slice summary. Percentages are based on the specified percent base. For a slice summary, only summary functions appropriate for the type of chart are available.

First Values. The value found in the first case for each category in the data file at the time the summary function was assigned.

Kurtosis. A measure of the extent to which observations cluster around a central point. For a normal distribution, the value of the kurtosis statistic is 0. Positive kurtosis indicates that the observations cluster more and have longer tails than those in the normal distribution, and negative kurtosis indicates that the observations cluster less and have shorter tails.

Last Values. The value found in the last case for each category in the data file that created it.

Maximum Values. The largest value for each category.

Means. The arithmetic average for each category.

Medians. The value below which half of the cases fall in each category. If there is an even number of cases, the median is the average of the two middle cases when they are sorted in ascending or descending order.

Minimum Values. The smallest value within the category.

Modes. The most frequently occurring value within each category. If multiple modes exist, the smallest value is used.

Number of Cases Above (N of Cases >). The number of cases having values above the specified value.

Number of Cases Between (N Between). The number of cases between two specified values.

Number of Cases Equal to (N of Cases =). The number of cases equal to the specified value.

Number of Cases Greater Than or Equal to (N of Cases >=). The number of cases having values above or equal to the specified value.

Number of Cases Less Than (N of Cases <). The number of cases below the specified value.

Number of Cases Less Than or Equal to (N of Cases <=). The number of cases below or equal to the specified value.

Percentage of Cases Above (% of Cases >). The percentage of cases having values above the specified value.

Percentage of Cases Between (N Between). The percentage of cases between two specified values.

Percentage of Cases Between (% Between). The percentage of cases having values between two specified values.

Percentage of Cases Equal to (% of Cases =). The percentage of cases equal to the specified value.

Percentage of Cases Greater Than or Equal to (% of Cases >=). The percentage of cases having values above or equal to the specified value.

Percentage of Cases Less Than (% of Cases <). The percentage of cases having values below the specified value.

Percentage of Cases Less Than or Equal to (% of Cases <=). The percentage of cases having values below or equal to the specified value.

Percentiles. The data value below which the specified percentage of values fall within each category.

Skewness. A measure of the asymmetry of a distribution. The normal distribution is symmetric and has a skewness value of 0. A distribution with a significant positive skewness has a long right tail. A distribution with a significant negative skewness has a long left tail.

Standard Deviations (SD). A measure of dispersion around the mean, expressed in the same unit of measurement as the observations, equal to the square root of the variance. In a normal distribution, 68% of cases fall within one standard deviation of the mean and 95% of cases fall within two standard deviations.

Standard Errors of Kurtosis (S.E. of Kurtosis). The ratio of kurtosis to its standard error can be used as a test of normality (that is, you can reject normality if the ratio is less than –2 or greater than +2). A large positive value for kurtosis indicates that the tails of the distribution are longer than those of a normal distribution; a negative value for kurtosis indicates shorter tails (becoming like those of a box-shaped uniform distribution).

Standard Errors of the Mean (S.E. of the Mean). A measure of how much the value of the mean may vary among samples taken from the same distribution. It can be used to roughly compare the observed mean to a hypothesized value (that is, you can conclude the two values are different if the ratio of the difference to the standard error is less than –2 or greater than +2).

Standard Errors of Skewness (S.E. of Skewness). The ratio of skewness to its standard error can be used as a test of normality (that is, you can reject normality if the ratio is less than –2 or greater than +2). A large positive value for skewness indicates a long right tail; an extreme negative value, a long left tail.

Sums. The sums of the values within each category.

Sums of Absolute Values. The sums of the absolute values within each category.

Sums of Squares. The sums of the squares of the values within each category.

Variances. A measure of how much observations vary from the mean, expressed in squared units.

Chapter

2

Working with Charts Interactively

Starting with a blank interactive chart or with an interactive chart already created, you can add and delete various chart elements and objects and change the data summary function until you have exactly the right combination to illustrate the characteristics of your data. With interactive charts, you don't have to make a new chart to add data or change the role of a variable—you can simply change the variable assignments.

This chapter discusses elements and text that can be inserted into a chart. See Chapter 12 for information about how to modify elements and objects that have already been inserted into a chart and how to rearrange them.

Creating an Interactive Chart

Charts can be created interactively, starting with a blank chart and adding one or more chart elements simply by clicking buttons and dragging variables.

Example. A blank 2-D chart is inserted, and variables are assigned to the *x* and *y* axes. A scatterplot cloud is inserted from the drop-down list obtained by clicking the Insert Element tool. Following each mouse action, changes in the chart are immediately displayed.

Figure 2-1
Blank 2-D chart and variable assignments

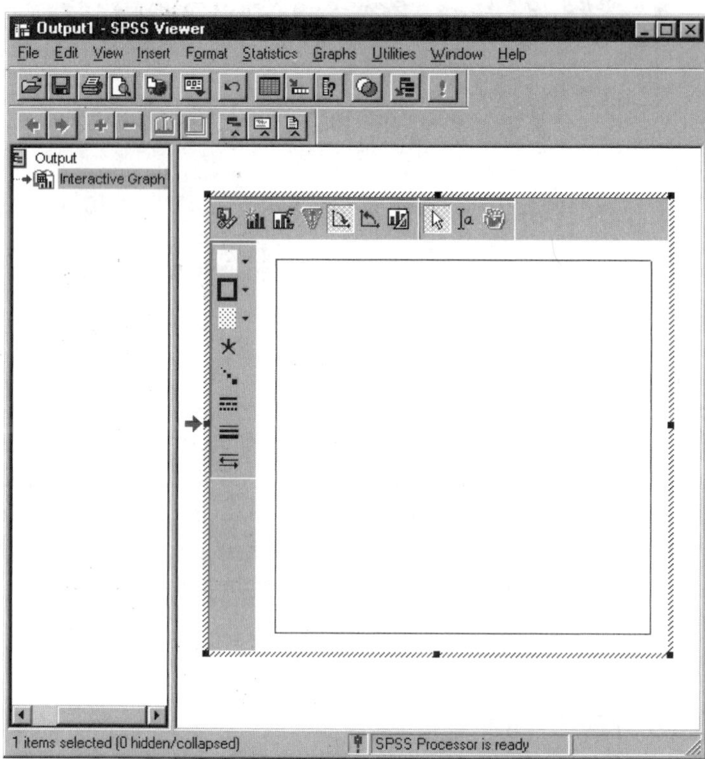

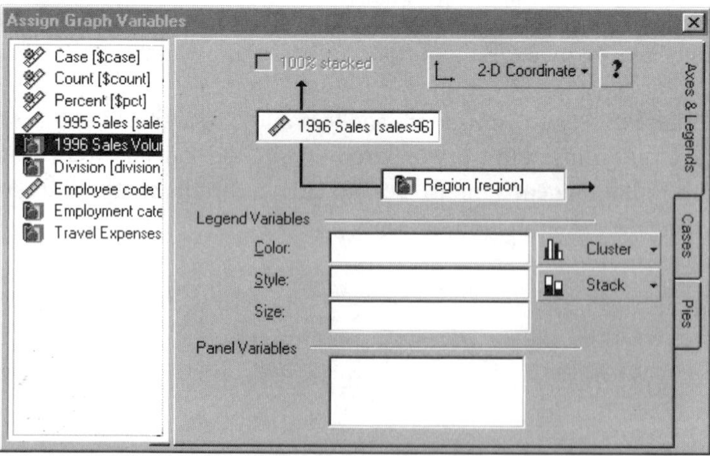

Figure 2-2
Scatterplot cloud added

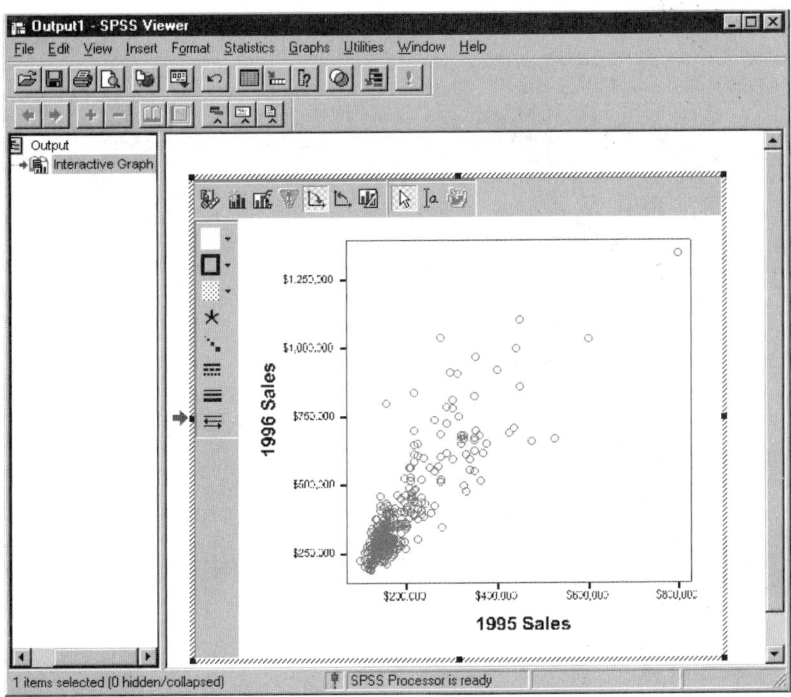

Next, to group the symbols by style, a categorical variable is assigned to Legend Variables Style.

Figure 2-3
Scatterplot grouped by a variable assigned to Legend Variables Style

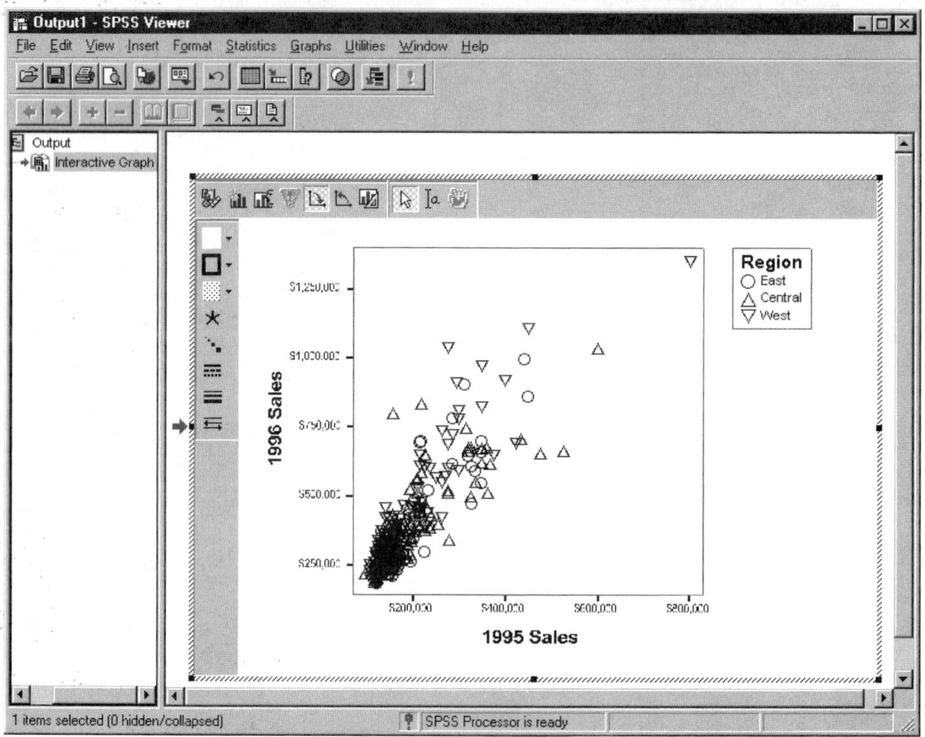

Finally, a smoother (LLR fit line) is added for the total group of points.

Figure 2-4
Scatterplot with smoother added

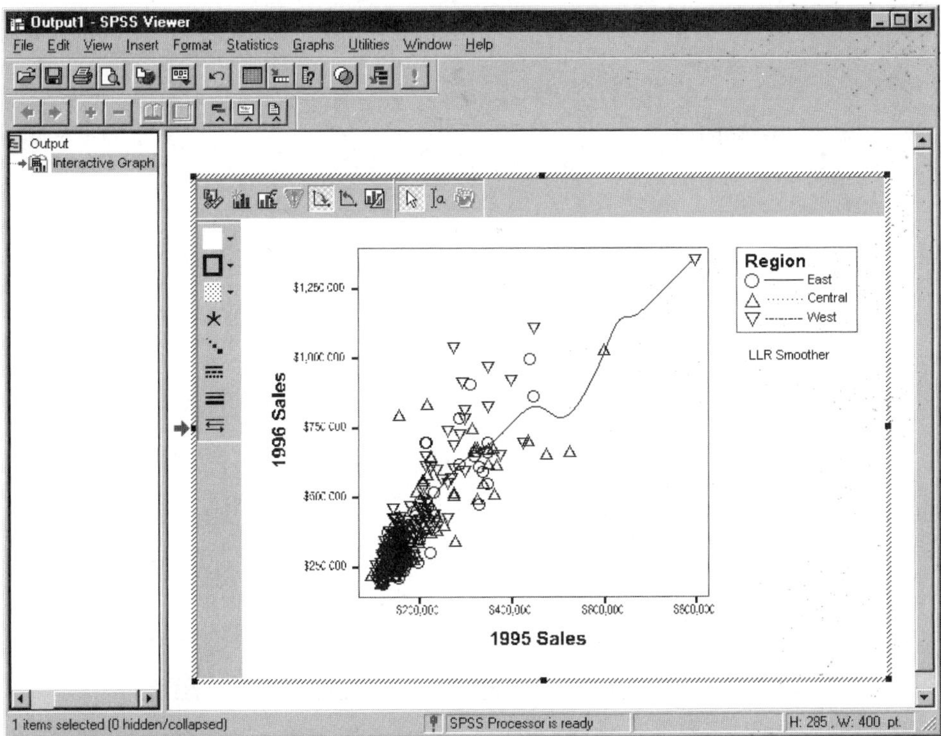

Adding more elements. Other elements can be added to the chart. Smoothers can be added for the subgroups assigned in the legend. In a bar chart, a line element could be added; error bars might be added to a bar chart or a line chart. Each additional chart element responds to the same assignment of variables.

To Create a 2-D Chart Interactively

▶ From the Viewer menus choose:

Insert
  Interactive 2-D Graph

This produces an activated blank 2-D chart, with interactive graph menus displayed at the top of the Viewer.

Figure 2-5
Blank 2-D chart

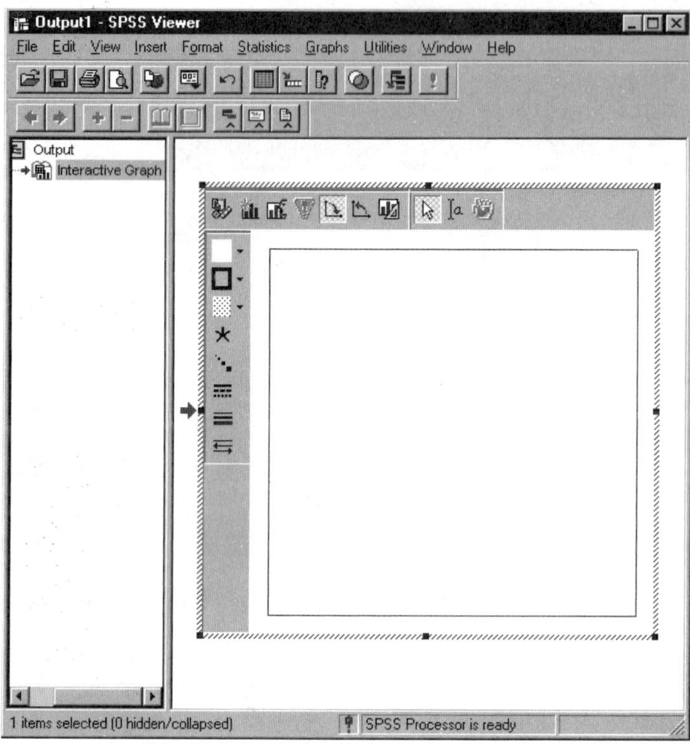

- From the menus choose:

  Insert

  or

- Click the Insert Element tool on the chart toolbar.

- Select a graphical element, such as Bar or Cloud.

▶ From the menus choose:

Edit
 Assign Variables

or

▶ Click the Assign Graph Variables tool on the chart toolbar.

▶ Drag variables from the source list to the appropriate targets: axes, legend, or panel.

The chart changes as you assign each variable.

You can add more than one element to the chart. The variable assignments apply to all elements. If you pay attention to the current assignment of variables before assigning new elements, you can avoid charts containing a multitude of elements (for example, hundreds of plotted pies because of a scale variable assigned to an axis).

To Create a 3-D Chart Interactively

▶ From the Viewer menus choose:

Insert
  Interactive 3-D Graph

This produces an activated blank 3-D chart, with interactive graph menus displayed.

Figure 2-6
Blank 3-D chart

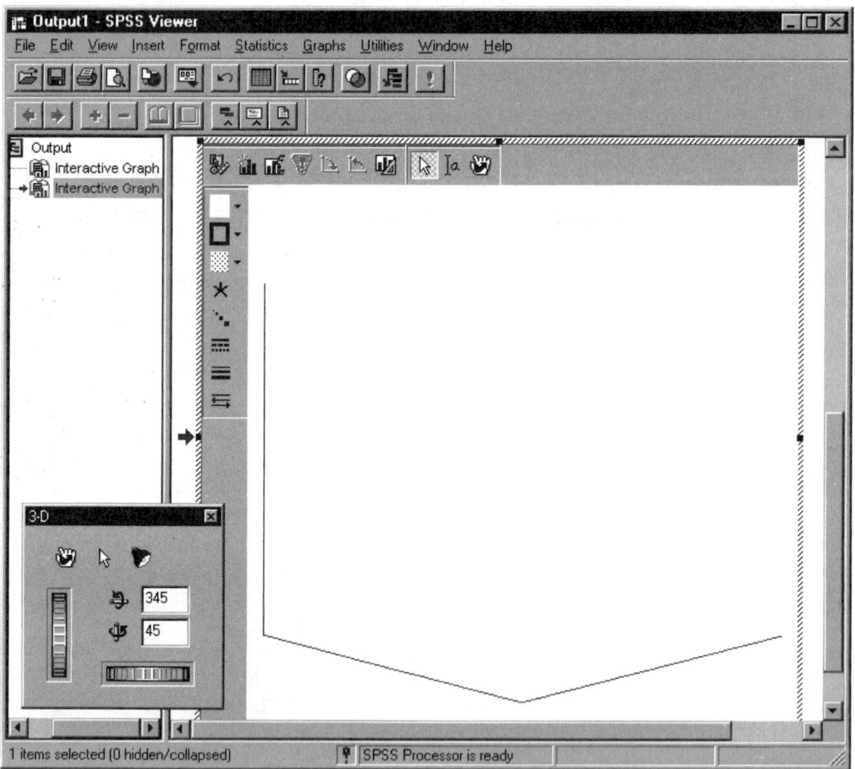

▶ From the menus choose:

Insert

or

▶ Click the Insert Element tool.

▶ Select a graphical element, such as Bar or Cloud.

▶ From the menus choose:

Edit
  Assign Variables

or

▶ Click the Assign Graph Variables tool.

▶ Drag variables from the source list to the appropriate targets: axes, legend, or panel.

The chart changes as you assign each variable.

You can add more than one element to the chart. The variable assignments apply to all elements. If you pay attention to the current assignment of variables before inserting new elements, you can avoid charts containing a multitude of elements (for example, hundreds of plotted pies because of a scale variable assigned to an axis).

Assign Graph Variables: Axes and Legends

In the Assign Graph Variables dialog box, you can assign variables to various roles in a chart. The chart changes as soon as you drag the variables to their new targets. On the Axes & Legends tab, variables can be assigned to axes, to color, style, and size legends, or to panels.

Figure 2-7
Assign Graph Variables dialog boxes for 2-D and 3-D charts

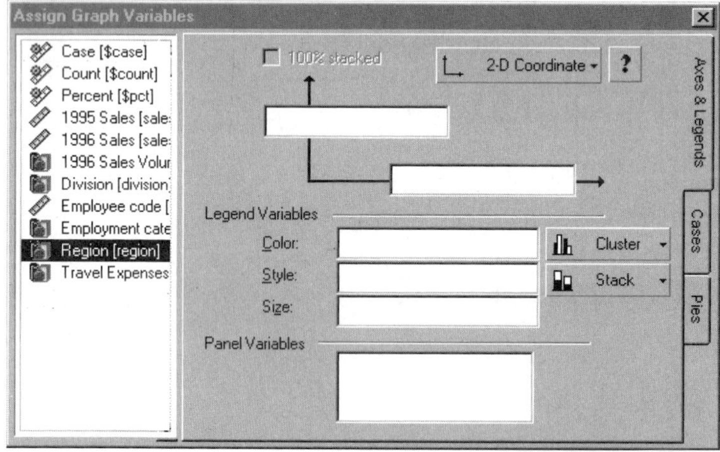

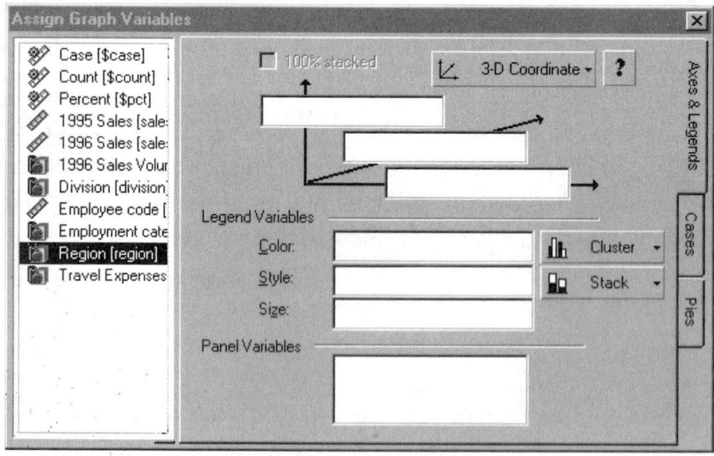

Coordinate systems. Choosing a 2-D or 3-D coordinate system determines the number of axis targets available. Selecting 3-D Effect displays each 2-D element in the chart as a three-dimensional solid object, but no variable is assigned to the third axis.

Variables. The variable list contains scale variables, categorical variables, and built-in variables, distinguishable by their icons. You can switch a scale variable to a categorical variable and vice versa by using the context menu (right-click on the variable and select Categorical or Scale). Reassigning the variable type applies only to the current chart.

Be careful when assigning variables with a large number of distinct values. You could get such a large number of bars, for example, that you couldn't distinguish them. If you add a pie element when a scale variable is assigned to one of the axes, a large number of tiny plotted pies may be generated. If the chart is not what you expected, try looking at the Chart Manager to see what elements are actually in the chart and what warnings have been posted.

Summary Functions. If a scale variable is assigned to the dependent axis, the summary function (means, medians, sums, etc.) is determined by the graphical element inserted into the chart. For example, bars could represent means and lines could represent maximum values in the same chart.

Legend Variables. In the legend, color, style, and size can be used to show group membership by assigning categorical variables. Color and Style are the targets used to split categories in various charts or to slice pies. Also, scale variables can be assigned to Color or Size. With a scale variable assigned in a chart with a summary function (for example, bars represent means), the legend displays a gradient that represents means of the scale variable.

The Color and Style legends can be set to Cluster or Stack. Stacking applies only to bar or area elements. Other types of elements ignore it. If a stacked element is present, it can be stacked as percentages with the 100% stacked option.

Panel Variables. For easy comparison of groups, you can create separate panel charts for each category or combination of categories by assigning one or more categorical variables to Panel Variables.

This dialog box can remain open while you change element and object properties.

To Assign Graph Variables

- ▶ Activate a chart or insert a new 2-D or 3-D chart.

- ▶ From the menus choose:

  Edit
    Assign Variables

  or

- ▶ Click the Assign Graph Variables tool.

- ▶ Drag the desired variables to the appropriate targets. Use the Shift-click method to drag more than one variable.

- ▶ If you want a stacked element, select Stack from the drop-down list for Color or Style.

- ▶ If you want a paneled chart, drag one or more variables to the Panel Variables box.

If you drag a variable to a target that already has a variable assigned, the variables swap places.

Assign Graph Variables: Cases

Figure 2-8
Assign Graph Variables: Cases tab

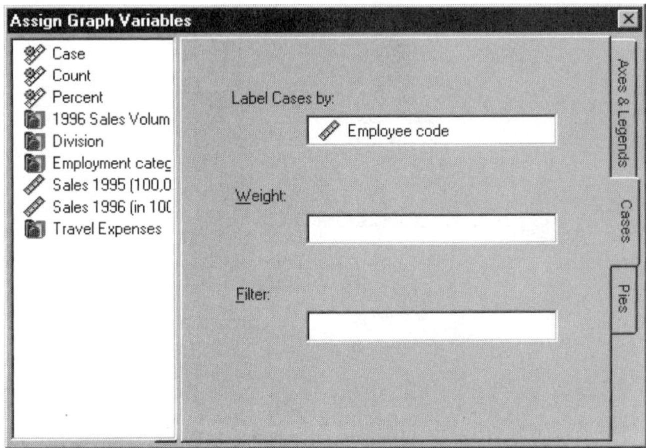

Label Cases by. Labels can be assigned for individual points or for cases plotted along an axis. The values of a variable assigned to Identify Points by are used to label plotted points in scatterplots and boxplots.

When a variable is assigned to Label Cases by, the values are used to label the ticks along an axis to which the built-in variable *$case* has been assigned. These values are ignored if the *$case* variable is not assigned.

Weight. The weight variable should represent the number of observations represented by each case. In any calculations, each case value is multiplied by the value in the weight variable for the case. A scale or categorical variable can be used.

Filter. If a case has a value of 0 for the filter variable, that case is not used in the chart. A scale or categorical variable can be used.

Assign Graph Variables: Pies

Figure 2-9
Assign Graph Variables: Pies tab

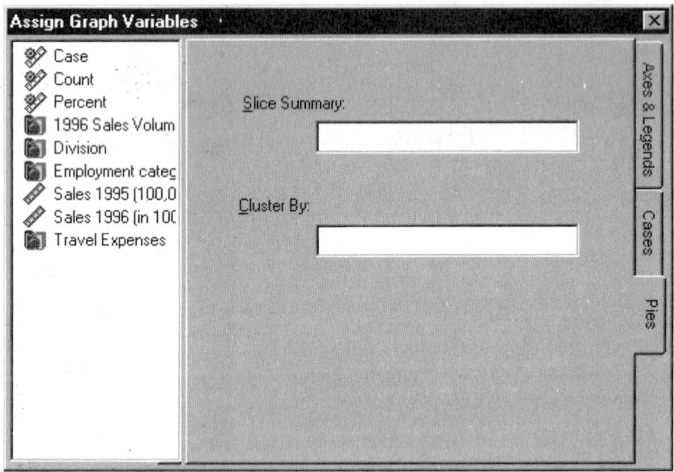

Variables can be assigned or changed for pie charts through this dialog box. These changes affect all pie elements in the chart. Pie slices can be changed on the Axes & Legends tab of this dialog box.

Slice Summary. One of the built-in variables (*$count* or *$pct*) or a scale variable can be assigned to the Slice Summary target. For a scale variable, the default summary function is *Sums*.

Cluster By. Only categorical variables can be assigned to Cluster By. In a clustered pie stack, each category is represented by one pie.

Inserting a Chart Title

A title, subtitle, or caption can be inserted into the chart. The text of the inserted object can then be edited. A title, subtitle, or caption cannot be inserted if the object already exists.

To Insert a Title, Subtitle, or Caption into a Chart

▶ Activate the chart.

▶ From the menus choose:

Insert
 Title

or

Insert
 Subtitle

or

Insert
 Caption

A title, subtitle, or caption is inserted into the chart.

▶ Double-click to edit the title, subtitle, or caption in place.

Optionally, you can drag the title, subtitle, or caption to a new position.

Inserting Text into a Chart

Using the Insert menu, you can add text to a chart and then drag it to another position. Another way to insert text is to click the Text tool and then click the chart at the position at which you want the text to be placed. You can later drag the text to a new position in the chart.

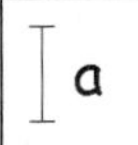

To Insert Text into a Chart

▶ Activate the chart (double-click it).

▶ From the menus choose:

Insert
 Text

or

▶ Click the Text tool.

▶ Click where you want the text to start.

A text object is placed on the chart.

▶ Enter the desired text.

Optionally, you can drag the text to a new position in the chart.

Editing Text in a Chart

You can edit text in a chart, including titles, subtitles, captions, axis titles, legend titles, labels, and text added to the chart after creation.

To Edit Text in a Chart

▶ Activate the chart (double-click it).

▶ Use the Arrow pointer to select the text object that you want to edit.

▶ Click once to get an insertion point, and then enter or edit the text.

Optionally, you can select part of the text and delete or replace the selection.

Chapter

3

Area Charts

A simple area chart is like a line chart with the space below the line filled in. Areas for several categories can be stacked on top of one another, with data values additive from one category to the next. A stacked area chart emphasizes the categories as components of the whole. If you want to show how the percentage contribution of each category changes, as opposed to how the sum of values changes, you can create a chart showing a total of 100% for each value along the independent axis.

Another way to represent categories is with a clustered area chart in which the areas for all categories of the legend variable have the same baseline. This representation is most useful in 3-D.

Sample Output

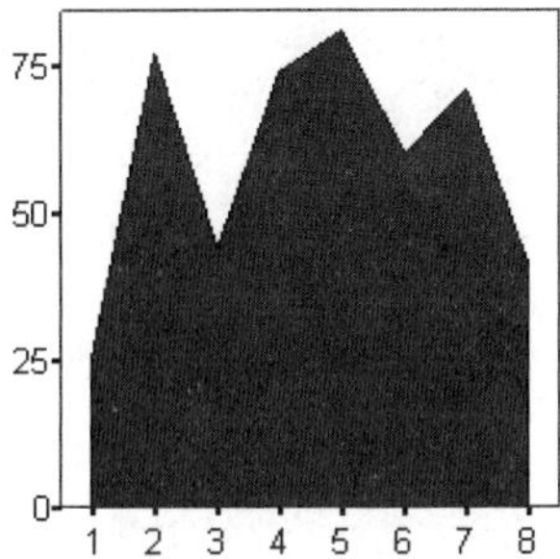

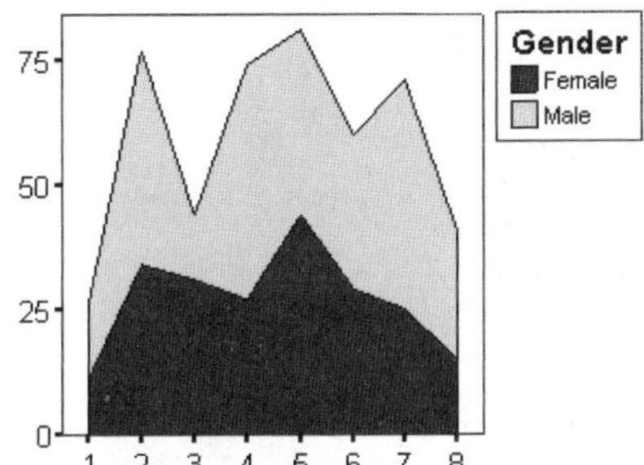

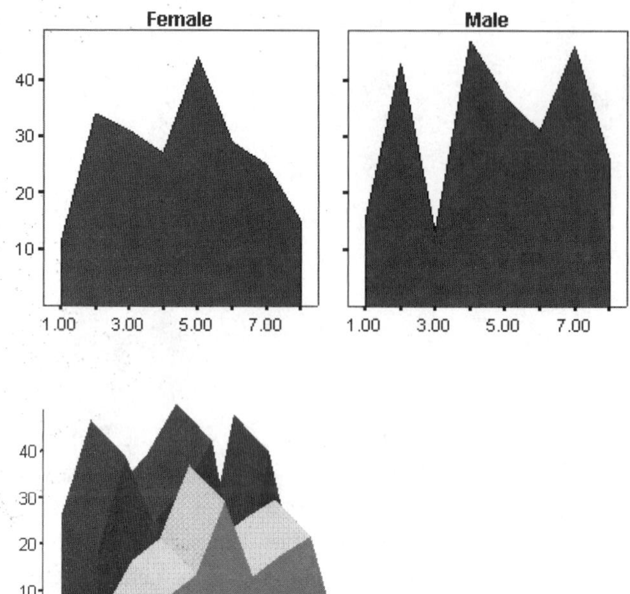

To Create an Interactive Area Chart

▶ From the menus choose:

Graphs
  Interactive
    Area...

Create Area Chart: Assign Variables

Figure 3-1
Create Area Chart: Assign Variables tab

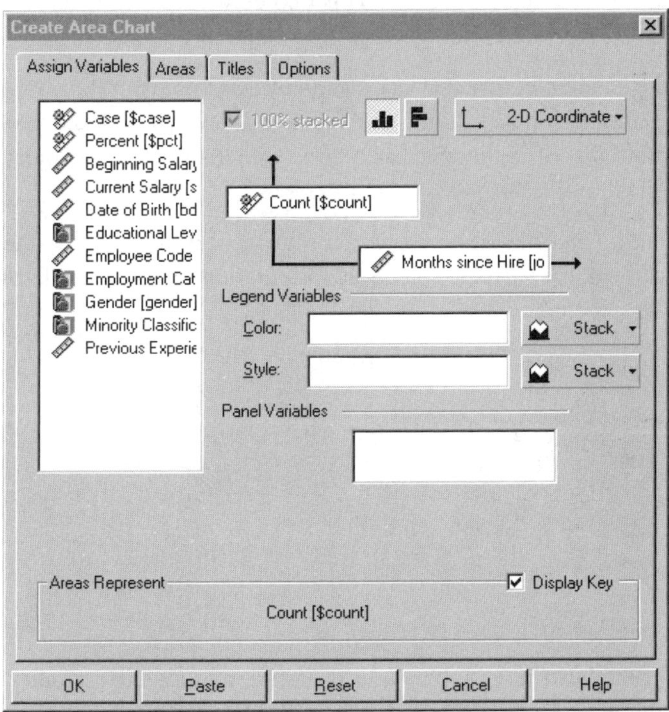

In a simple area chart, the points are plotted and joined with lines, and the area is filled in between the data line and the baseline. One common use is to show the continuity of a summary variable (dependent) through time (independent variable). The summary function can be changed near the bottom of the dialog box, and a key can be displayed to identify the function. Legend categories define stacked or clustered area charts.

Stacked area charts. Areas for categories can be stacked. The top of the previous category forms the base for the next category. This type of chart emphasizes the sum of the categories and the flow along the independent axis. However, in this representation, specific values of individual categories cannot be easily determined.

100% stacked area charts. If an area chart is stacked, you can change the dependent axis to represent 100%. The areas show the percentage contributed by each category of the legend variable, but, in contrast to a regular stacked area chart, the 100% stacked chart does not indicate increases or decreases in the totals.

Clustered area charts. The categories of a color or style variable divide a clustered chart into areas that have a common baseline. This choice works best when used with 3-D coordinates or 3-D effect. (Clustering may hide some of the areas behind other areas.)

Number of dimensions. Selecting 2-D Coordinate or 3-D Coordinate from the drop-down list changes the number of axis targets for variable selection. Selecting 3-D Effect displays each plotted area in the chart as a three-dimensional solid object, but no variable is assigned to the third axis.

Orientation. Clicking an orientation (vertical or horizontal) icon sets up the appropriate axis targets, as shown, for variable selection. Orientation icons are available only when 2-D Coordinate is selected.

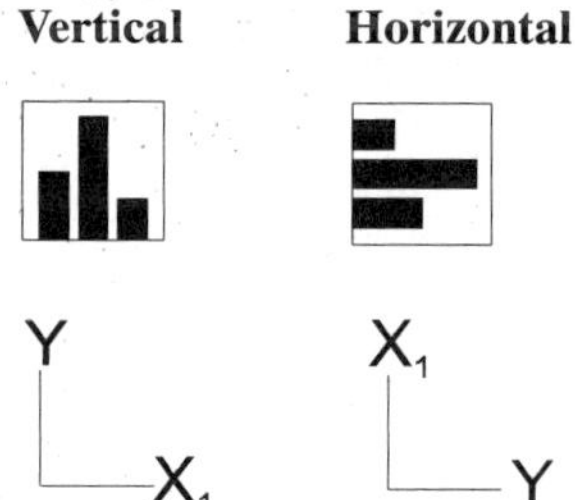

Case Variable. If the built-in variable *Case* is assigned to an axis, another target becomes available where you can assign a variable for labeling cases. For example, the labels might be days of the week or months.

Many of the charts shown below are vertical. To create a horizontal chart, click the horizontal icon before or after dragging variables.

To Create a Simple Area Chart

- Drag one or more variables (usually categorical) to the *x1* axis. This will be the base of the areas.

- Drag *Count* or a scale variable to the *y* axis (if not there by default).

  For another summary chart, you can use the built-in variable *Percent*.

  Optionally, you can:

  - Swap the axes by clicking the orientation icon. Currently assigned variables swap along with the axes.
  - Change the area baseline on the Areas tab.

To Create an Area Chart Summarizing a Scale Variable

- Drag a variable (usually categorical) to the *x1* axis.

- Drag a scale variable to the *y* axis.

  By default, the data points represent the mean of the scale variable.

  Optionally, you can:

  - Select another summary function from the Areas Represent drop-down list near the bottom of the dialog box.

To Create a Stacked or Clustered Area Chart

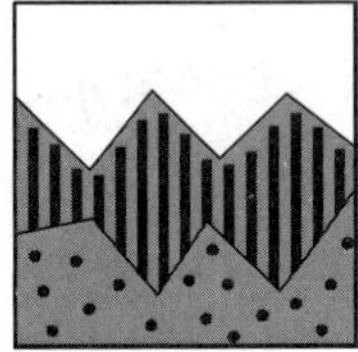

▶ Drag a variable (usually categorical) to the *x1* axis.

▶ Drag a scale variable to the *y* axis.

▶ Drag a categorical variable to Color or Style and select Stack or Cluster from the drop-down list.

In a stacked chart, the top of one category forms the base for the next category. In a clustered area chart, all areas have the same baseline.

Optionally, you can:

- Swap the axes by clicking the orientation icon. Currently assigned variables swap along with the axes.

To Create a 100% Stacked Area Chart

▶ Drag a variable (usually categorical) to the *x1* axis.

▶ Drag a scale variable to the *y* axis.

▶ Drag a categorical variable to Color or Style and select Stack from the drop-down list.

This enables the 100% Stacked check box.

▶ Select 100% Stacked.

Optionally, you can:

- Swap the axes by clicking the orientation icon. Currently assigned variables swap along with the axes.

To Create an Area Chart with Colors Assigned by a Summary of a Scale Variable

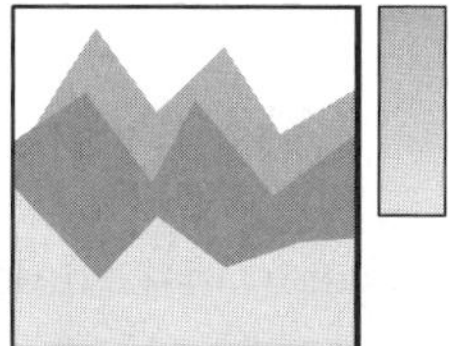

▶ Drag a variable (usually categorical) to the *x1* axis.

▶ Drag a scale variable to the *y* axis.

▶ Drag a scale variable to Color.

The color of each area indicates the mean of the color variable for the category represented by the area.

To Create Area Chart Panels for Categories

▶ Drag a variable (usually categorical) to the *x1* axis.

▶ Drag a scale variable to the *y* axis.

▶ Drag one or more categorical variables to Panel Variables.

To Create a 3-D Effect Clustered Area Chart

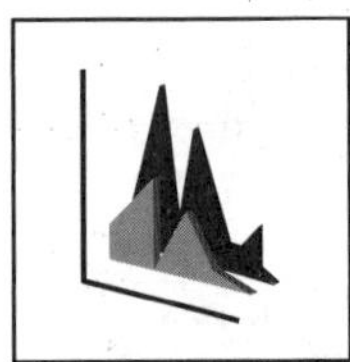

- Drag a variable (usually categorical) to the *x1* axis.
- Drag a scale variable to the *y* axis.
- Drag a categorical variable to Color or Style and select Cluster from the drop-down list.
- Select 3-D Effect from the dimensions drop-down list.

To Create a 3-D Area Chart

- Select 3-D Coordinate from the dimensions drop-down list.

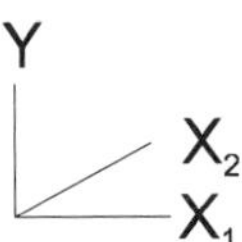

- Drag a scale variable to the *y* axis.
- Drag variables (usually categorical) to the *x1* and *x2* axes.

Create Area Chart: Areas

Figure 3-2
Create Area Chart: Areas tab

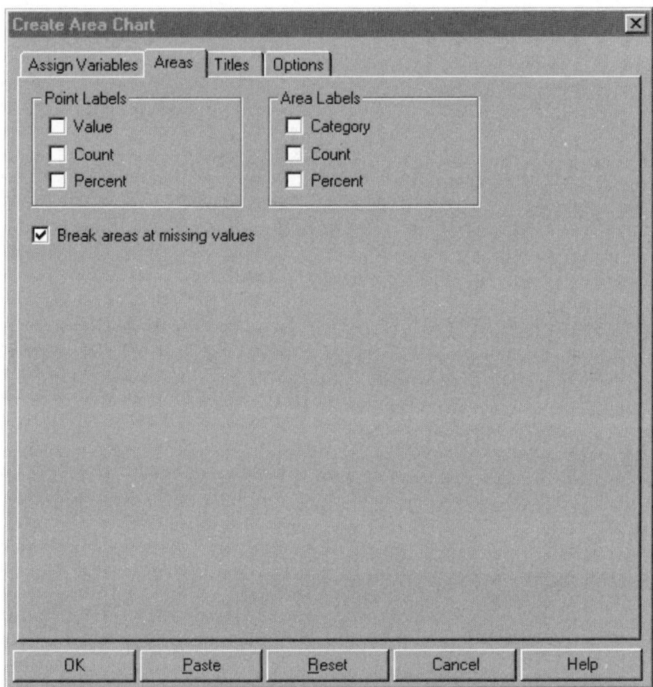

Several options are available to enhance areas.

Point Labels. The data points that define the edge of the area polygon can be labeled. Values, counts, and percentages are available. Any combination of these is allowed.

Area Labels. The area polygons can be labeled with the category name, the percentage of total cases, and the number of cases included in each area. Any combination is allowed.

Break areas at missing values. When this item is selected, the area is interrupted at any point along the independent axis where there is a missing value. If this item is deselected, the edge of the area is interpolated through the missing value and the area is filled in.

Modifying Areas

To modify the area element (all areas) in an existing chart:

- Activate the chart (double-click it).
- From the menus choose:

Format
  Graph Elements
    Area

or

- Right-click an area and from the context menu choose:

Areas...

- Select the desired changes.

Areas: Area Options

Figure 3-3
Areas: Area Options tab

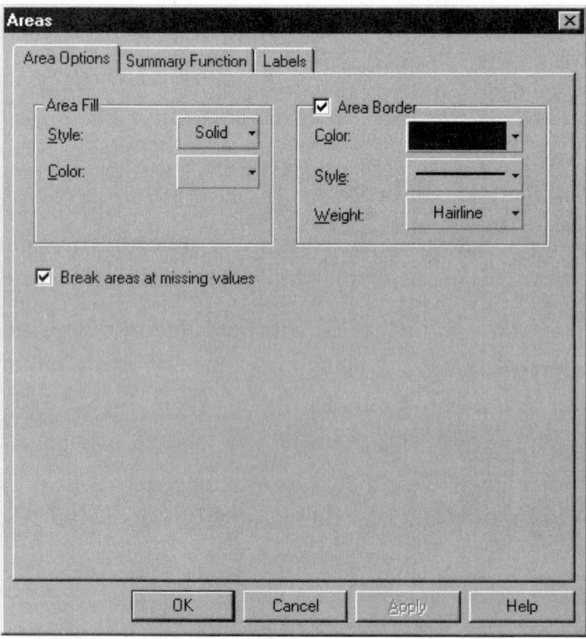

Several options are available to enhance areas.

Area Fill. Fills all areas in the chart with the selected style and color. If style or color is controlled by the data, it cannot be changed.

Area Border. Sets the border style, color, and weight for all areas in the chart. This option is available only for 2-D charts.

Break areas at missing values. When this item is selected, the area is interrupted when there is a missing value along the independent axis. If this item is deselected, the edge of the area is interpolated through the missing value and the area is filled in.

Areas: Summary Function

Figure 3-4
Areas: Summary Function tab

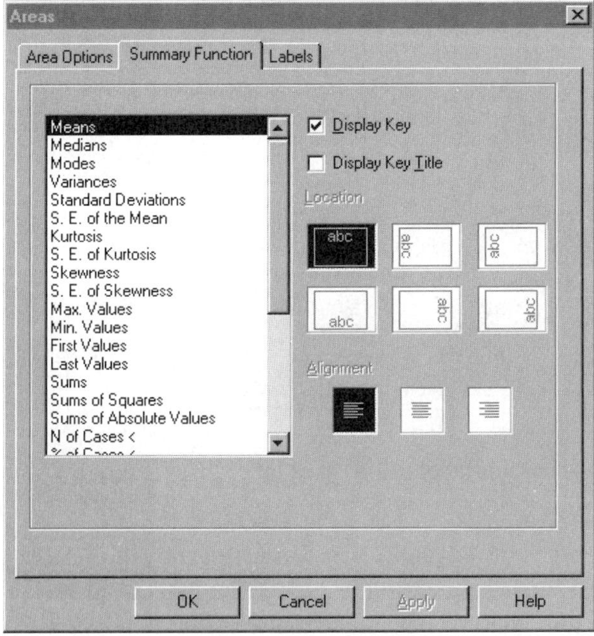

For an existing chart, if there is a scale variable on the dependent axis, you can change the summary function. For example, if the original areas represent the *means* of a variable, you can change to the *maximum values* of the same variable.

Key display options. These selections change the way summary information is displayed in the chart. You can display the key and determine the alignment and location of the key title.

Areas: Labels

Figure 3-5
Areas: Labels tab

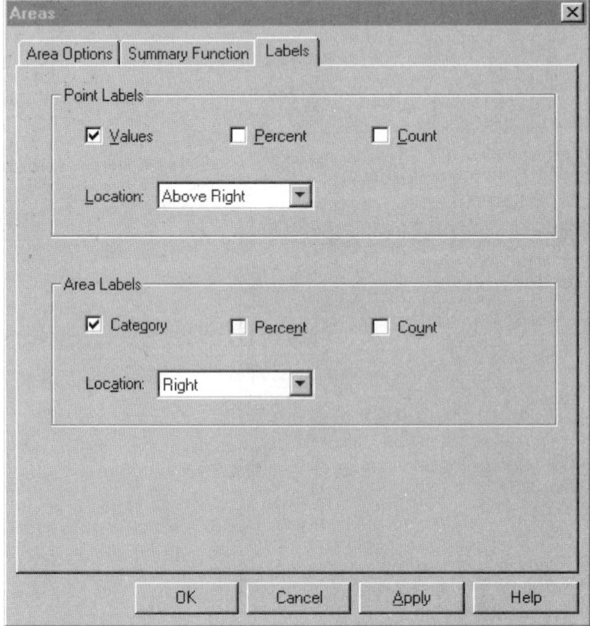

These controls apply to all point labels or all area labels. Several types of labels can be displayed simultaneously.

Point Labels. Labels on each of the points that define the edge of the area polygon. Values, counts, and percentages are available. A percent label displays the percentage of all cases in the area polygon that contribute to the point.

Area Labels. The area polygons can be labeled with the category name, the percentage of cases, and the number of cases included in each area. A percent label displays the percentage that contributes to the area out of the total number of cases.

Areas: Area Width

Figure 3-6
Areas: Area Width tab

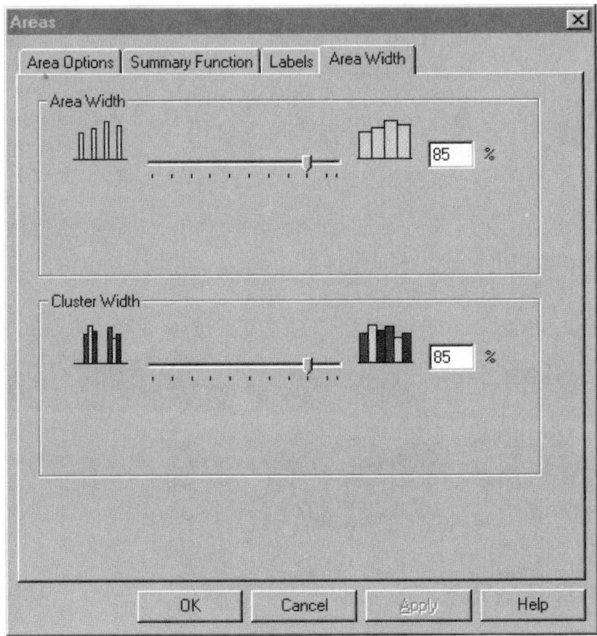

For 3-D or 3-D Effect area charts, you can change the width of the areas or the width of clusters of areas by dragging a slider. The cluster-width slider is available only if the chart is clustered.

Changing Area Properties

Individual areas or a selection of several areas have the properties Fill, Border, and Labels, which can be changed if the property is not controlled by assigned variables. However, in a stacked area chart in which color is used to distinguish categories, the color of a group of areas in one category can be changed only for the whole group (using the legend).

In addition to selecting the areas in the display, you can also select labels.

To Change Area Properties

▶ Activate the chart (double-click it).

▶ Select one or more areas.

▶ From the menus choose:

Edit
  Area Properties...

or

▶ Right-click an area or selected group of areas and choose Properties.

Optionally, you can:

- Change the fill and border.
- Turn labels on or off for points or areas.

Area Properties

Figure 3-7
Area Properties dialog box

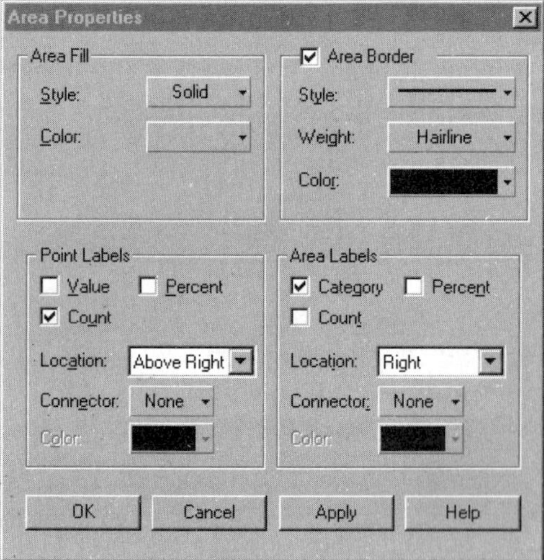

The properties apply only to currently selected areas.

Area Fill. The style and color of the selected areas can be changed, if not controlled by the data.

Area Border. If borders are on (selected), you can change the style, color, or weight.

Point Labels. Labels on each of the points that define the edge of the area polygon. Values, counts, and percentages are available. A percent label displays the percentage of all cases in the area polygon that contributes to the point.

Area Labels. An area polygon can be labeled with the category name, a percentage, and the number of cases included in each area. A percent label displays the percentage of cases that contributes to the area out of the total number of cases.

Point Label Properties

Figure 3-8
Point Label Properties dialog box

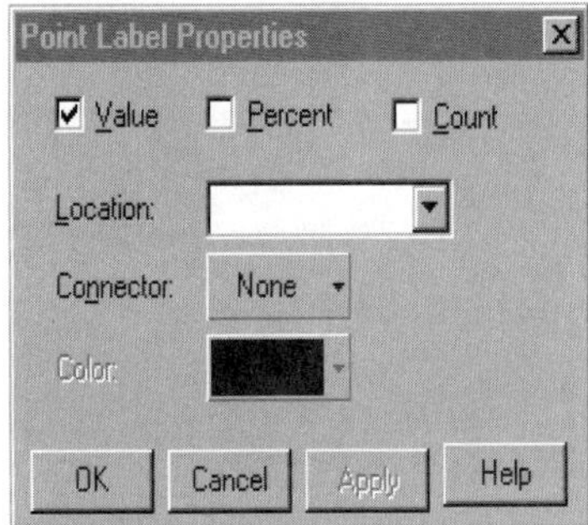

The properties apply only to currently selected point labels.

A data point can be labeled with the value represented, the percentage of cases in the area that contribute to the point, and the count of cases in the area that contribute to the point. You can control the location of a label with respect to the data point, the style of connector, and its color.

Area Label Properties

Figure 3-9
Area Label Properties dialog box

The properties apply only to currently selected area labels.

An area can be labeled with the category name, the percentage of all cases that contribute to the area, and the count (number of cases) represented in the area. You can control the location of a label with respect to the data point, the style of connector, and its color.

Chapter

4

Bar Charts

A simple bar chart presents a summary variable divided into discrete categories, making it easy to compare categories visually. A glance at a bar chart tells you the relative sizes of the quantities represented by the bars, which can be drawn vertically or horizontally. Bars can be subdivided into clusters by a category variable and further subdivided by placing another category variable in the third dimension. Categories can also be stacked. Many other variations are possible.

Sample Output

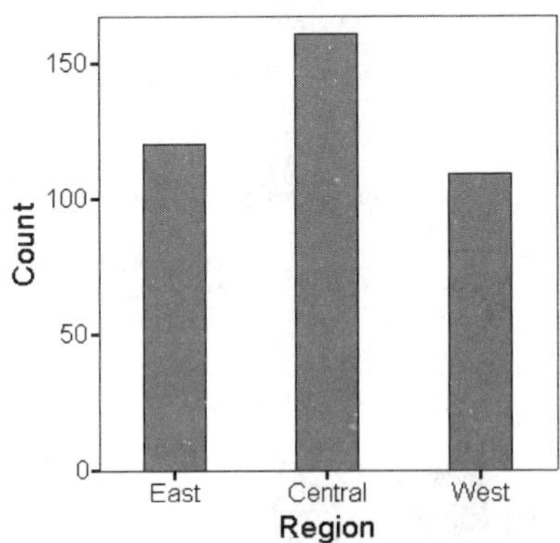

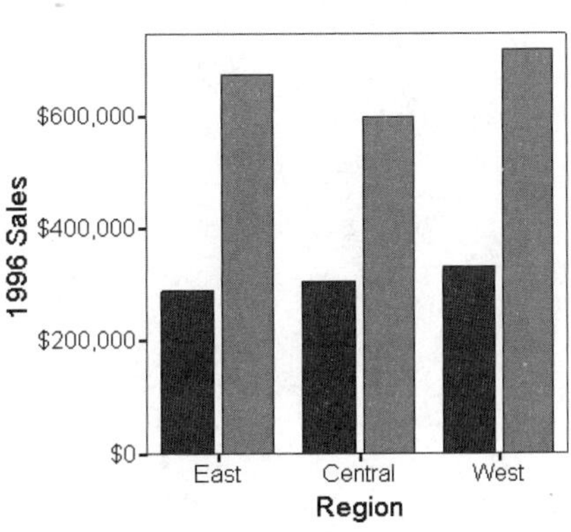

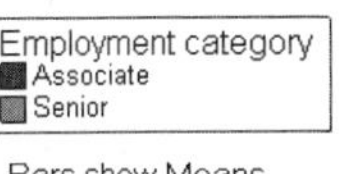

Bars show Means

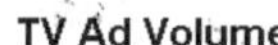

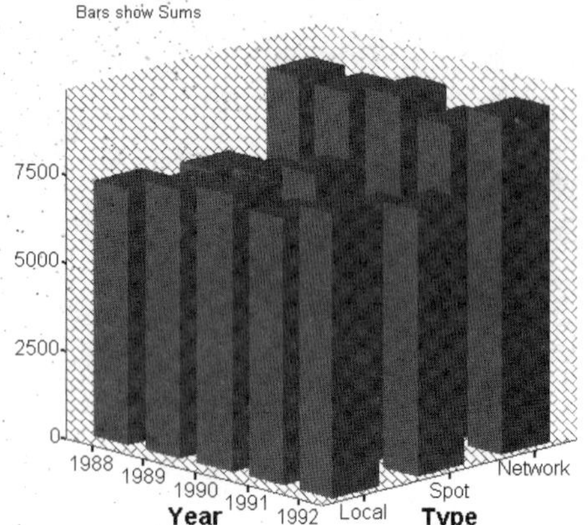
TV Ad Volume
Bars show Sums
7500
5000
2500
0
1988
1989
1990
1991
1992
Year
Local
Spot
Network
Type

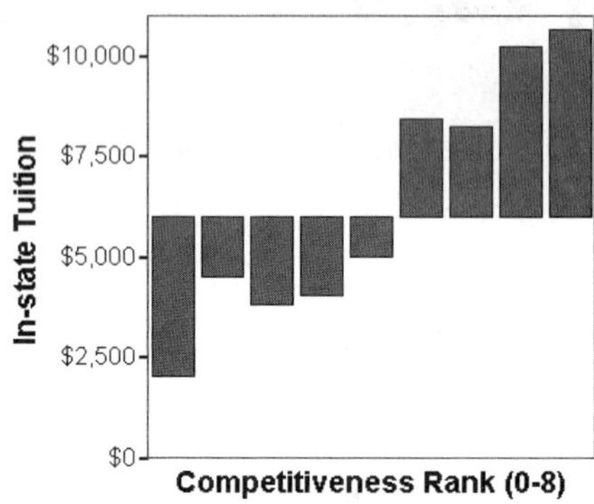
$10,000
$7,500
$5,000
$2,500
$0
In-state Tuition
Competitiveness Rank (0-8)

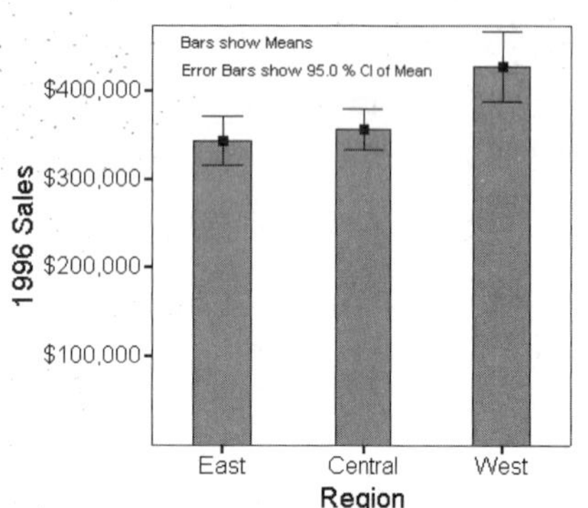
Bars show Means
Error Bars show 95.0 % CI of Mean
$400,000
$300,000
$200,000
$100,000
1996 Sales
East
Central
West
Region

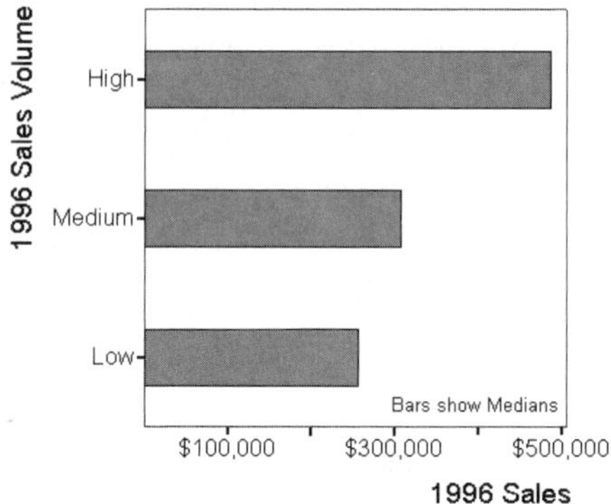
High
Medium
Low
1996 Sales Volume
Bars show Medians
$100,000
$300,000
$500,000
1996 Sales

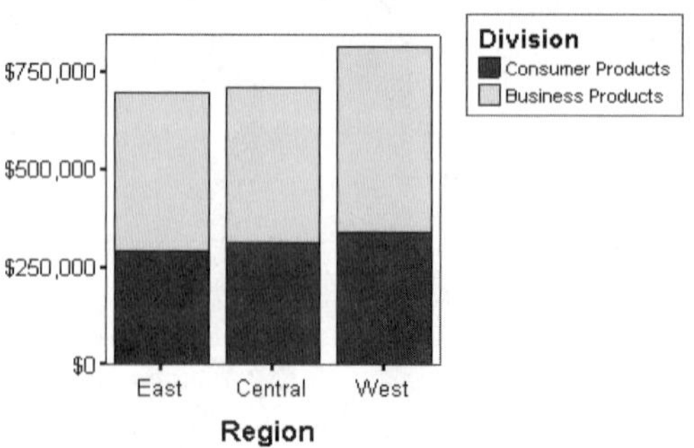
Average Sales by Region and Division
Division
Consumer Products
Business Products
$750,000
$500,000
$250,000
$0
East
Central
West
Region

To Create a Bar Chart

▶ From the menus choose:

Graphs
 Interactive
  Bar...

Create Bar Chart: Assign Variables

Figure 4-1
Create Bar Chart: Assign Variables tab

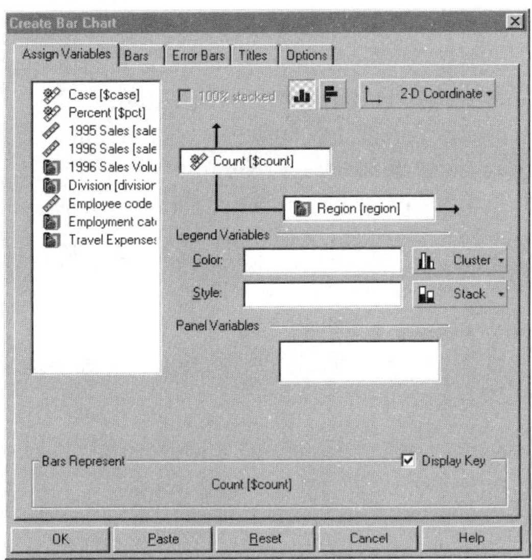

A bar chart presents summary statistics for one or more variables, most often within groups defined by one or two categorical variables. Bar length commonly represents a count of cases for each category, a percentage of the total number of cases, or a function of another variable (for example, the mean value for each category). The function can be changed near the bottom of the dialog box, and you can display a key that identifies the function.

Number of dimensions. Selecting 2-D Coordinate or 3-D Coordinate changes the number of axis targets for variable selection. Selecting 3-D Effect specifies that the bars are three-dimensional objects, lined up along one axis.

Orientation. Clicking the vertical or horizontal orientation icon sets up the appropriate axis targets for variable selection. Orientation icons are available only when 2-D Coordinate is selected.

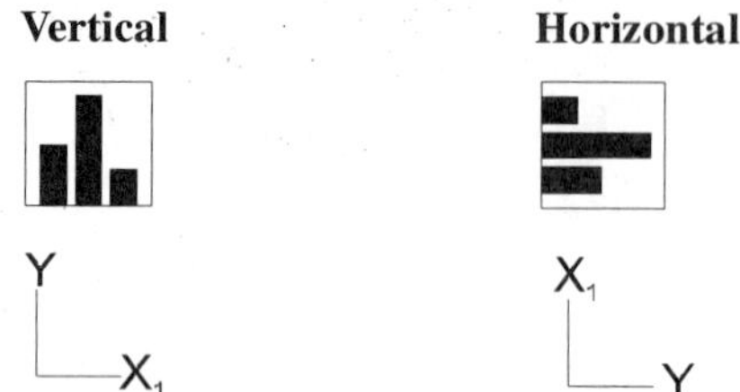

Clustered and Stacked Bars. If a categorical variable is assigned to Color or Style, the bars for categories can be clustered next to one another or stacked. In a stacked bar, the categories of the legend variable are stacked on top of one another. The top of one segment forms the base for the next segment. Because this type of chart emphasizes the sum of the categories, only functions appropriate for summation should be selected for stacking in Bars Represent. If a color or style stack legend has been selected, you can change the dependent axis to represent 100%. The segments then represent the percentage contributed by each category.

Case Variable. If the built-in variable *Case* is assigned to an axis, another target becomes available where you can assign a variable for labeling cases. For example, the labels might be days of the week or months.

Most of the charts shown below are vertical. To create a horizontal chart, click the horizontal orientation icon before or after dragging variables.

To Create a Simple Bar Chart

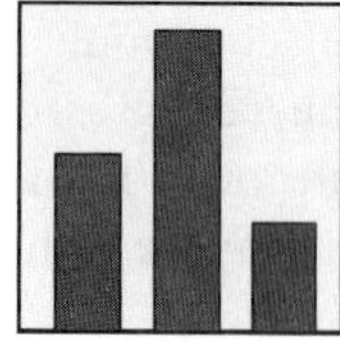 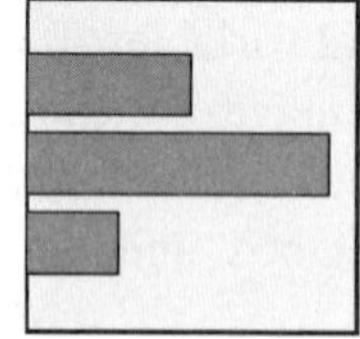 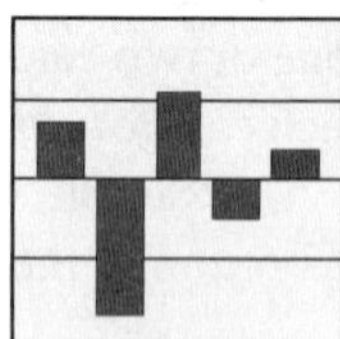

- ▶ Drag a variable (usually categorical) to the *x1* axis. This will be the base of the bars.
- ▶ Drag *Count* or a scale variable to the *y* axis (if one is not already there by default).

For another summary chart, you can use the built-in variable *Percent*.

Optionally, you can:

- Assign multiple variables to each axis by Shift-clicking.
- Swap the axes by clicking the orientation icon. The currently assigned variables swap with the axes.
- Change the bar baseline on the Bars tab.

To Create a Bar Chart Summarizing a Scale Variable

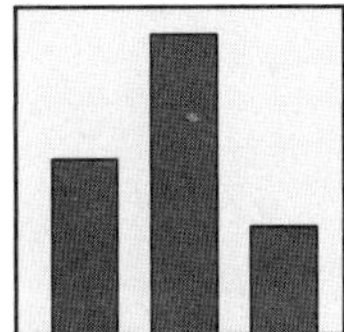

▶ Drag a variable (usually categorical) to the *x1* axis.

▶ Drag a scale variable to the *y* axis.

By default, the bars represent the mean of the scale variable.

Optionally, you can:

- Select another summary function from the Bars Represent drop-down list near the bottom of the dialog box.
- Choose whether to display the key. The key displays the name of the summary function on the chart.

To Create a Clustered Bar Chart

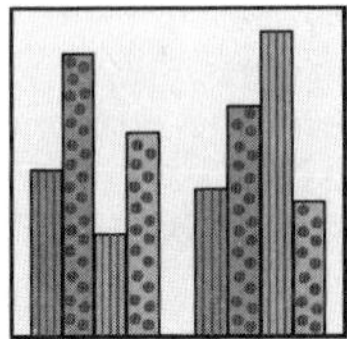

- Drag a variable (usually categorical) to the *x1* axis.
- Drag another variable to the *y* axis.
- Drag a categorical variable to Color or Style.

To Create a 3-D Bar Chart

- Select 3-D Coordinate from the drop-down list.

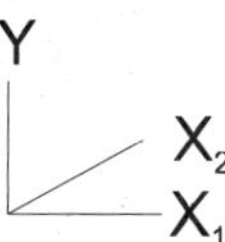

- Drag *Count* or another variable to the *y* axis.
- Drag variables (usually categorical) to the *x1* and *x2* axes. Assigning a scale variable to the *x1* or *x2* axis can result in a large number of bars.

To Create a Bar Chart of Individual Cases

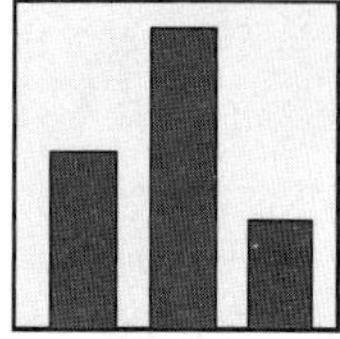

- Drag *Case* to the *x1* axis. The number of bars is equal to the number of cases.
- Right-click on *Case* and select Categorical (to avoid overlapping bars).

▶ Drag a variable (usually a scale variable) to the *y* axis.

Optionally, you can:

- Swap the axes by clicking the orientation icon. The currently assigned variables swap with the axes.
- Assign a variable for case labels.

Note: Bar charts that display values for individual cases are meaningful only if you select a summary variable for the dependent (*y*) axis. Summary functions such as mean, median, or mode will result in bars that display the value of the summary variable for each case. Counts, percentages, and summary functions that represent the number of cases or percentage of cases above or below a specified value will not reveal any particularly useful information when charting cases, since every case has a count of exactly 1.

To Create Bar Chart Panels for Categories

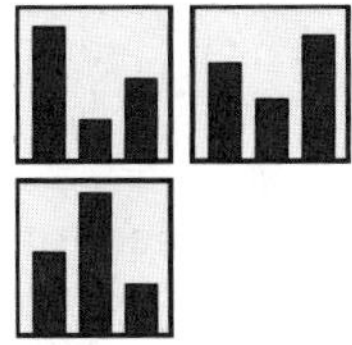

▶ Drag a variable (usually categorical) to the *x1* axis.

▶ Drag a scale variable or a built-in variable to the *y* axis.

▶ Drag one or more categorical variables to Panel Variables.

To Create a Bar Chart with Colors Assigned by a Scale Variable

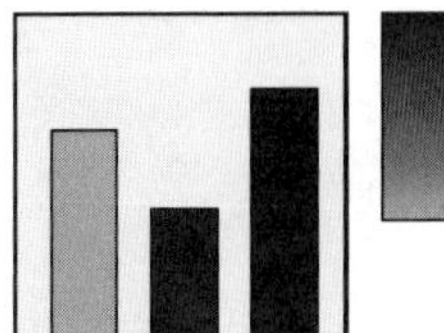

- Drag a variable (usually categorical) to the *x1* axis.
- Drag a scale variable or a built-in variable to the *y* axis.
- Drag a scale variable to Color.

  The color of each bar indicates the mean of the legend color variable for the category represented by the bar.

To Create a Bar Chart with a Scale Variable on the Independent Axis

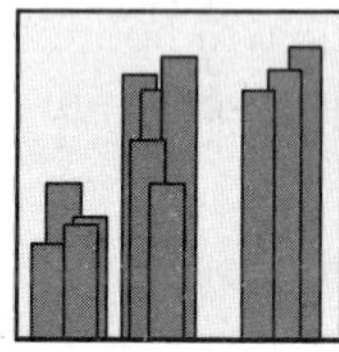

- Drag a scale variable to the *x1* axis.
- Drag a scale variable or a built-in variable to the *y* axis.

  The bars are spaced along the independent axis according to the values of the scale variable.

To Create a Bar Chart with Error Bars

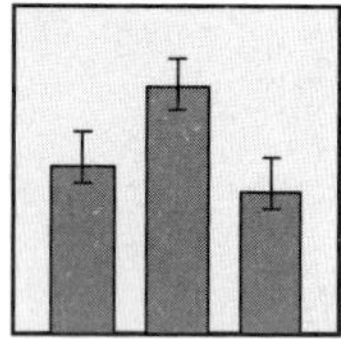

- Drag a categorical variable to the *x1* axis.
- Drag a scale variable to the *y* axis.
- Select Means as the summary function.

- Click the Error Bars tab and select Display Error Bars.
- Specify the properties of the error bars.

  Optionally, you can:

  - Specify a confidence interval or the number of standard deviations or the number of standard errors of the mean.
  - Specify the direction in relation to the bars in the chart.
  - Specify the look of the error bars.

To Create a Stacked Bar Chart

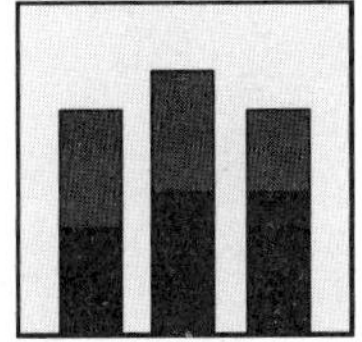 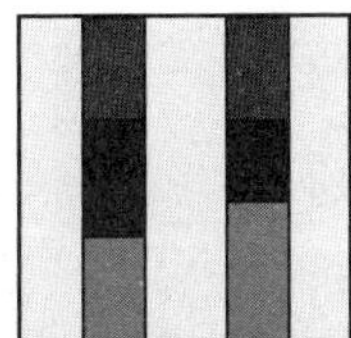

- Drag a categorical variable to the *x1* axis.
- Drag a scale variable to the *y* axis.
- Select Sums or another appropriate summary function.
- Drag a categorical variable to Color or Style and select Stack from the corresponding drop-down list.

  Optionally, you can display bar segments as percentages by selecting 100% Stacked.

To Create a Bar Chart with 3-D Effect

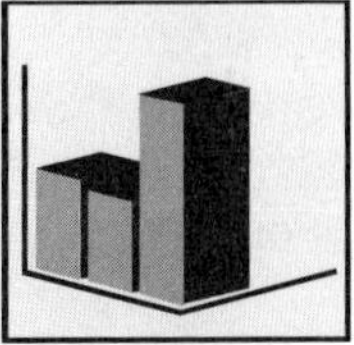

- Select the vertical orientation icon.
- Select 3-D Effect from the orientation drop-down list.
- Drag a categorical variable to the *x1* axis.
- Drag a built-in or scale variable to the *y* axis.

Optionally, you can activate the chart and rotate the axes.

Create Bar Chart: Bars

Figure 4-2
Create Bar Chart: Bars tab

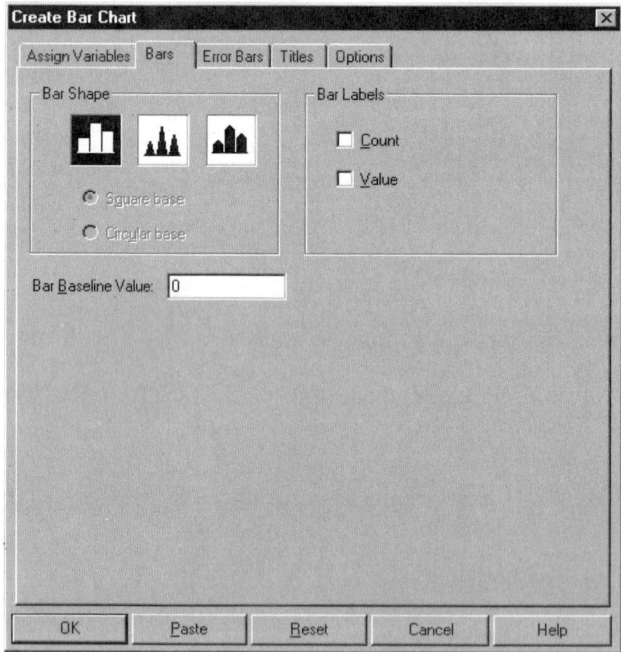

Several options are available to enhance bar charts.

Bar Shape. Displays rectangles, pyramids, or monuments. For 3-D bars, the shape of the base can be round or square.

Bar Labels. Displays labels giving the count (number of cases) and the value represented by the length of the bar.

Bar Baseline Value. Sets the location of the baseline from which bars will hang (vertical bars) or extend (horizontal bars). The baseline emphasizes the differences between the groups below and above the baseline.

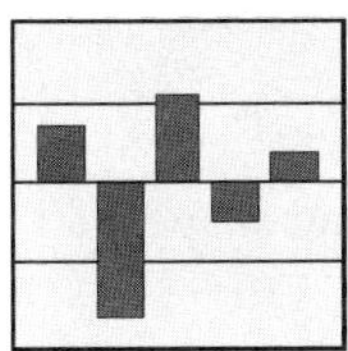

Create Bar Chart: Error Bars

Figure 4-3
Create Bar Chart: Error Bars tab

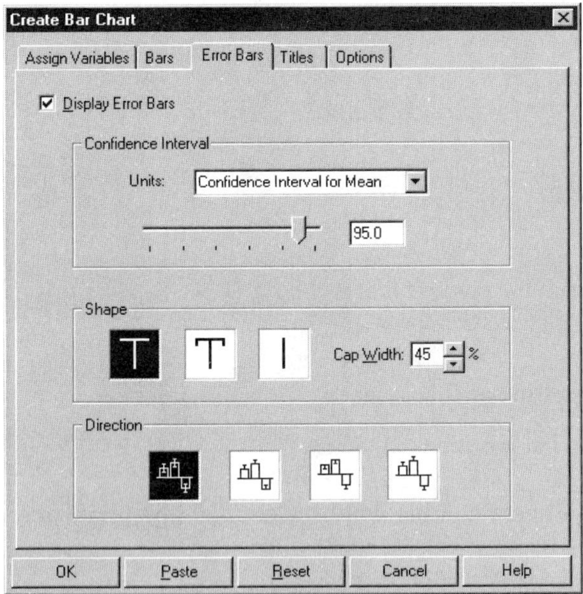

Error bars, indicating the variability of the measure displayed, are available when the dependent variable is a scale variable and bars or lines represent the summary function *Means*. The length of an error bar represents the amount of variability. The length of the error bars is displayed as the lower and upper limits of a confidence interval (at a specified percentage level) or in standard deviations or standard errors of the mean.

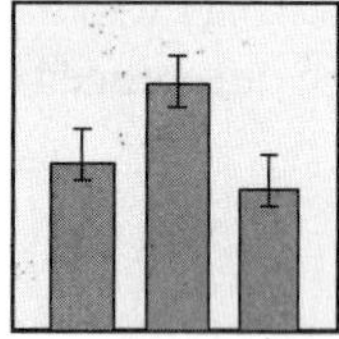

You can specify the confidence interval's level, direction, and shape, and change the appearance of error bars.

Modifying Bars

To modify the bar element (all bars) in an existing chart:

▶ Activate the chart by clicking it.

▶ From the menus choose:

Format
  Graph Elements
    Bars

or

▶ Right-click a bar and from the context menu choose:

Bars...

▶ Select the desired changes in bar shape, labels, fill, and borders.

You can also change the bar baseline.

To change the summary function or bar width, select the appropriate tabs in the Bars dialog box.

Bars: Bar Options

Figure 4-4
Bars: Bar Options tab

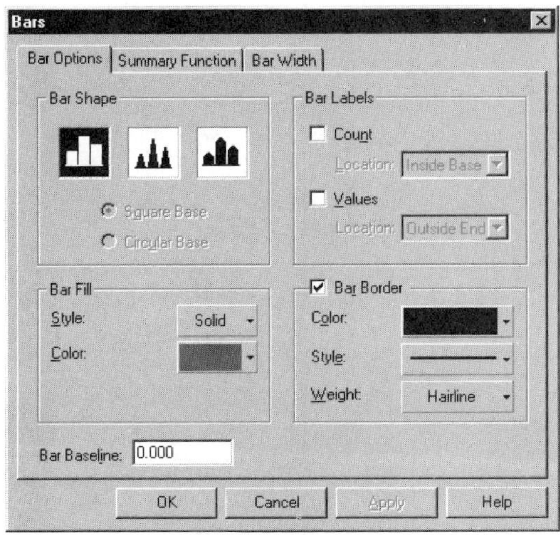

Several options are available to enhance bar charts.

Bar Shape. Displays rectangles, pyramids, or monuments. For 3-D bars, the shape of the base can be round or square.

Bar Labels. Displays labels giving the number of cases or the value represented by the length of each bar.

Bar Fill. Fills all bars in the chart with the selected style and color. Style or color that is controlled by the data is not available for change.

Bar Border. Sets the border style, color, and weight for all bars in the chart.

Bar Baseline. Sets the location of the baseline from which bars will hang (vertical bars) or extend (horizontal bars). The baseline emphasizes the differences between the groups below and above the baseline.

Bars: Summary Function

Figure 4-5
Bars: Summary Function tab

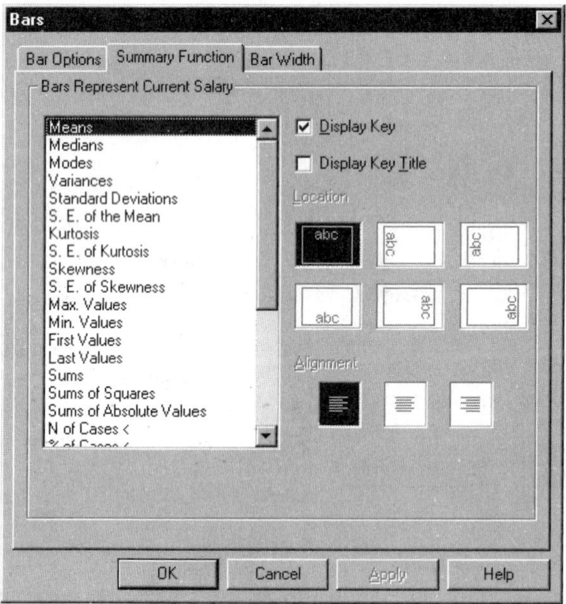

For an existing chart, if there is a scale variable on the dependent axis, you can change the summary function. For example, if the original bars represent the *means* of a variable, you can change to the *maximum values* of the same variable.

Key display options. These selections change the way summary information is displayed in the chart. You can display the key and determine the alignment and location of the key title.

Bars: Bar Width

Figure 4-6
Bars: Bar Width tab

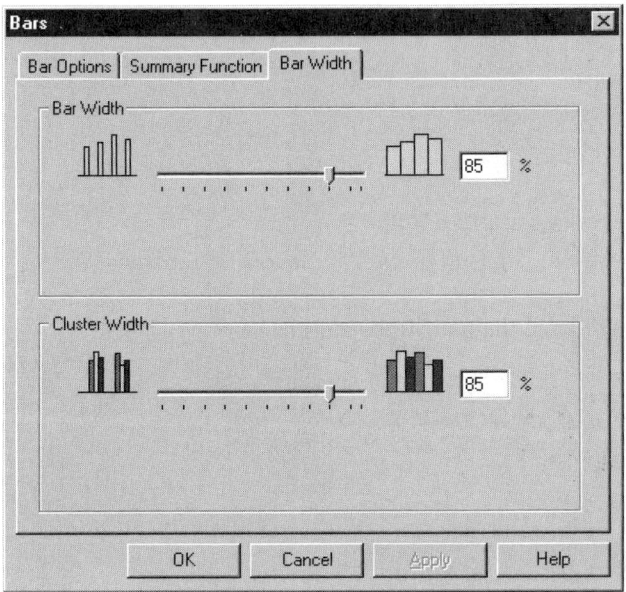

After bars are created, you can change the width of the bars or of clusters by dragging the appropriate slider.

Changing Individual Bar Properties

Individual bars or a selection of several bars have the properties Fill, Border, and Labels, which can be changed as long as the property is not controlled by the data. For example, in a simple bar chart, you can change the color of each bar. However, in a clustered bar chart in which color is used to distinguish categories, the color of a group of bars in one category can be changed only for the whole group in the legend.

To Change Bar Properties

- ▶ Activate the chart by clicking it.
- ▶ Select one or more bars in a bar chart.
- ▶ From the menus choose:

  Edit
   Bar Properties...

  or

- ▶ Right-click a bar or selected group of bars and choose Properties.

Optionally, you can change the bar fill, border, or labels.

Bar Properties

Figure 4-7
Bar Properties dialog box

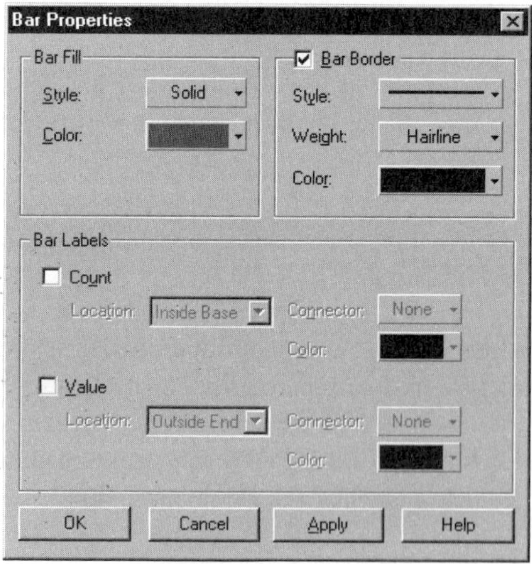

Changes to the properties apply only to currently selected bars.

Bar Fill. The style and color of the selected bars can be changed, if they are not controlled by the data assignments.

Bar Border. If borders are on (selected), you can change the style, color, or weight.

Bar Labels. Labels can show the number of cases (count) used to calculate the value for each bar and the value represented by each bar. For each type of label, the location, type of connector, and connector color can be set.

Chapter

5

Boxplots

A boxplot characterizes the distribution and dispersion of a variable, displaying its median and quartiles. Special symbols identify the position of outliers and extreme values, if any. Simple boxplots display boxes for a single scale variable. The cases can be grouped by the values of a categorical variable. Clustered boxplots display a cluster of boxes for each value of another categorical variable.

Sample Output

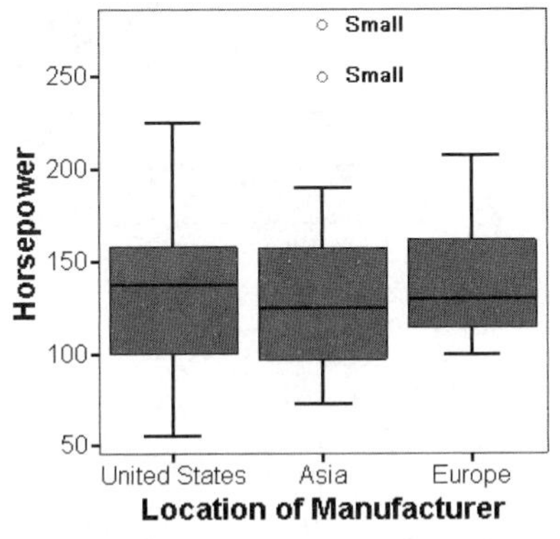

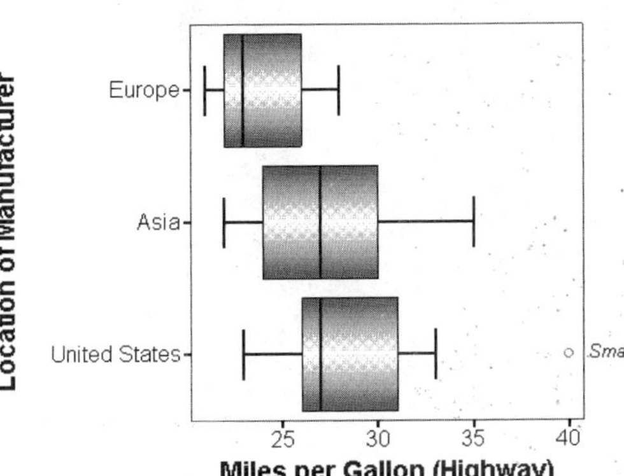

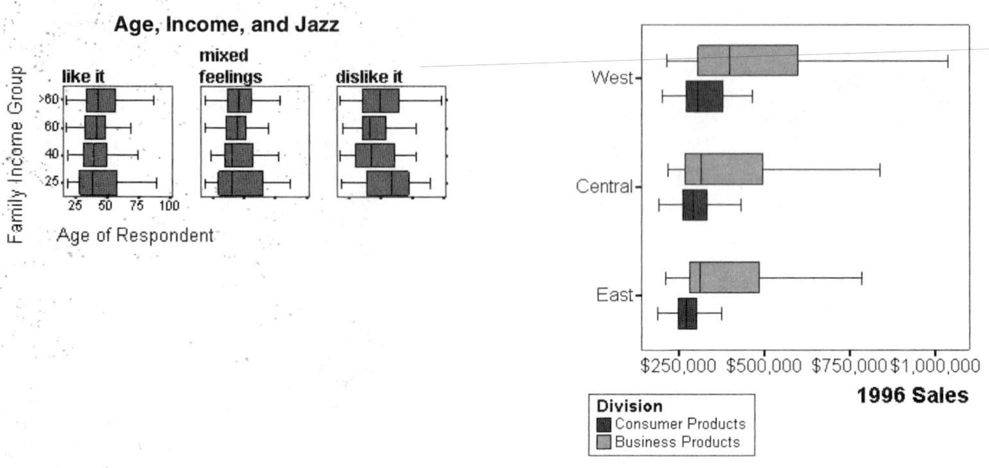
Age, Income, and Jazz
like it
mixed feelings
dislike it
Family Income Group
>60
60
40
25
25 50 75 100
Age of Respondent
West
Central
East
$250,000 $500,000 $750,000 $1,000,000
1996 Sales
Division
Consumer Products
Business Products

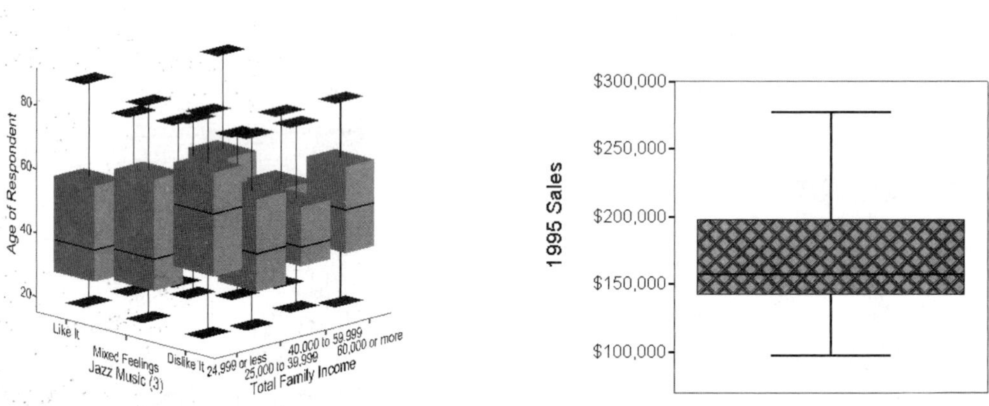
Age of Respondent
80
60
40
20
Like It
Mixed Feelings
Dislike It
Jazz Music (3)
24,999 or less
25,000 to 39,999
40,000 to 59,999
60,000 or more
Total Family Income
1995 Sales
$300,000
$250,000
$200,000
$150,000
$100,000

To Create an Interactive Boxplot

▶ From the menus choose:

Graphs
  Interactive
    Boxplot...

Create Boxplot: Assign Variables

Figure 5-1
Create Boxplot: Assign Variables tab

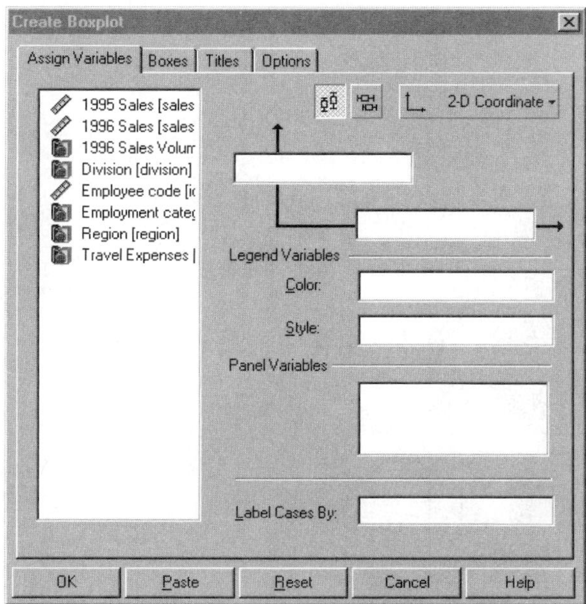

A boxplot, sometimes called a box-and-whiskers plot, shows the median, quartiles, and outlier and extreme values for a scale variable. It can be split into categories and clusters.

Number of dimensions. Selecting 2-D Coordinate or 3-D Coordinate changes the number of axis targets for variable selection. Selecting 3-D Effect specifies that the boxes are three-dimensional objects, lined up along one axis.

Orientation. Clicking an orientation (vertical or horizontal) icon sets up the appropriate axis targets, as shown, for variable selection. Orientation icons are available only when 2-D Coordinate is selected.

Many of the charts shown below are horizontal. To create a vertical chart, click the vertical icon before or after dragging variables.

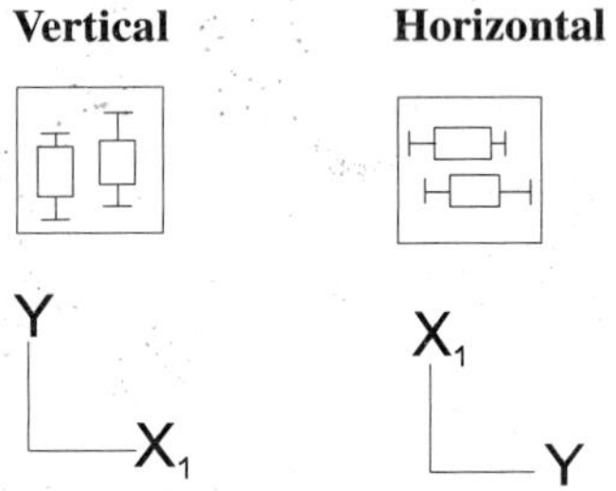

To Create a Simple Boxplot

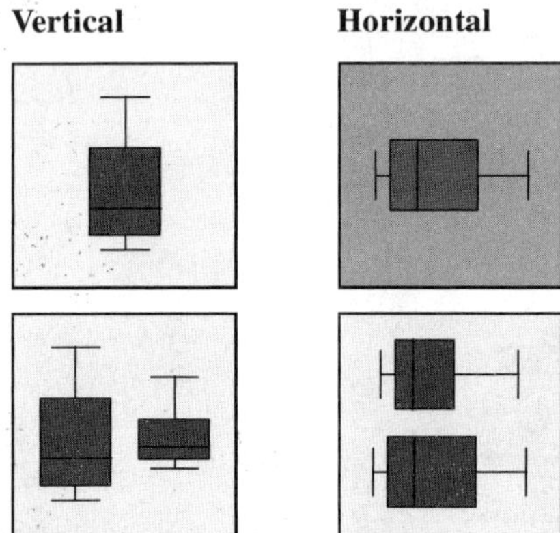

- ▶ Drag a scale variable to the *y* axis. This is sufficient to draw a boxplot of a single variable.

- ▶ To display boxes for separate categories, drag a categorical variable to the *x1* axis.

Optionally, you can:

- Drag a variable to Label Cases By, for identifying the outliers and extremes.

- Swap the axes by clicking the orientation icon. Currently assigned variables swap, along with the axes.
- Use a scale variable on the *x1* axis, although this assignment can create a large number of boxes.

To Create a Clustered Boxplot

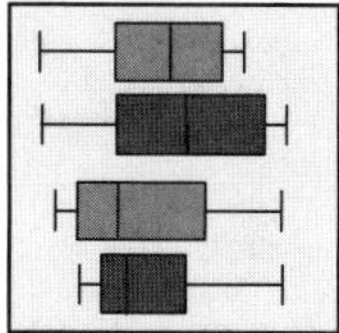

- ▶ Drag a variable (usually categorical) to the *x1* axis.
- ▶ Drag a scale variable to the *y* axis.
- ▶ Drag a categorical variable to Color or Style (or both).

Optionally, you can:

- Swap the axes by clicking the orientation icon. Currently assigned variables swap, along with the axes.

To Create a 3-D Boxplot

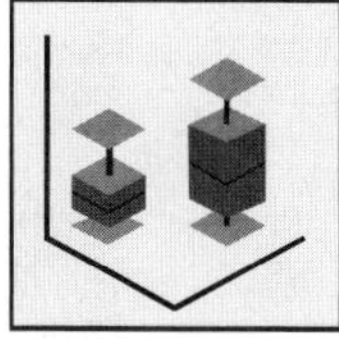

- ▶ Select 3-D Coordinate from the drop-down list.

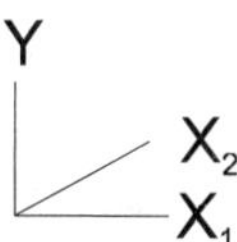

- Drag a scale variable to the *y* axis.
- Drag variables (usually categorical) to the *x1* and *x2* axes.

To Create Boxplot Panels for Categories

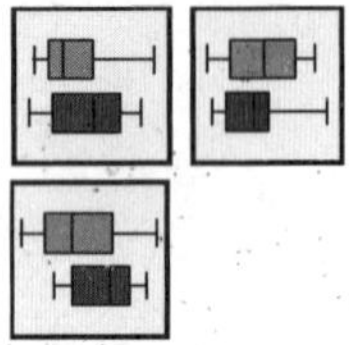

- Drag a variable (usually categorical) to the *x1* axis.
- Drag a scale variable to the *y* axis.
- Drag one or more categorical variables to Panel Variables.

To Create a Boxplot with Colors Assigned by a Summary of a Scale Variable

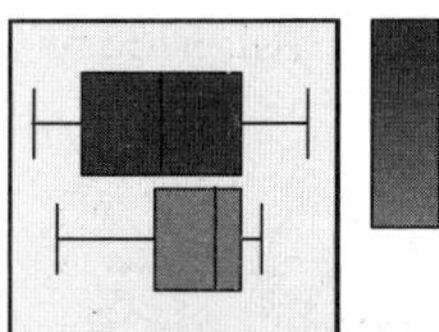

- Drag a variable (usually categorical) to the *x1* axis.
- Drag a scale variable to the *y* axis.
- Drag a scale variable to Color.

  The color of each box indicates the mean of the color variable for the category represented by the box.

Create Boxplot: Boxes

Figure 5-2
Create Boxplot: Boxes tab

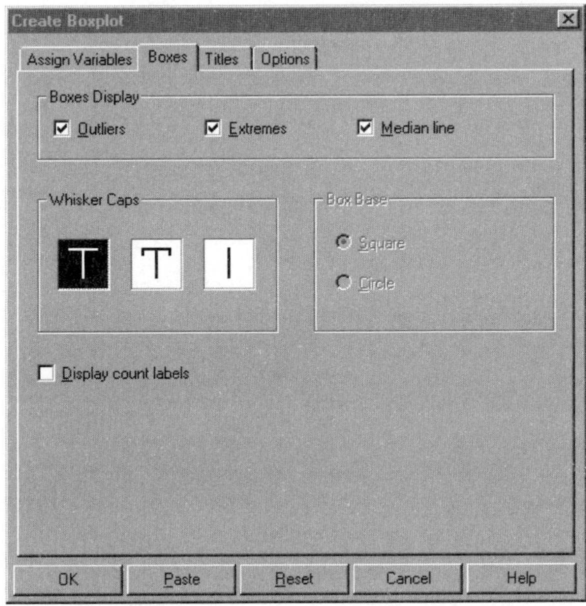

Several options are available to enhance boxplots.

Boxes Display. Outliers, extremes, and the median line can be displayed for each box. Outliers are between 1.5 box lengths and 3 box lengths from the end of the box. Extremes are more than 3 box lengths from the end of the box.

Whisker Caps. Several shapes are available for the cap at the end of each whisker in a 2-D boxplot.

Box Base. The bases of 3-D boxes can be square or circular.

Display count labels. When selected, the number of cases included in each category is displayed.

Modifying Boxes

To modify the box element (all boxes) in an existing chart:

- ▶ Activate the chart (double-click it).
- ▶ From the menus choose:

Format
  Graph Elements
    Box

or

- ▶ Right-click a box and from the context menu choose:

Boxes...

- ▶ Select the desired changes.

Boxes: Box Options

Figure 5-3
Boxes: Box Options tab

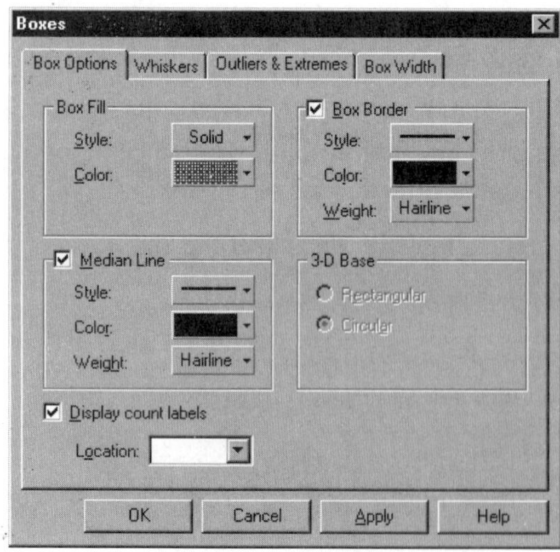

Several options are available to enhance boxes.

Box Fill. Fills all boxes in the chart with the selected style and color. If style or color is controlled by the data, it cannot be changed.

Box Border. Sets the border style, color, and weight for all boxes in the chart. This option is available only for 2-D charts.

Median Line. Displays the median line in each box. You can change style, weight, and color.

Display count labels. Count labels show how many cases contribute to each box. If count labels have been dragged to another position, you can use the location to bring them back to the base.

3-D Base. The base for 3-D boxes can be rectangular or circular.

Boxes: Whiskers

Figure 5-4
Boxes: Whiskers tab

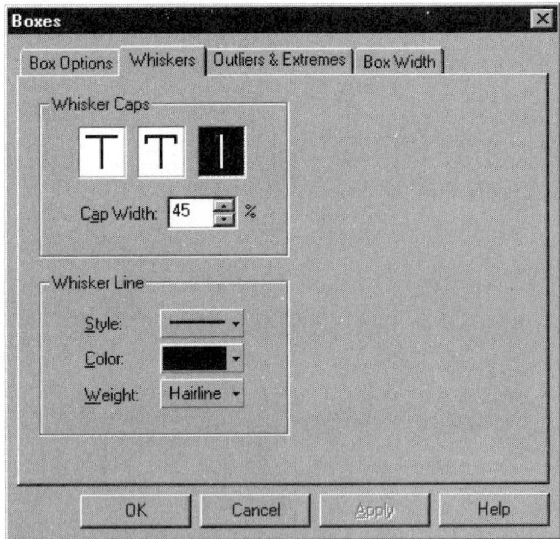

Whiskers at the ends of the box show the distance from the end of the box to the largest and smallest observed values that are less than 1.5 box lengths from either end of the box.

Whisker Caps. The whisker caps can have different shapes. The width of the cap is set as a percentage of the width of a box.

Whisker Line. The line extending from the end of each box can have style, color, and weight assigned.

Boxes: Outliers and Extremes

Figure 5-5
Boxes: Outliers & Extremes tab

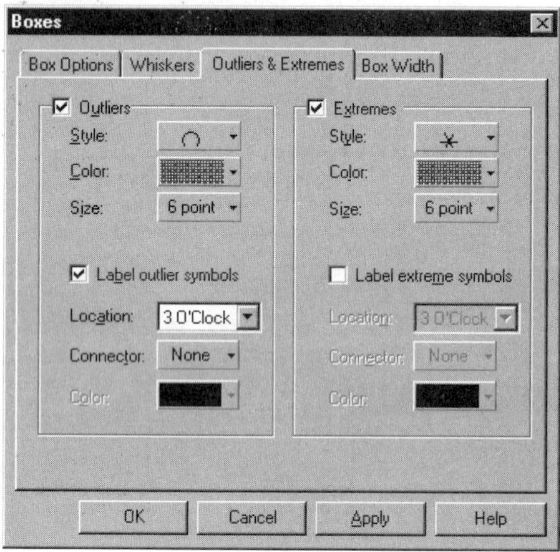

Cases far from the box on either end can be displayed or suppressed. Also, their styles, labels, and label connectors can be changed.

Outliers. Cases with values that are between 1.5 and 3 box lengths from either end of the box.

Extremes. Cases with values more than 3 box lengths from either end of the box.

Boxes: Box Width

Figure 5-6
Boxes: Box Width tab

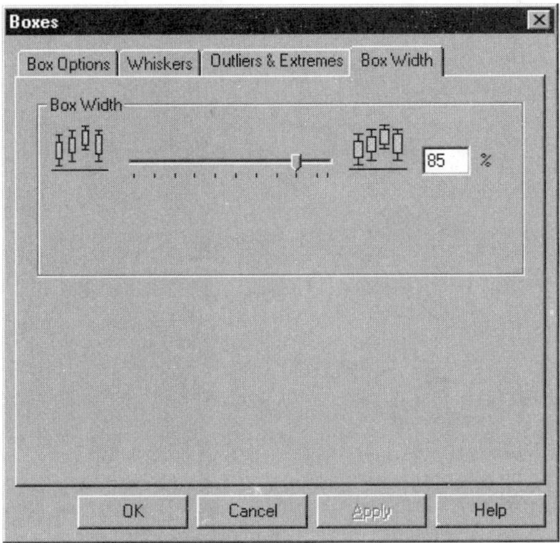

After boxes are created, you can change the width of the boxes or the width of clusters of boxes by dragging a slider.

Changing Individual Box Properties

Individual boxes or a selection of several boxes have the properties Fill, Border, and Median Line, which can be changed if the property is not controlled by the data. For example, in a simple boxplot, you can change the color of each individual box. However, in a clustered boxplot in which color is used to distinguish categories, the color of a group of boxes in one category can be changed only for the whole group in the legend.

In addition to selecting the boxes in the display, you can also select whiskers of a box, the confidence interval, or individual outlier or extreme symbols. Boxes are unique elements in that their individual parts can be selected, but a box, whiskers, and median cannot be selected by using Shift-click. You can select several whiskers, several extremes, several boxes, or several medians.

To Change Box Properties

▶ Activate the chart (double-click it).

▶ Select one or more boxes, medians, or whiskers.

▶ From the menus choose:

Edit
  Box Properties

or

▶ Right-click a box or selected group of boxes or whiskers or medians, and choose Properties.

Depending on which part is selected, you can:

- Change the fill, border, or median line, or display count labels.
- Change the whisker style, color, or weight.
- Change the symbol label properties.

Box Properties

Figure 5-7
Box Properties dialog box

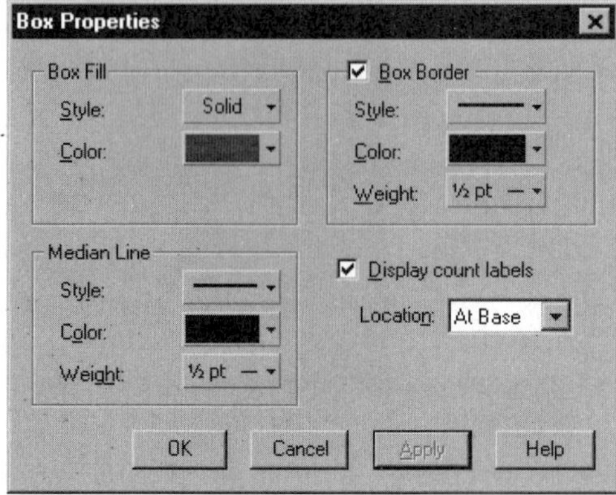

The properties apply only to currently selected boxes or median lines.

Box Fill. The style and color of the selected boxes can be changed, if not controlled by the data.

Box Border. If borders are on (selected), you can change the style, color, or weight.

Median Line. The style, color, and weight of the median lines can be changed.

Display count labels. Labels can show the number of cases for each box.

Box Symbol Properties

Figure 5-8
Box Symbol Properties dialog box

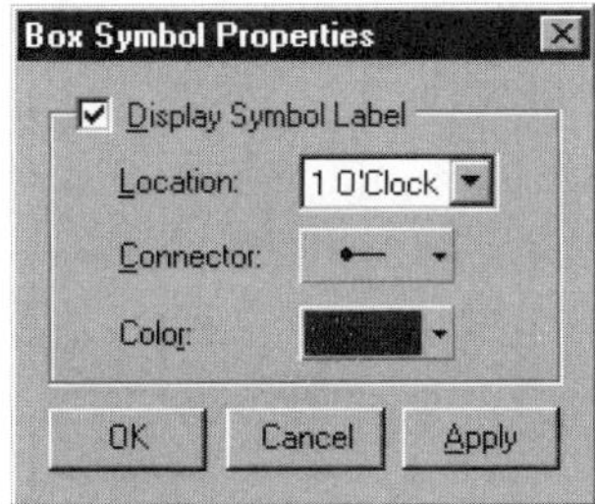

The properties apply only to currently selected extremes and outliers.

Display Symbol Label. Symbols are labeled with values of the label variable (assigned when the chart was created). If no variable was specified, the extremes and outliers are labeled with case numbers.

Changing the label variable. If the chart is live (still connected to the original data), the label variable can be changed in Assign Variables.

Box Whisker Properties

Figure 5-9
Box Whisker Properties dialog box

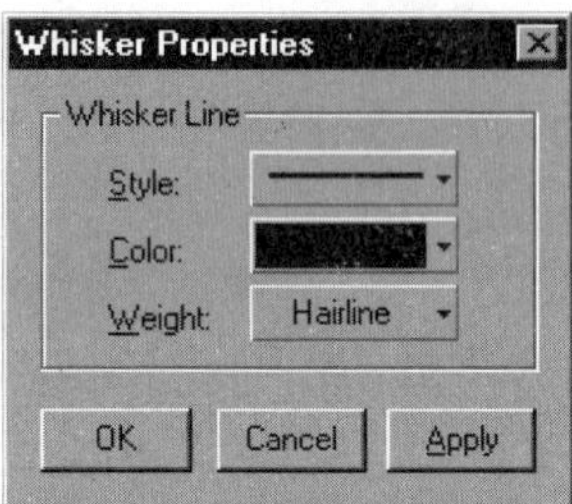

The properties apply only to currently selected whiskers.

Whisker Line. You can change the style, color, or weight of the lines that make up the whiskers.

Chapter

6

Error Bars

Error bars indicate the variability of the measure displayed. Error bars can be built around the mean. They are often used in conjunction with other elements—for example, an error bar element can be added to a bar chart.

Sample Output

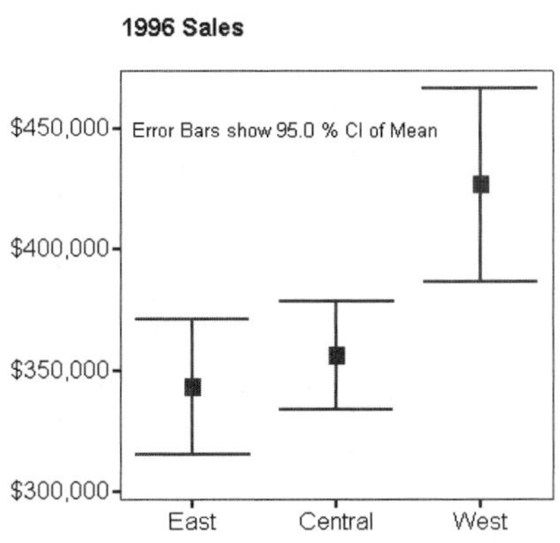

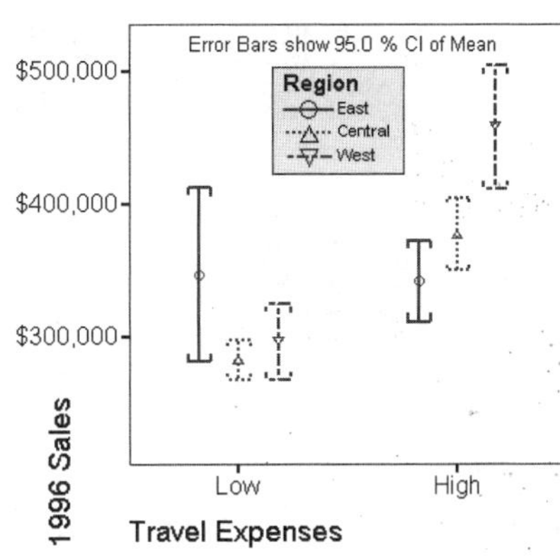

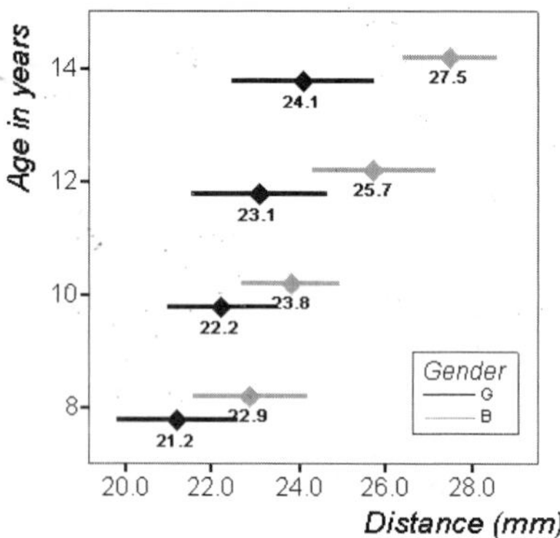

Error Bar Charts with Other Graph Elements

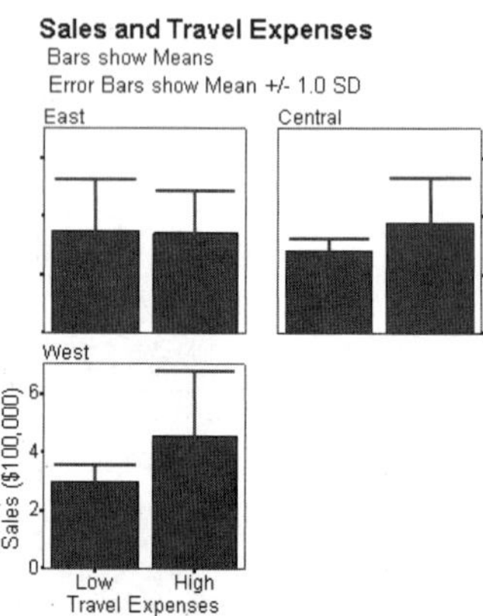

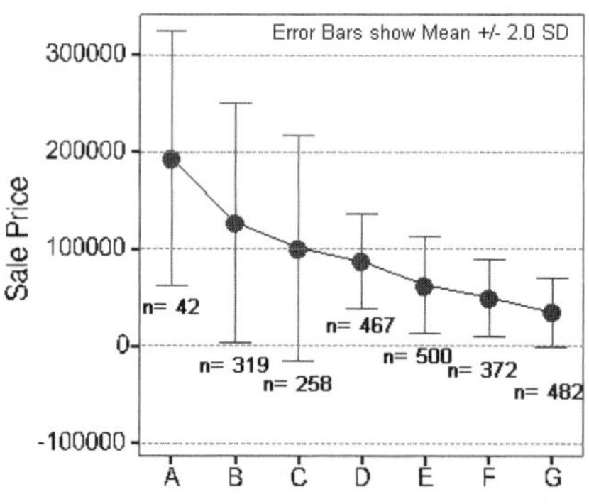

To Create an Error Bar Chart

▶ From the menus choose:

Graphs
  Interactive
    Error Bar...

Create Error Bar Chart: Assign Variables

Figure 6-1
Create Error Bar Chart: Assign Variables tab

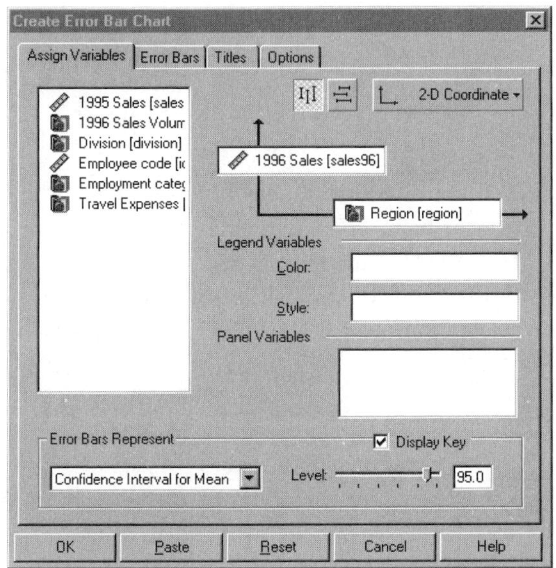

Error bars help you visualize distributions and dispersion by indicating the variability of the measure being displayed. The mean of a scale variable is plotted for a set of categories, and the length of an error bar on either side of the mean value indicates a confidence interval or a specified number of standard errors or standard deviations. Error bars can extend in one direction or both directions from the mean.

Error bars are sometimes displayed in the same chart with other chart elements such as bars or lines.

Number of dimensions. Selecting 2-D Coordinate or 3-D Coordinate changes the number of axis targets for variable selection. Selecting 3-D Effect specifies that the error bars are three-dimensional objects, displayed in a row.

Orientation. Clicking an orientation (vertical or horizontal) icon sets up the appropriate axis targets for variable selection. Orientation icons are available only when 2-D Coordinate is selected.

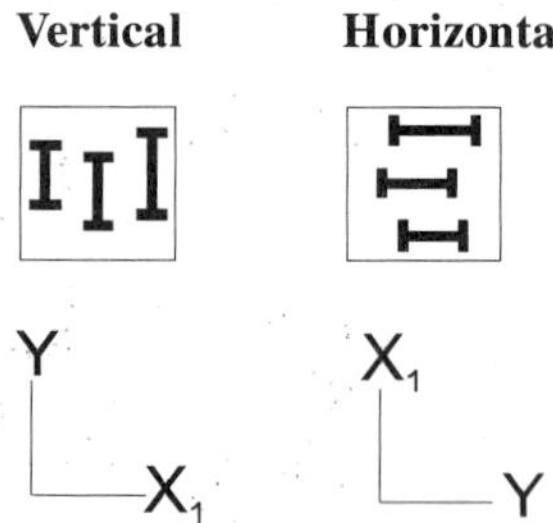

Error Bars Represent. Lists the statistics and summary functions available for determining the lengths of the error bars. You can display a key that identifies the function. On a confidence interval for the mean, you can specify a percentage for the level. The number of standard deviations or standard errors represented is determined by the multiplier, which can be any number greater than 0 and less than or equal to 6.

To Create a Simple Error Bar Chart

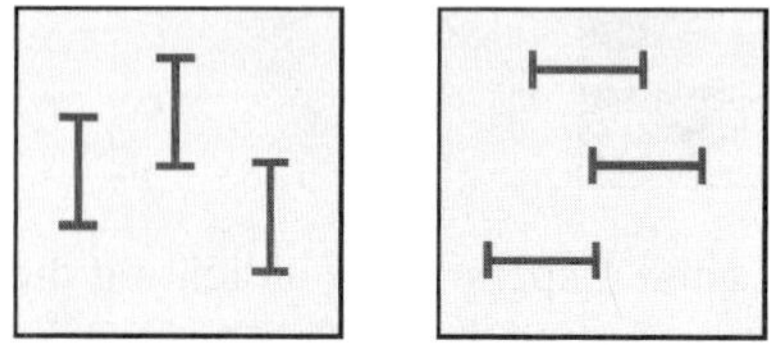

▶ Drag a variable (usually categorical) to the *x1* axis.

▶ Drag a scale variable to the *y* axis.

By default, the length of the error bars represents the confidence interval around the mean.

Optionally, you can:

- Change the statistic used to determine the length of the error bars.
- Change the multiplier for standard deviation or standard error.
- Change the percentage level of the confidence interval.
- Swap the axes by clicking the orientation icon. Previously assigned variables swap, along with the axes.

To Create a Clustered Error Bar Chart

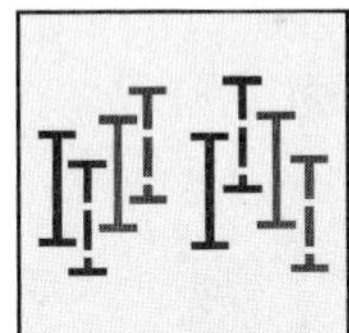

- Drag a categorical variable to the *x1* axis.
- Drag a scale variable to the *y* axis.
- Drag categorical variables to Color, Style, or both.

To Create a 3-D Error Bar Chart

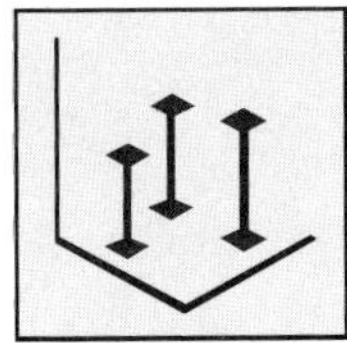

- Select 3-D Coordinate from the drop-down list.

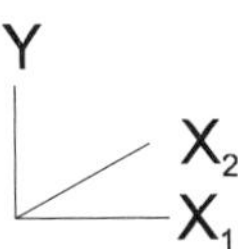

- Drag a scale variable to the *y* axis.
- Drag categorical variables to the *x1* and *x2* axes.

To Create an Error Bar Chart with Colors Assigned by a Summary of a Scale Variable

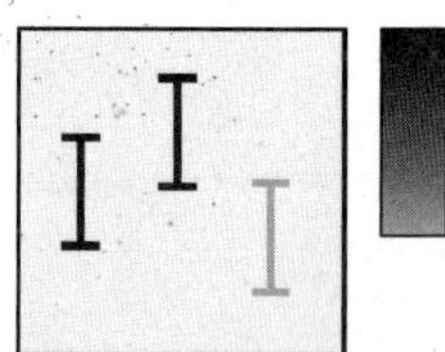

- Drag a categorical variable to the *x1* axis.
- Drag a scale variable to the *y* axis.
- Drag a scale variable to Color.

  The color of each error bar indicates the mean of the legend color variable for the category represented by the error bar.

To Create Error Bar Panels for Categories

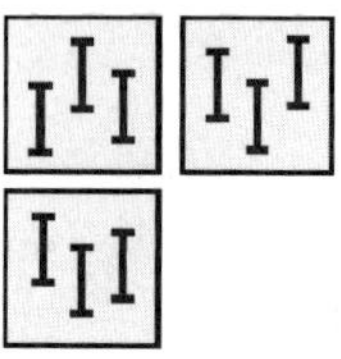

- Drag a variable to the *x1* axis.
- Drag a scale variable to the *y* axis.
- Drag one or more categorical variables to Panel Variables.

Create Error Bar Chart: Error Bars

Figure 6-2
Create Error Bar Chart: Error Bars tab

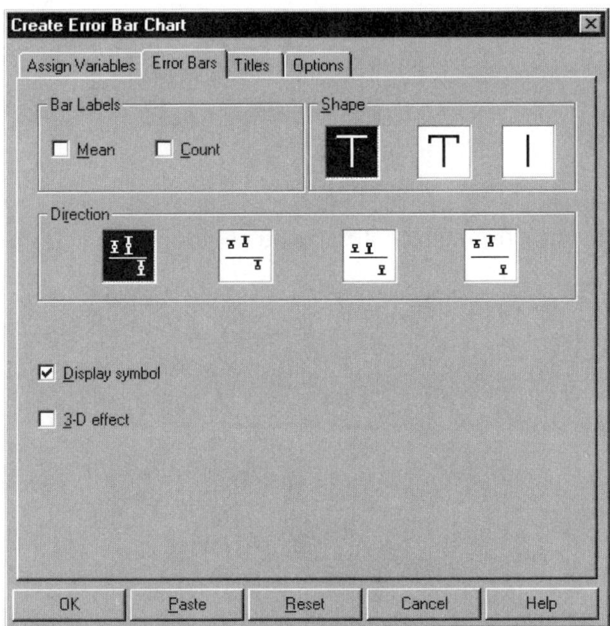

Several options are available to enhance error bar charts.

Bar Labels. The number of cases (count) and the value of the mean can be displayed.

Direction. Arranges the error bars. Error bars can show the part above the mean, the part below the mean, or both. Error bars can also be based on values above or below the baseline.

Shape. Various shapes are available for the caps at the ends of the error bars.

Display symbol. Determines whether a marker is displayed at the mean value for each error bar.

Modifying Error Bars

To modify the error bar element (all error bars) in an existing chart:

▶ From the menus choose:

Format
  Graph Elements
    Error Bar

or

▶ Right-click an error bar and from the context menu choose:

Error Bars...

▶ Select the desired changes.

Error Bar: Error Bar Options

Figure 6-3
Error Bar: Error Bar Options tab

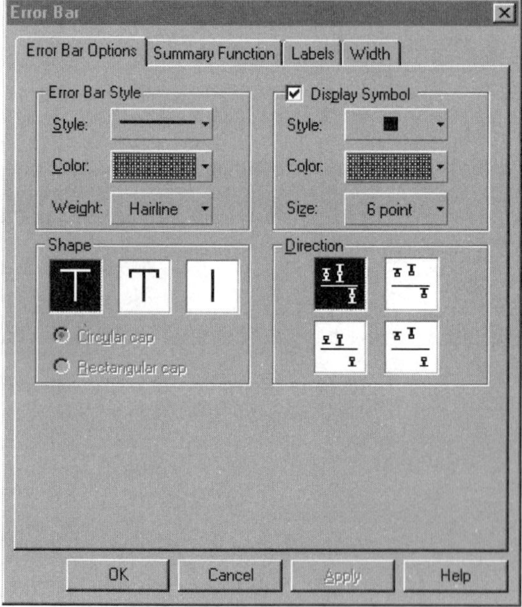

Several options are available to enhance error bars.

Error Bar Style. Changes the style, color, or weight for all error bars in the chart. If the color or style is controlled by the data, you cannot change them with this option.

Display Symbol. Changes the symbol marker, color, and size of the symbols at the mean values. If the color or style is controlled by the data, you cannot change them with this option.

Shape. Various shapes are available for the caps on the ends of the error bars.

Direction. Arranges the error bars. Error bars can show the part above the mean, the part below the mean, or both. Error bars can also be based on values above or below the baseline.

Error Bar: Summary Function

Figure 6-4
Error Bar: Summary Function tab

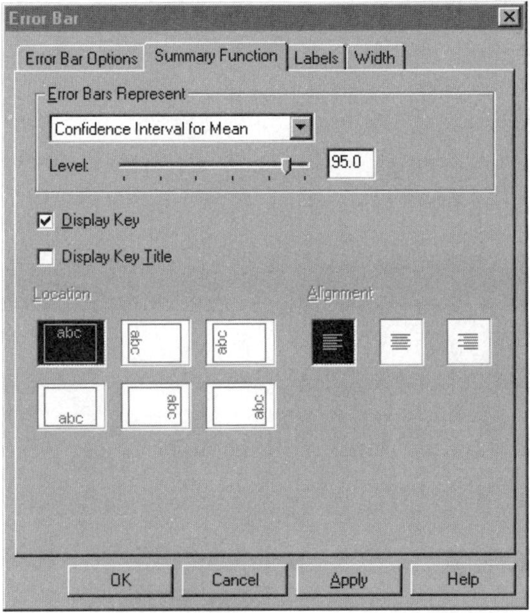

Error Bars Represent. Lists the statistics available for determining the lengths of the error bars. On a confidence interval for the mean, you can specify a percentage for the level. The number of standard deviations or standard errors represented is determined by the multiplier, which can be any number greater than 0 and less than or equal to 6.

Display key options. These selections change the way summary information is displayed in the chart. You can display the key and determine the alignment and location of the key title.

Error Bar: Labels

Figure 6-5
Error Bar: Labels tab

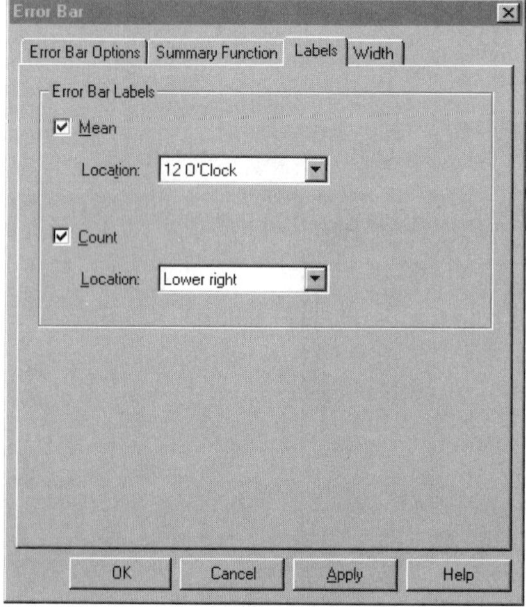

Labels can be displayed that show the values of the count or mean for each category. Each type of label can have its own location within the chart.

Error Bar: Width

Figure 6-6
Error Bar: Width tab

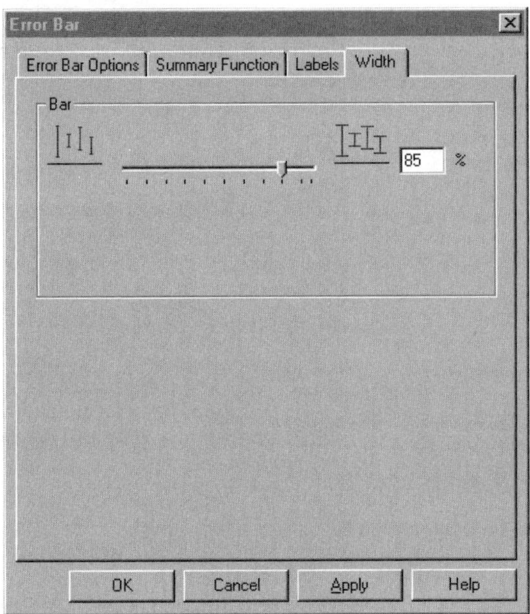

After error bars are created, you can change the width of the bar caps or the width of clusters by dragging the slider.

Changing Error Bar Properties

Individual error bars or a selection of several error bars have a style, symbol, and labels that can be changed as long as the property is not controlled by the data.

To Change Error Bar Properties

- Select one or more error bars.

▶ From the menus choose:

Format
  Properties...

or

▶ Right-click an error bar or selected group of error bars and choose Properties.

Optionally, you can:

- Change the line style or symbol.
- Turn labels and their connectors on or off.

Error Bar Properties

Figure 6-7
Error Bar Properties dialog box

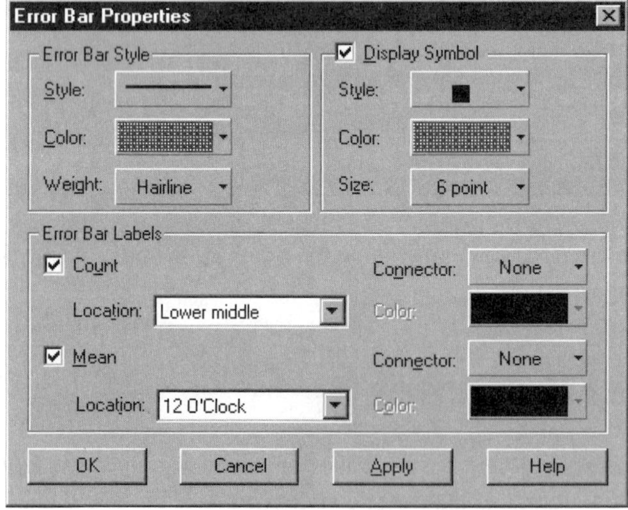

The properties apply only to currently selected error bars.

Error Bar Style. The style, color, and weight of the selected error bars can be changed, if they are not controlled by the data.

Display Symbol. A symbol style can be selected and its color and size specified. This symbol is at the mean value.

Error Bar Labels. Bar labels can be turned on or off and their locations specified. For each type of label, the connector style and color can be specified.

Chapter

7

Histograms

Often, an investigator wants to know how data are distributed across a range of values. A **histogram** shows the distribution of values in a quantitative variable by dividing the range into equally spaced intervals and plotting the count of cases in each interval as a bar. Instead of the count of cases, you can also plot the percentage. A cumulative option is also available.

Sample Output

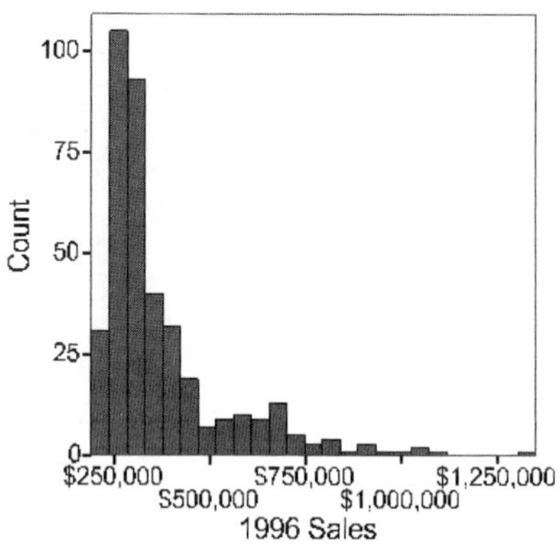

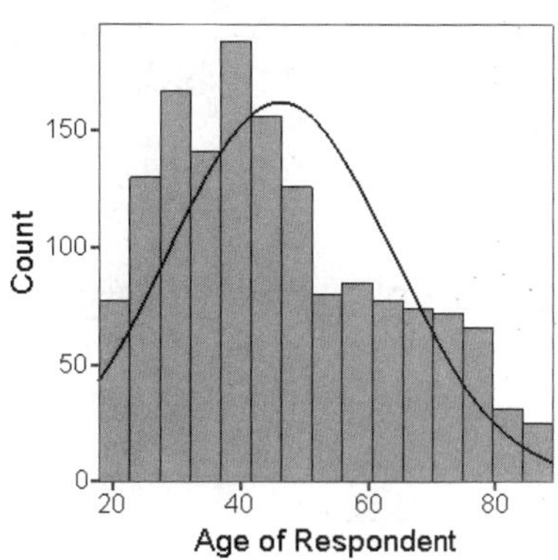

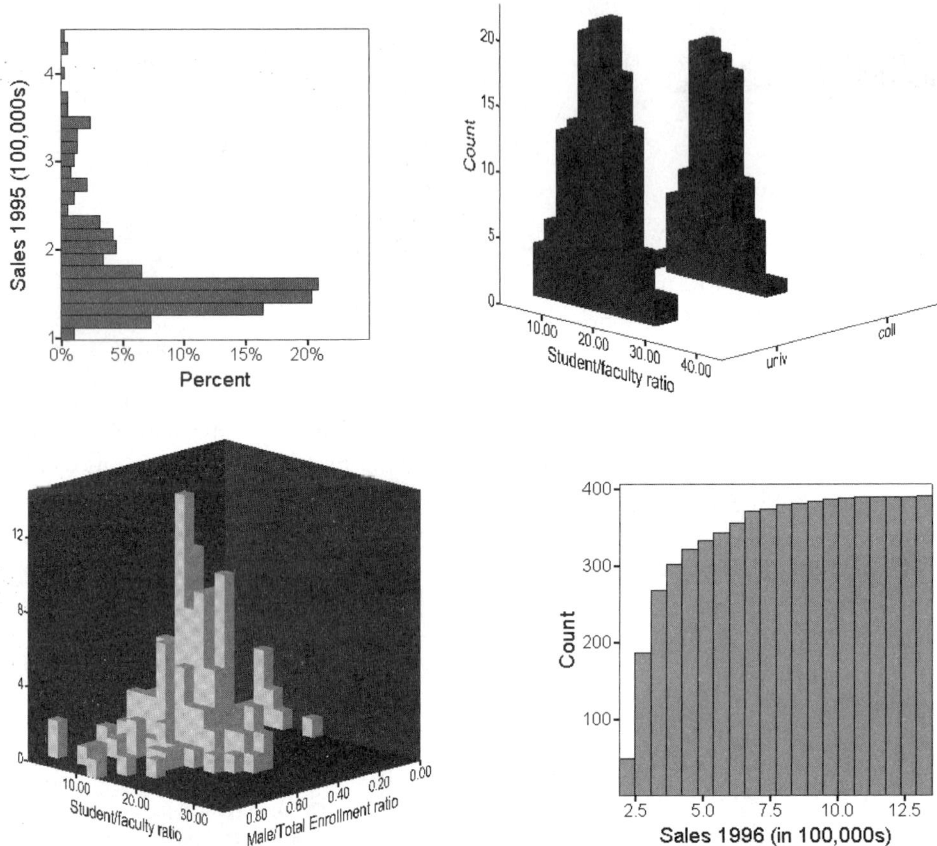

To Create a Histogram

▶ From the menus choose:

Graphs
  Interactive
    Histogram...

Create Histogram: Assign Variables

Figure 7-1
Create Histogram: Assign Variables tab

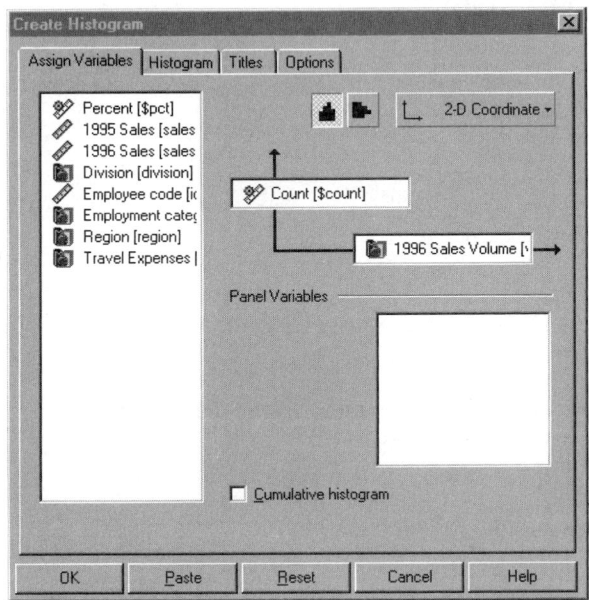

A histogram groups the values of a variable into evenly spaced groups (intervals or bins) and plots a count of the number of cases in each group. The count can be expressed as a percentage. Percentages are useful for comparing data sets of different sizes. The count or percentage can also be accumulated across the groups.

A histogram can indicate outliers and deviations from symmetry. Such deviations can indicate that a variable is unsuitable for analysis by a procedure that assumes a normal distribution.

Number of dimensions. Selecting 2-D Coordinate or 3-D Coordinate changes the number of axis targets for variable selection. Selecting 3-D Effect specifies that the histograms are three-dimensional objects.

Orientation. Clicking an orientation (vertical or horizontal) icon sets up the appropriate axis targets for variable selection. Orientation icons are available only when 2-D Coordinate is selected.

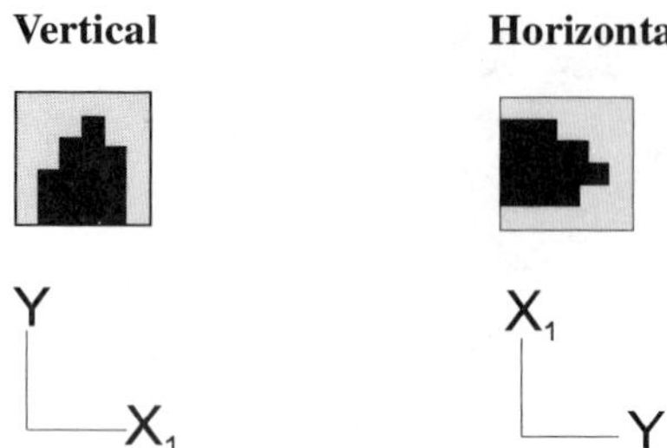

Variables. Only *Count* or *Percent* can be assigned to the *y* axis. For the *x1* axis, assign a scale variable.

Cumulative histogram. In a cumulative histogram, each bar represents the sum of the previous intervals plus the current interval.

To Create a Simple Histogram

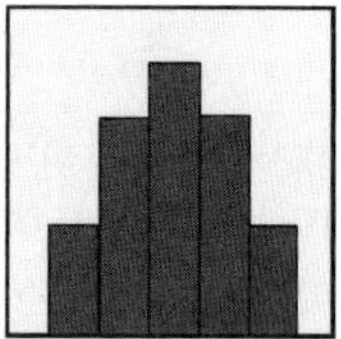 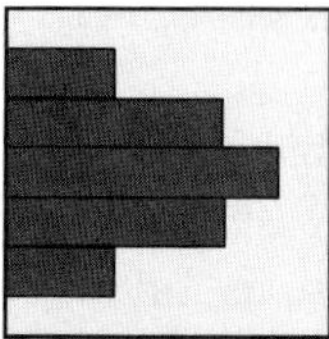 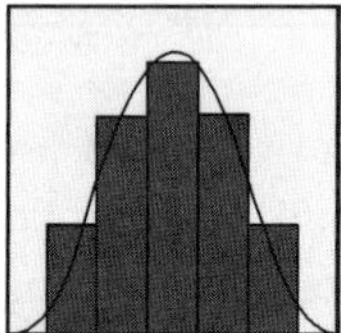

- Select the vertical or horizontal orientation icon.
- Drag *Count* to the *y* axis (if it is not there by default).
- Drag a scale variable to the *x1* axis.

Optionally, you can:

- Add a normal curve (Histogram tab).
- Swap the axes by clicking the orientation icon. Previously assigned variables swap, along with the axes.

- Use the built-in variable *Percent*.
- Create a cumulative histogram.

To Create a Categorical 3-D Histogram

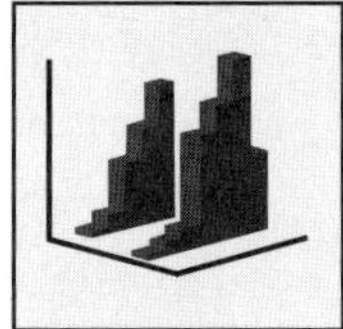

- ▶ Select 3-D Coordinate from the drop-down list.

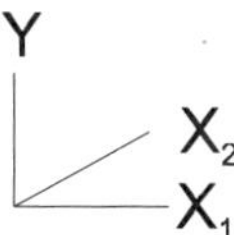

- ▶ Drag *Count* or *Percent* to the *y* axis.
- ▶ Drag a scale variable to the *x2* axis.
- ▶ Drag a categorical variable to the *x1* axis.

Optionally, you can:

- Assign a scale variable to *x1* and a categorical variable to *x2*.

To Create a Bivariate Histogram

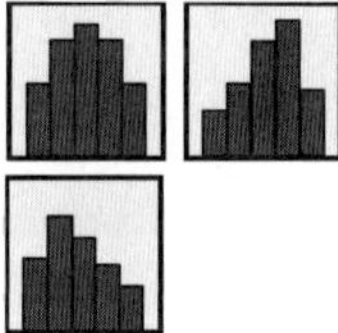

- Select 3-D Coordinate from the drop-down list.

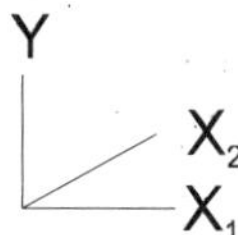

- Drag *Count* or *Percent* to the *y* axis.
- Drag scale variables to the *x1* and *x2* axes.

To Create a Cumulative Histogram

- Drag *Count* or *Percent* to the *y* axis.
- Drag a scale variable to the *x1* axis.
- Select Cumulative histogram.

To Create Histogram Panels for Categories

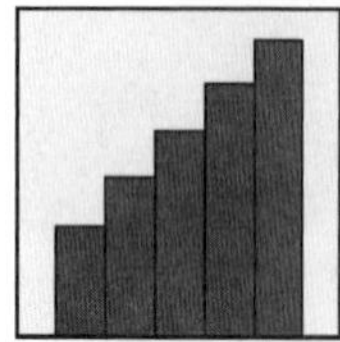

- Drag a scale variable to the *x1* axis.
- Drag *Count* or *Percent* to the *y* axis.

▶ Drag one or more categorical variables to Panel Variables.

Create Histogram: Histogram

Figure 7-2
Histogram tab

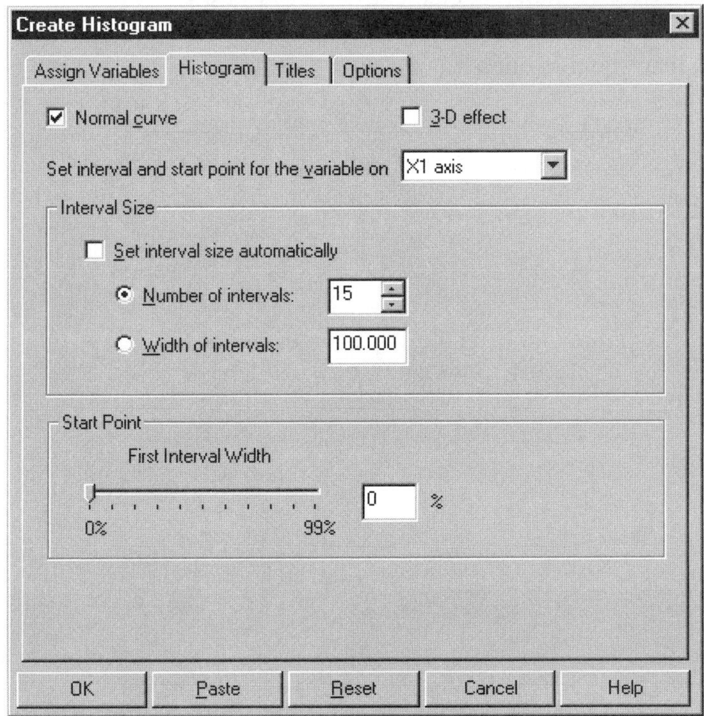

Several options are available to enhance histograms.

Normal curve. A normal curve can be superimposed onto the histogram, with the same mean and variance as the data. The normal curve is available only for a 2-D histogram.

Set interval and start point for the variable. This choice determines the axis for which you are setting the interval size and start point. If the chart is not 3-D, the settings for a second axis are ignored.

Interval Size. To set either the number of intervals or the width of intervals, deselect Set interval size automatically and enter the number. The maximum number of intervals is 250.

Start Point. The start point of the first interval can be set anywhere from the minimum scale value up to the minimum value plus the width of one interval.

Modifying a Histogram

To modify an existing histogram element:

- Activate the chart (double-click it).
- From the menus choose:

Format
  Graph Elements
    Histogram

or

- Right-click a histogram and from the context menu choose:

Histogram...

Histogram: Histogram

Figure 7-3
Histogram tab

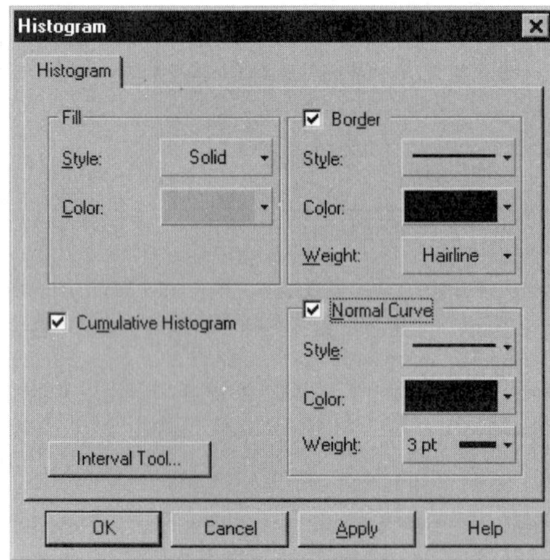

Several options are available to enhance histograms.

Fill. The style and color of the inside of the histogram.

Border. (2-D only.) The appearance of the borders of the bars that make up the histogram, including the base line.

Cumulative Histogram. In a cumulative histogram, each bar represents the sum of the previous intervals plus the current interval.

Normal Curve. (2-D only.) Displays a normal curve based on the mean and variance of your data. The style, color, and weight of the normal curve can be changed.

Interval Tool. Changes the interval size, number, and start point for a histogram.

Histogram: 3-D Depth

Figure 7-4
Histogram 3-D Depth tab

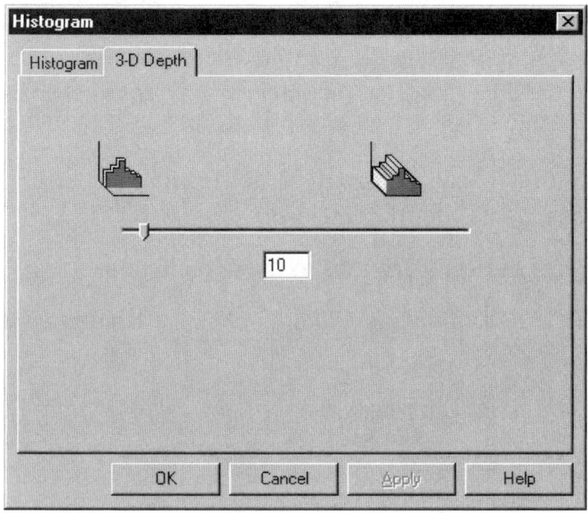

The slider controls the depth of 3-D histograms in the chart.

Histogram: Interval Tool

Figure 7-5
Interval Tool dialog box

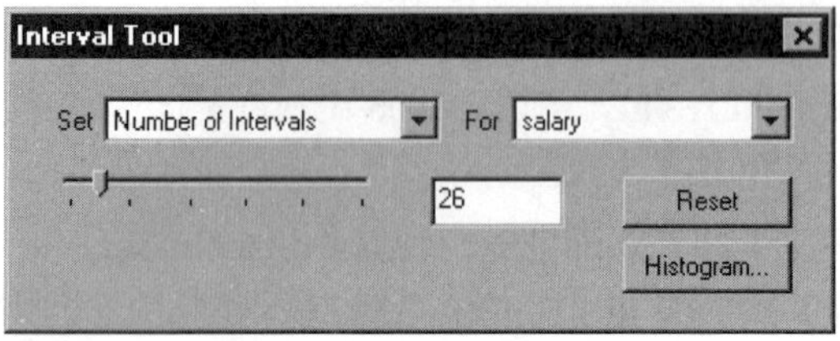

The Interval Tool dialog box is used to dynamically change the size of intervals in a histogram. You can either use the slider or enter a number. To view changes, press Enter on your keyboard.

Set. Using the Set drop-down list, you can specify options for the number of intervals, the interval size, and the start point of the first interval. The start point ranges from the scale minimum to the scale minimum plus the width of one interval.

You can specify from 1 to 250 intervals. If a specified interval size is not evenly divisible into the current data range, the last (partial) bar of the histogram is not displayed. If you change the data range for the interval axis, interval sizes are recomputed.

For. In a bivariate histogram, you can change the specifications for each axis independently by choosing a variable from the drop-down list.

Reset. The Reset button sets the specifications to the default values.

Histogram. Closes the Interval Tool dialog box and opens the Histogram dialog box.

To Change Interval Specifications in a Histogram

- Activate the chart.

- From the menus choose:

  Edit
   Interval...

  or

- Right-click the histogram and choose Interval Tool.

▶ Select a variable from the For drop-down list.

▶ Choose a type of specification from the Set drop-down list.

Optionally, you can:

- Change the number of intervals.
- Change the interval size.
- Change the start point.

Press Enter to apply the new specifications.

Changing Histogram Properties

For selected histograms you can change the fill, border, and normal curve.

To Change Histogram Properties

▶ Select a histogram.

▶ From the menus choose:

Format
  Graph Elements
    Histogram

or

▶ Right-click a histogram and choose Properties.

Optionally, you can:

- Change the fill, border, or normal curve.

Histogram Properties

Figure 7-6
Histogram Properties dialog box

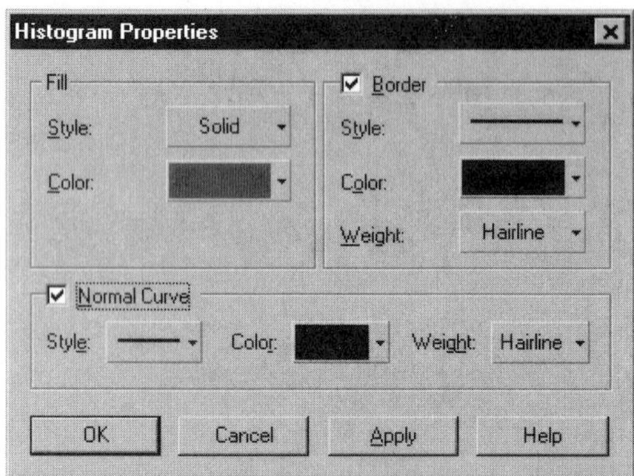

The properties listed apply only to the currently selected histogram. Single bars in the histogram cannot be selected individually.

Fill. The style and color of the histogram can be changed if not encoded by the data.

Border. The border is around the whole histogram. It can be turned on or off, and the style, weight, and color can be changed.

Normal Curve. If the normal curve is turned on, you can change the style, color, or weight.

Chapter

8

Line, Dot, and Ribbon Charts

A dot or line chart usually presents a summary function plotted against a categorical variable. A point is plotted for each value of the category variable. In a line chart, the points are connected by lines. A line chart is often used when the category axis is defined by an ordered series, although the points can represent any set of values.

The data can be connected with lines (ribbons in 3-D), and dot symbols can be displayed at the plotted points. Multiple-line charts can have drop lines connecting the categories. In a drop-line chart, the dots in each category are connected by a line.

Sample Output

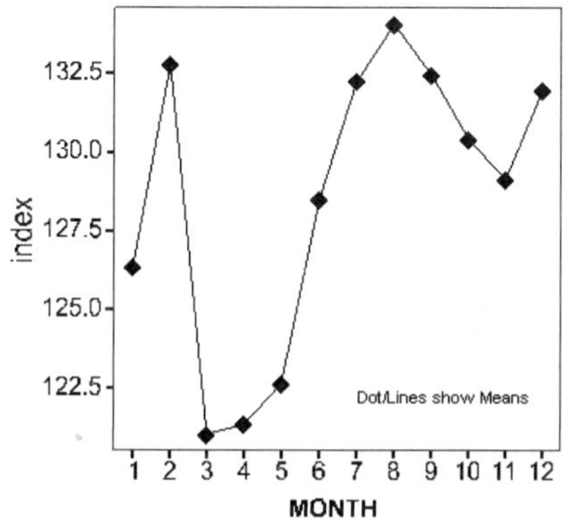

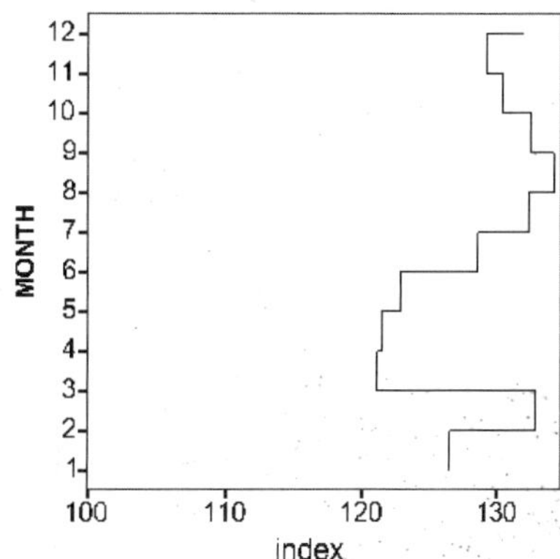

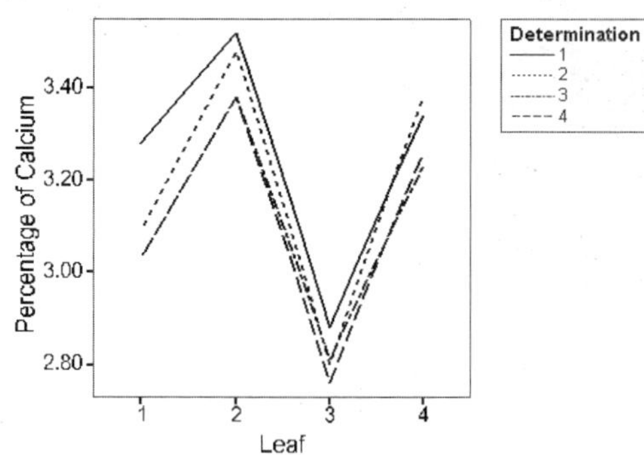
Determination
1
2
3
4
Percentage of Calcium
3.40
3.20
3.00
2.80
1
2
3
4
Leaf

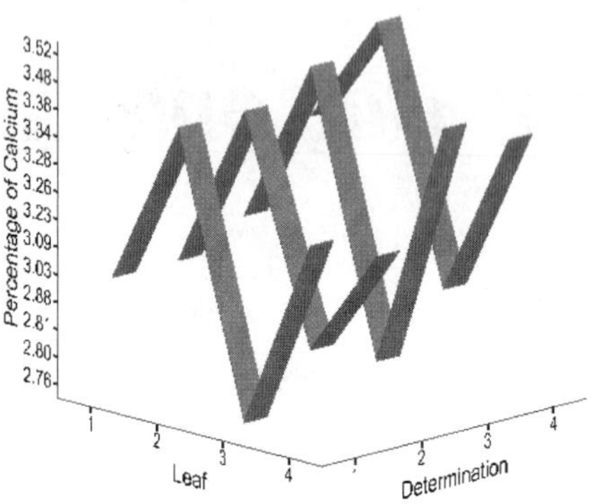
Percentage of Calcium
Leaf
Determination

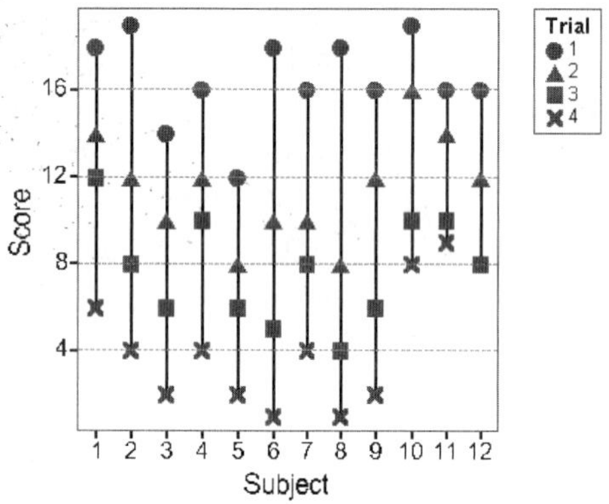
Trial
1
2
3
4
Score
16
12
8
4
1 2 3 4 5 6 7 8 9 10 11 12
Subject

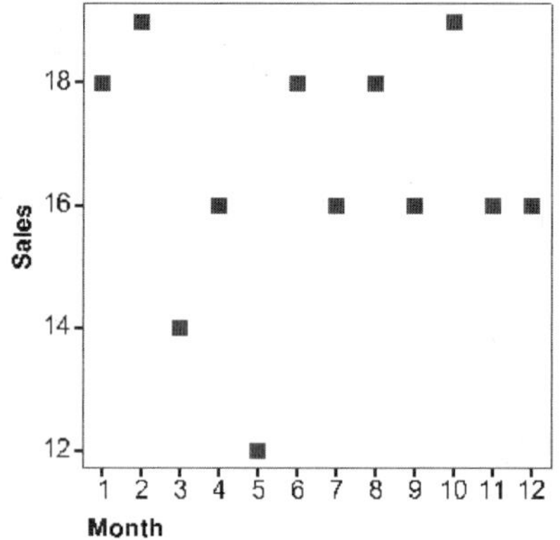
Sales
18
16
14
12
1 2 3 4 5 6 7 8 9 10 11 12
Month
Dot/Lines show Max Values

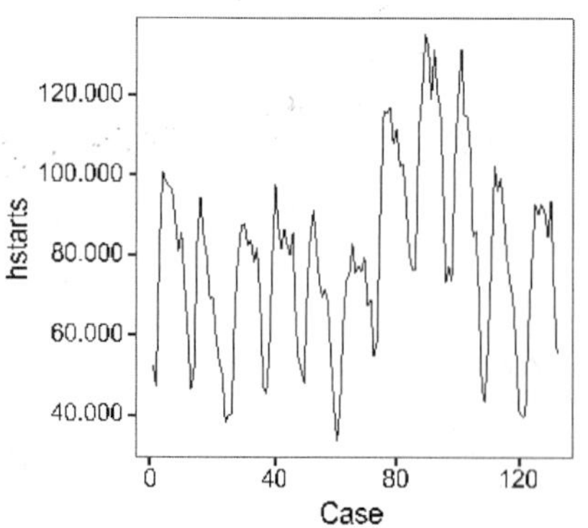
hstarts
120.000
100.000
80.000
60.000
40.000
0
40
80
120
Case

To Create a Line or Dot Chart

▶ From the menus choose:

Graphs
Interactive
Line...

Related options include Dot, Ribbon, and Drop-Line.

Create Dots, Lines, Ribbons, or Drop Lines: Assign Variables

Figure 8-1
Create Lines: Assign Variables tab

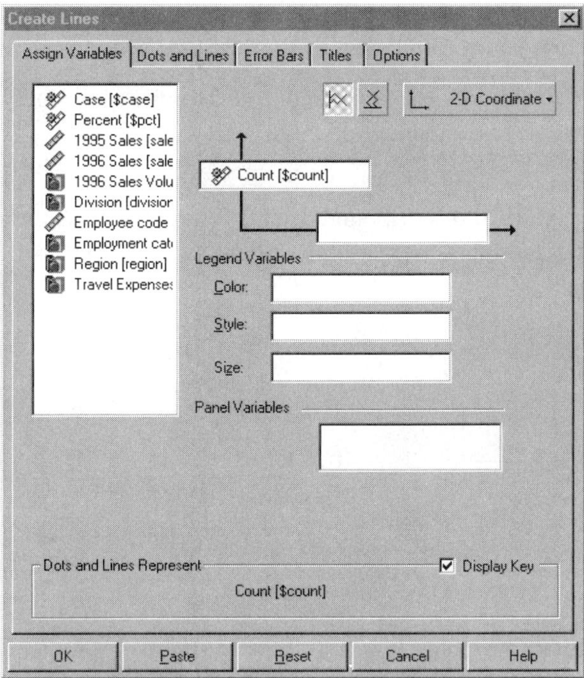

Dot charts, line charts, ribbon charts, and drop-line charts are all created by similar methods.

Lines. A line chart summarizes categories of one or more variables. Line charts tend to emphasize flow or movement instead of individual values. They are commonly used to display data over time and therefore can be used to give a good sense of trends. Line charts are especially effective for presenting a large number of values in a compact space. Dots can be displayed at the data points.

Dots. The display can show dots at the data points, lines connecting the points, or both dots and lines.

Ribbons. A ribbon chart is similar to a line chart, with the lines displayed as ribbons in a third dimension. Ribbon charts can be two-dimensional (displayed with a 3-D effect) or three-dimensional.

Drop Lines. For multiple-line or dot charts, where a category variable is assigned to Color or Style, drop lines are available between color or style dots in the same axis category.

Summary function. For a dependent scale variable, the summary function can be changed from the Dots and Lines Represent drop-down list.

Number of dimensions. Selecting 2-D Coordinate or 3-D Coordinate changes the number of axis targets for variable selection. Selecting 3-D Effect specifies that the lines become ribbons.

Orientation. Clicking the vertical or horizontal orientation icon sets up the appropriate axis targets for variable selection. Orientation icons are available only when 2-D Coordinate is selected.

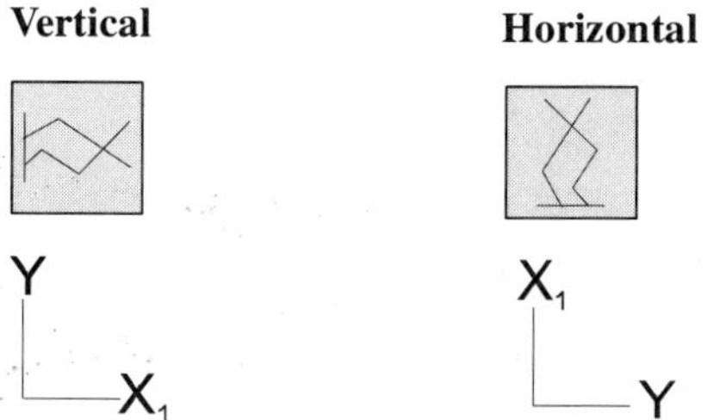

Case Variable. If the built-in variable *Case* is assigned to an axis, another target becomes available where you can assign a variable for labeling cases. For example, the labels might be days of the week or months.

To Create a Simple Line or Dot Chart

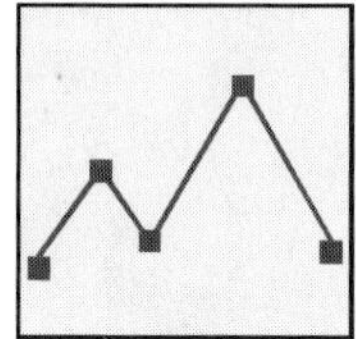 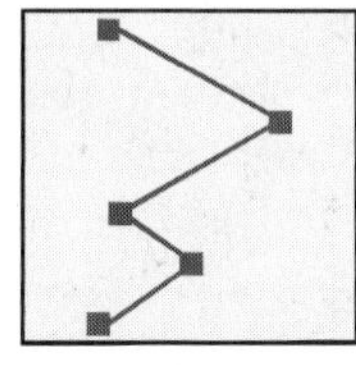 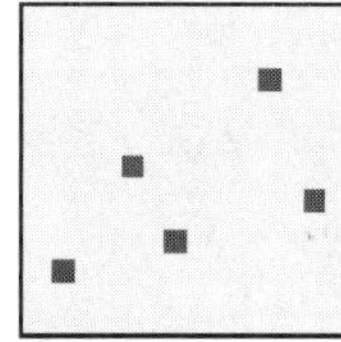

▶ Drag a variable (often categorical) to the *x1* axis.

▶ Drag *Count, Percent,* or a scale variable to the *y* axis (if one is not already there by default).

Optionally, you can:

- Swap the axes by clicking the orientation icon. The currently assigned variables swap with the axes.
- Display dots or lines or both (in the Dots and Lines tab).

To Create a Line Chart Summarizing a Scale Variable

▶ Drag a scale variable to the *y* axis.

▶ Drag a variable (often categorical) to the *x1* axis.

By default, the points represent the mean of the scale variable. Optionally, you can select another summary function in the Dots and Lines Represent drop-down list.

To Create a Multiple-Line Chart

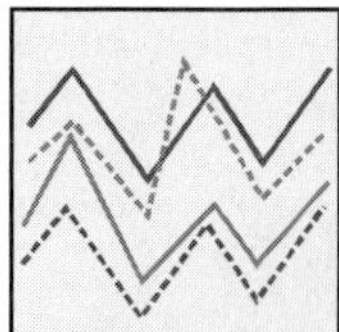

- ▶ Drag a variable (often categorical) to the *x1* axis.
- ▶ Drag another variable to the *y* axis.
- ▶ Drag a categorical variable to Color or Style or Size.

  Size can apply to symbol size for dots or line weight for lines.

To Create a Line or Dot Chart of Individual Cases

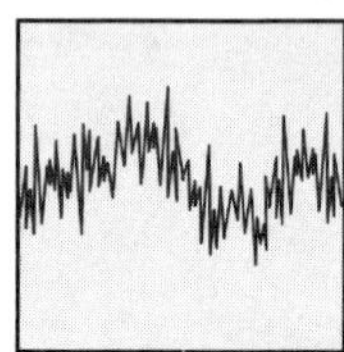

- ▶ Drag *Cases* to the *x1* axis.
- ▶ Drag a variable (usually a scale variable) to the *y* axis.

  Note: Charts that display values for individual cases are meaningful only if you select a summary variable for the dependent (*y*) axis. Summary functions such as mean, median, or mode will result in dots or points on a line that display the value of the summary variable for each case. Counts, percentages, and summary functions that represent the number of cases or percentage of cases above or below a specified value will not reveal any particularly useful information when charting cases, since every case has a count of exactly 1.

To Create a Drop-Line Chart

▶ From the menus choose:

Graphs
 Interactive
  Drop-Line...

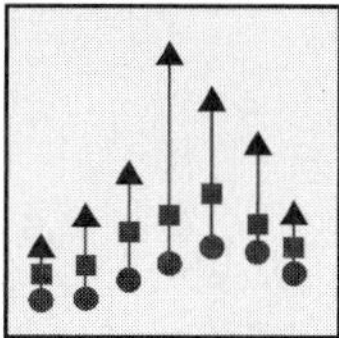

▶ Drag a variable (often categorical) to the *x1* axis.

▶ Drag *Count*, *Percent*, or a scale variable to the *y* axis (if one is not already there by default).

▶ Drag a categorical variable to Color, Style, or Size.

▶ On the Dots and Lines tab, select Drop Lines.

To Create a 2-D Ribbon Chart

▶ From the menus choose:

Graphs
 Interactive
  Ribbon...

▶ Drag a variable (usually categorical) to the *x1* axis.

▶ Drag *Count, Percent,* or a scale variable to the *y* axis (if one is not already there by default).

Optionally, you can:

- Swap the axes by clicking the orientation icon. The currently assigned variables swap with the axes.
- Display dots (Ribbons tab).
- Change the interpolation style (Ribbons tab).

To Create a 3-D Ribbon Chart

▶ From the menus choose:

Graphs
  Interactive
    Ribbon...

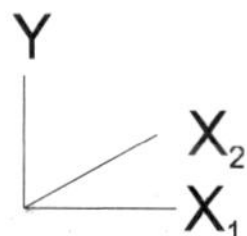

▶ Select 3-D Coordinate from the drop-down list.

▶ Drag variables to the *x1* and *x2* axes.

▶ Drag *Count* or another variable to the *y* axis (if one is not already there by default).

To Create Line or Dot Chart Panels for Categories

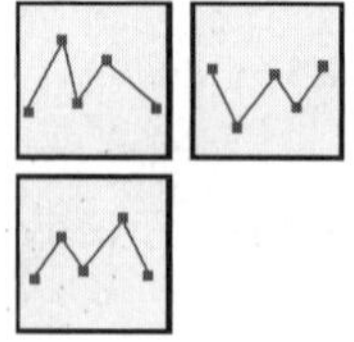

▶ Drag a categorical variable to the *x1* axis.

▶ Drag a scale variable or a built-in variable to the *y* axis.

▶ Drag one or more categorical variables to Panel Variables.

Dots and Lines

Figure 8-2
Create Lines: Dots and Lines tab

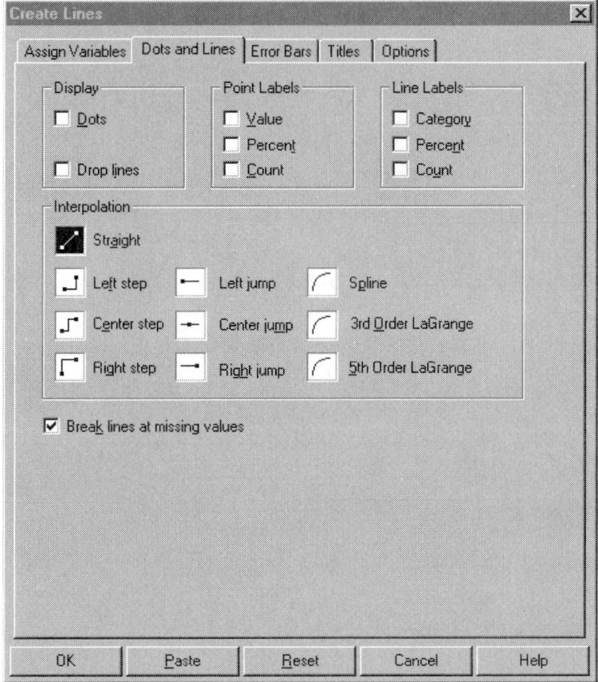

Several options are available to enhance dot, line, and ribbon charts.

Display. Dots, lines, or both can be displayed. The choices depend on the type of chart. Drop lines join the points in a single category on a multiple-line chart.

Point Labels and Line Labels. Point labels display the number of cases, percentage of cases, or the value represented by the distance of the point from the axis. Labels for each line are also available, showing the category, percentage, or count.

Interpolation. Controls how the lines are drawn between data points. Choices include straight lines; left, center, and right steps (horizontal lines through the points, with risers); and left, center, and right jumps (no risers). Also available are spline, 3rd order LaGrange, and 5th order LaGrange lines.

Break lines at missing values. With this option selected, lines are not drawn through categories that have no values.

Create Line Chart: Error Bars

Figure 8-3
Create Line Chart: Error Bars tab

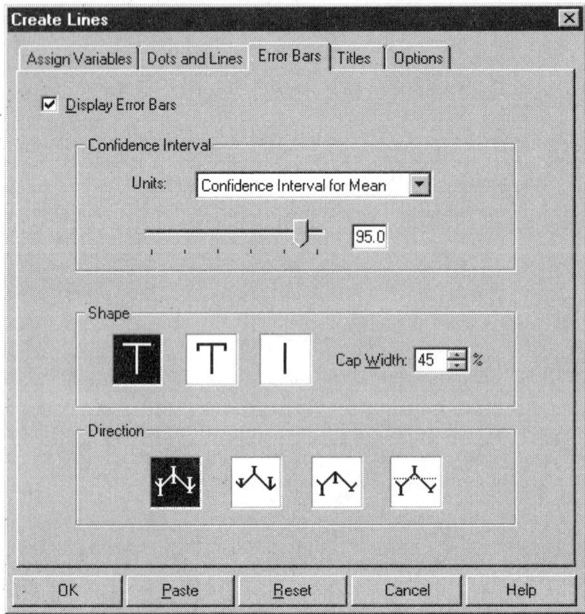

Error bars, indicating the variability of the measure displayed, are available when the dependent variable is a scale variable, and bars or lines represent the summary function *Means*. The length of an error bar represents the amount of variability. The length of the error bars is displayed as the lower and upper limits of a confidence interval (at a specified percentage level) or in standard deviations or standard errors of the mean.

You can specify the confidence interval's level, direction, and shape, and change the appearance of error bars.

Modifying Dots, Lines, and Ribbons

To modify the lines and dots element (all lines, dots, and ribbons) in an existing chart:

▶ Activate the chart (double-click it).

▶ From the menus choose:

Format
  Graph Elements
    Line

or

▶ Right-click a line or dot, and from the context menu choose:

Dots and Lines...

▶ Select the desired options.

Dots and Lines: Options

Figure 8-4
Dots and Lines: Options tab

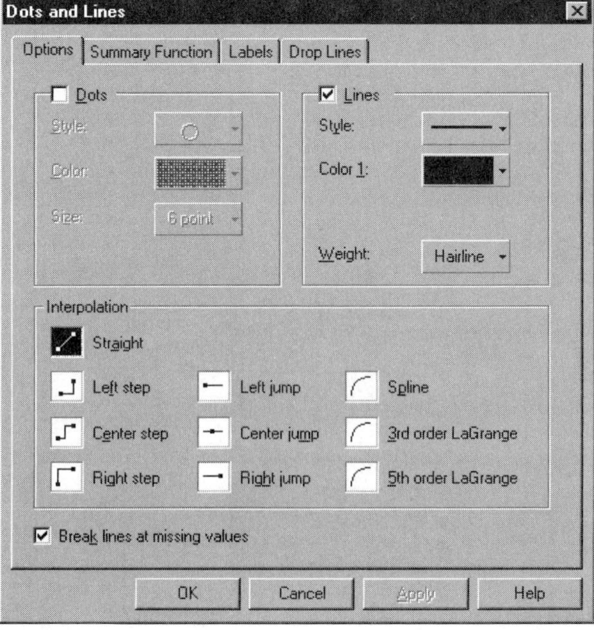

Several options are available for lines, dots, and ribbons.

Dots. The dots can be turned on or off. The style, color, and size can be changed if they have not been locked by variable assignments.

Lines. The lines can be turned on or off. The style, color, and weight can be changed if they have not been locked by variable assignments.

Interpolation. Controls how the lines are drawn between data points. Choices include straight lines; left, center, and right steps (horizontal lines through the points, with risers); and left, center, and right jumps (no risers). Also available are spline, 3rd order LaGrange, and 5th order LaGrange lines.

Break lines at missing values. With this option selected, lines are not drawn through categories that have no values.

Dots and Lines: Summary Function

Figure 8-5
Dots and Lines: Summary Function tab

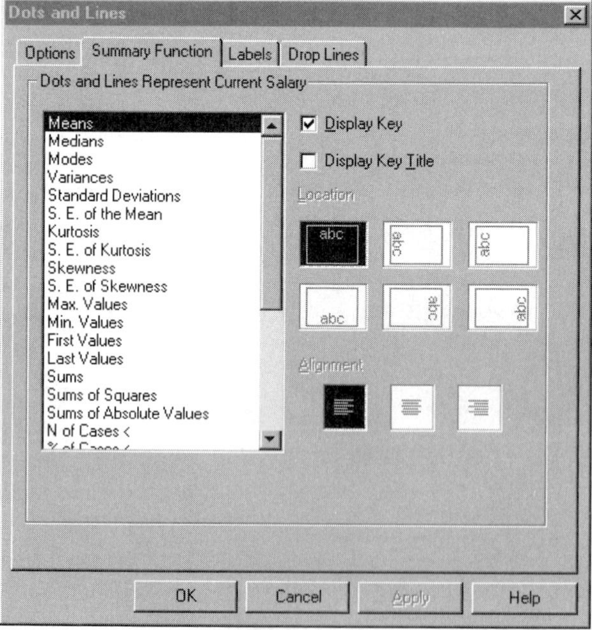

For an existing chart, if there is a scale variable on the dependent axis, you can change the summary function. For example, if the original lines represent the *Means* of a variable, you can change to the *Maximum values* of the same variable.

Display key options. These selections change the way summary information is displayed in the chart. You can display the key and determine the alignment and location of the key title.

Dots and Lines: Labels

Figure 8-6
Dots and Lines: Labels tab

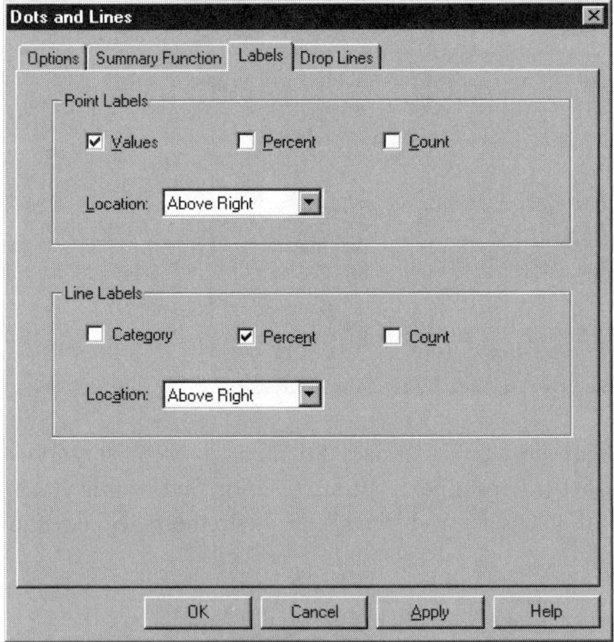

Point Labels. Value, percentage, and count labels can be displayed for data points.

Line Labels. Category, percentage, and count labels can be displayed for lines.

You can specify the position of the labels with respect to the points or lines.

Dots and Lines: Drop Lines

Figure 8-7
Dots and Lines: Drop Lines tab

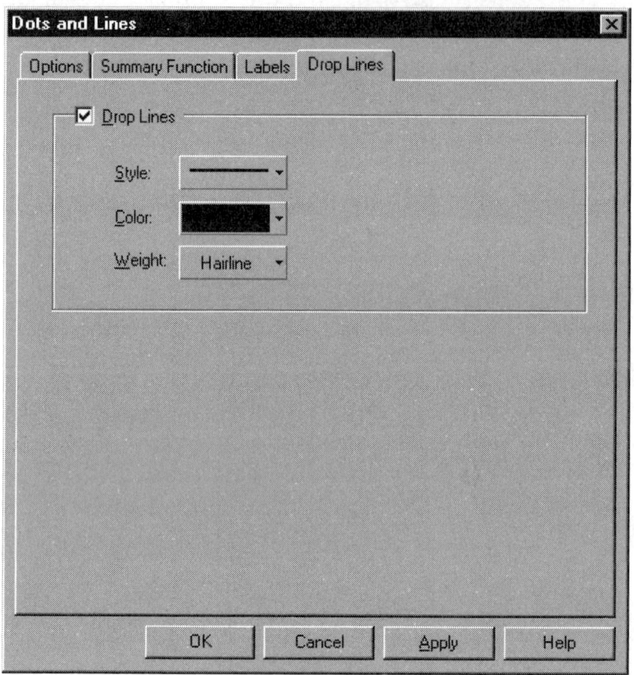

On a multiple-line chart, drop lines connect the points in each category across lines. Drop lines can be displayed or hidden. The style, color, and weight can be specified. Drop lines are not available when a scale variable is on the independent axis.

Dots and Lines: Ribbon Width

Figure 8-8
Dots and Lines: Ribbon Width tab

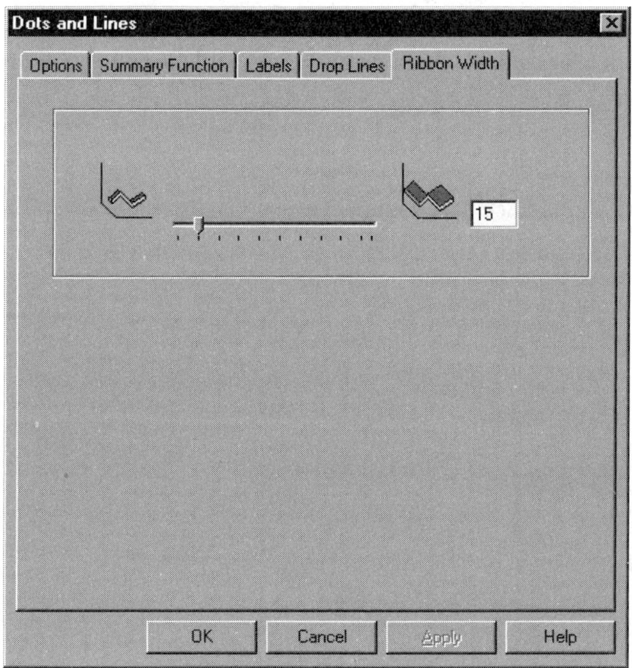

For three-dimensional line or ribbon charts, you can change the width of the ribbons.

To Change Line, Dot, or Ribbon Properties

A line or ribbon or dot set, or a selection of several lines or ribbons and dot sets, have properties that can be changed, as long as the property is not controlled by the data.

- ▶ Select one or more lines, ribbons, or dot sets in a line, ribbon, or dot chart.

▶ From the menus choose:

Edit
  Line Properties

or

▶ Right-click a line, dot, or ribbon (or selected group), and choose Properties from the context menu.

Optionally, you can:

- Change the line appearance and dot appearance.
- Change line labels and dot labels.

Dot and Line Properties

Figure 8-9
Dot and Line Properties dialog box

The properties listed here apply only to the lines, ribbons, or dot sets that are currently selected. A dot set consists of all of the dots that fall on the same line, whether or not the line is displayed.

Dots. Changes the style, color, and size of selected dot sets.

Lines. Changes the style, color, and weight of selected lines.

Point Labels. Displays the value represented by each data point. Also, labels can be displayed that show the number of cases used to calculate the value for each point or the percentage.

Line Labels. Displays the percentage or count of cases represented by the line, as well as the category.

To Change Point Label Properties

▶ Select one or more dot labels.

▶ From the menus choose:

Edit
  Line Properties

or

▶ Right-click a dot label and select Properties from the context menu.

Optionally, you can:

- Change the labels displayed.
- Change the location, connector, and color of the labels.

Point Label Properties

Figure 8-10
Point Label Properties dialog box

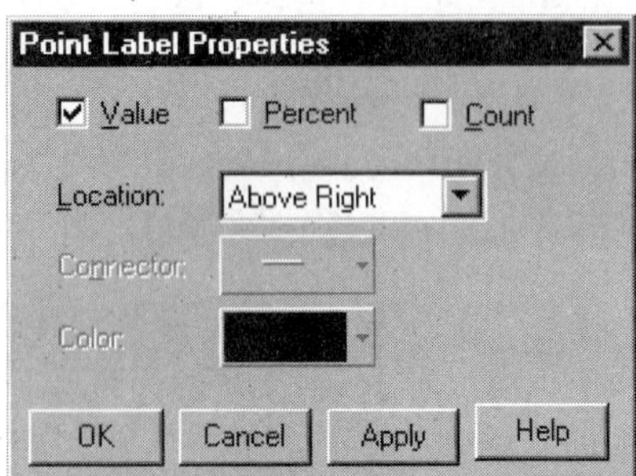

The properties listed here apply only to dot labels that are currently selected.

Value, Percent, Count. The display of three different labels can be selected or deselected.

Location. The location can be changed with respect to the selected dots.

Connector. The style of connector can be selected from the drop-down list.

Color. The color of the selected labels can be changed.

Chapter
9

Pie Charts

What proportion does each group contribute to the total? A pie chart demonstrates the contribution of parts to a whole. Each slice of the pie belongs to a group defined by a category of a variable. The size of a slice is proportional to the frequency (count) of its group or to a function of a summary variable. For example, one pie chart shows the number of employees in each department, making it easy to compare relative department sizes. In another pie, each slice shows the sum of sales for individuals in a group.

To compare separate categories, pie charts can be displayed separately in **panels** or stacked in a **cluster**. In a cluster, pies of different diameters are stacked to make comparison of slices easy. In another type of display, **plotted pies,** you can plot pies for subgroups defined by combinations of categories, using Cartesian coordinates (*x* and *y* axes) with a pie at each intersection of categories.

Sample Output

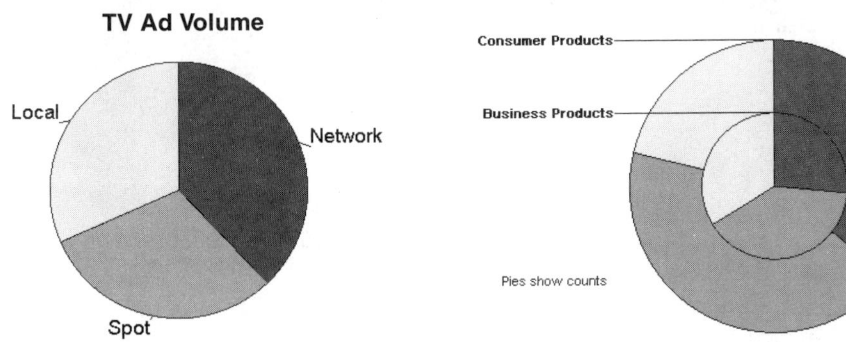

Business Products, West 18.21%
Consumer Products, East 16.41%
Consumer Products, Central 19.74%
Business Products, Central 21.54%
Consumer Products, West 9.74%
Business Products, East 14.36%

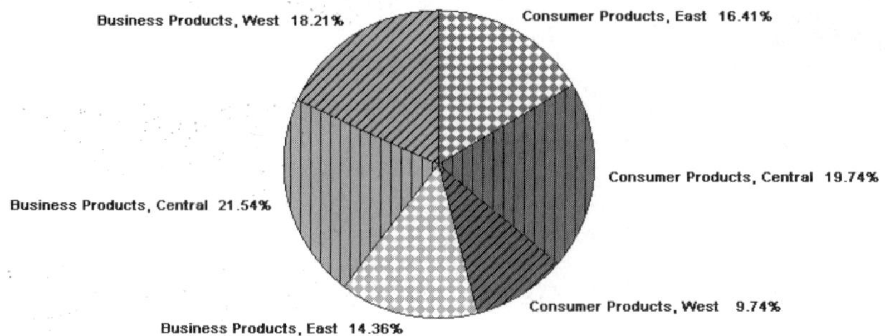

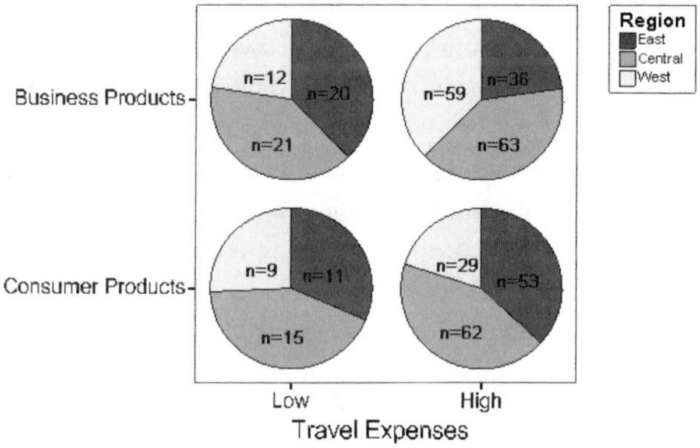

Region
East
Central
West
Business Products
n=12
n=20
n=21
n=59
n=36
n=63
Consumer Products
n=9
n=11
n=15
n=29
n=53
n=62
Low
High
Travel Expenses

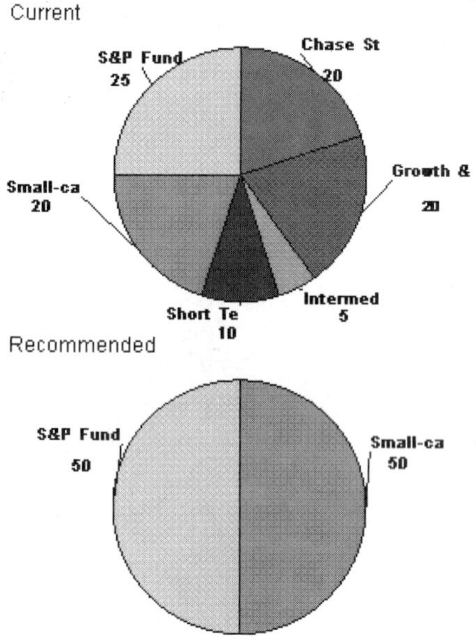

Current
S&P Fund 25
Chase St 20
Growth & 20
Small-ca 20
Short Te 10
Intermed 5
Recommended
S&P Fund 50
Small-ca 50

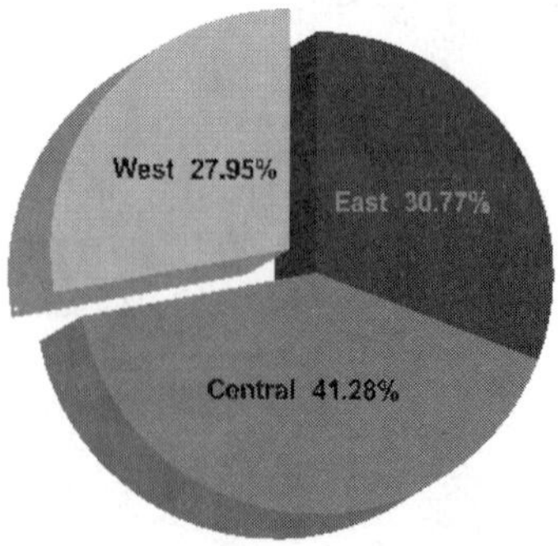

West 27.95%
East 30.77%
Central 41.28%

To Create a Pie Chart

▶ From the menus choose:

Graphs
 Interactive
  Pie
   Simple... *or* Clustered... *or* Plotted...

Create Simple Pie Chart: Assign Variables

Figure 9-1
Create Simple Pie Chart: Assign Variables tab

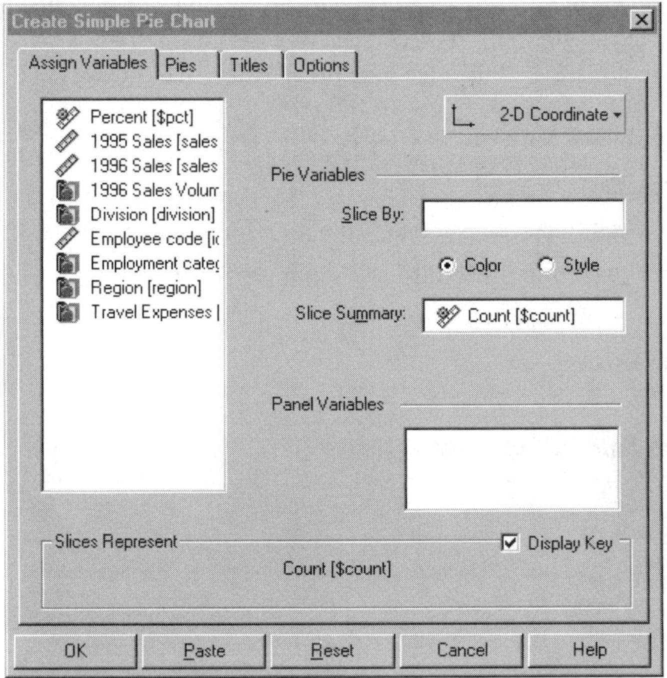

A simple pie chart summarizes categories defined by a single variable or by a group of related variables. For each category, the size of each slice represents the count, the percentage, or a summary function of a variable. You can display a key to identify the built-in or summary function. You can also create a paneled pie chart.

3-D Effect. Selecting this effect from the drop-down list gives the pie depth.

To Create a Simple Pie Chart Sliced by a Categorical Variable

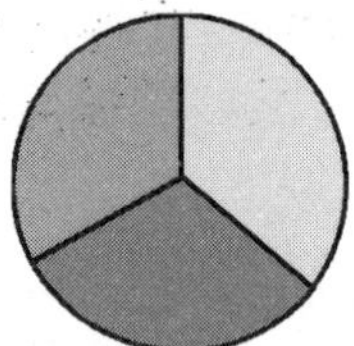
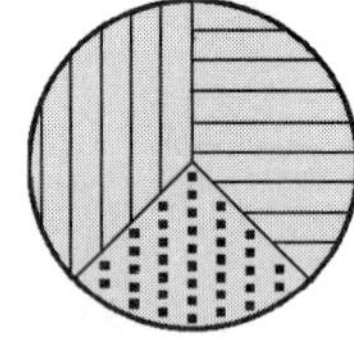

▶ Drag a categorical variable to Slice By.

▶ Drag *Count*, *Percent*, or a scale variable to Slice Summary (if it is not there by default).

In the Slice Summary, the *Count* or *Percent* built-in variables display the number of cases in each slice category or the percentage of cases. By default, a scale variable displays the sum of the Slice Summary variable in each slice category.

Optionally, you can:

- Slice by either Style or Color.
- Change the Slices Represent summary function for a scale variable.
- Display a key to identify the built-in or summary function.
- Assign one or more panel variables.
- Apply a 3-D effect.

To Create a Pie Chart Split by Color and Style

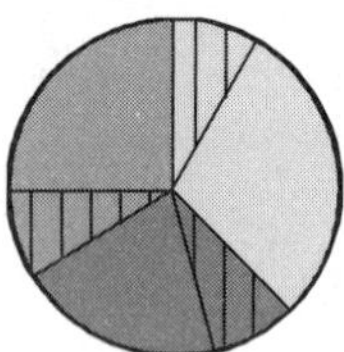

▶ Drag a category variable to Slice By and select Color.

▶ Click OK, and in the Viewer activate the pie chart (double-click it).

- From the menus choose:

  Edit
   Assign Variables

  or

- Click the Assign Graph Variables tool.

- Drag a categorical variable to Style.

  When a pie chart is split by both color and style, the primary split is always by color. That is, the pie is first divided by color, and then each color is divided by style.

To Create a Pie Chart Using a Scale Variable to Color Slices

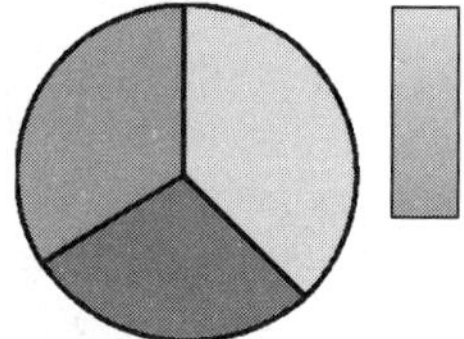

- Drag a categorical variable to Slice By.

- Select Style.

- Drag *Count*, *Percent*, or a scale variable to Slice Summary (if it is not there by default) and click OK.

- In the Viewer, activate the chart (double-click it).

- From the menus choose:

  Edit
   Assign Variables

  or

- Click the Assign Graph Variables tool.

- Drag a scale variable to Color.

  The colors are assigned by a summary function of the scale variable (the default is *Means*).

To Create Pie Chart Panels for Categories

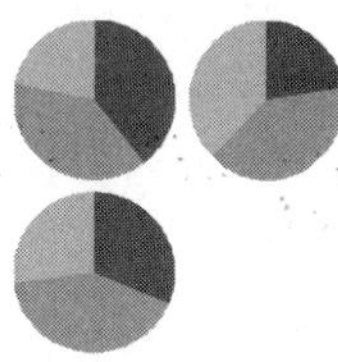

- Drag a categorical variable to Slice By.
- Drag *Count*, *Percent*, or a scale variable to Slice Summary (if it is not there by default).
- Drag one or more categorical variables to Panel Variables.

Create Simple Pie Chart: Pies

Figure 9-2
Create Simple Pie Chart: Pies tab

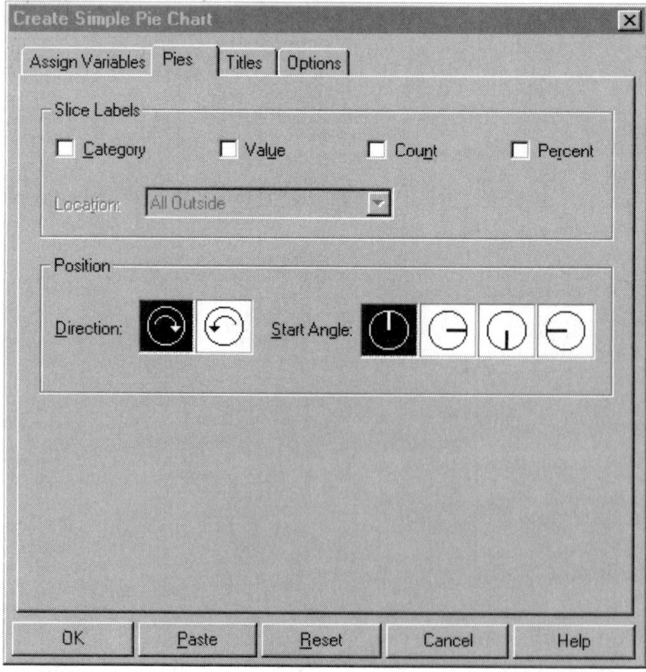

Slice Labels. Slices can have up to four types of labels. The initial appearance of labels is controlled in the ChartLook.

Position. Slices start at a position specified by a clock position: 12:00, 3:00, 6:00, or 9:00. After the first slice, the direction the slices follow is either clockwise or counterclockwise.

To Specify Enhancements for a New Simple Pie Chart

- Click the Pies tab.
- Select slice labels or position.

Create Clustered Pie Chart: Assign Variables

Figure 9-3
Create Clustered Pie Chart: Assign Variables tab

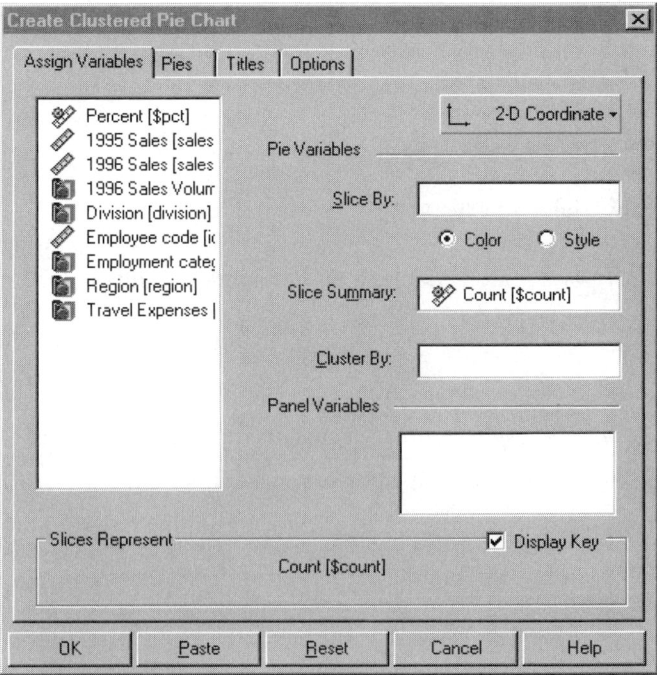

A clustered pie chart contains a cluster of simple pies, all of which are stacked into categories by the same variable. The pies are of different sizes and appear to be stacked on top of one another. The cluster contains as many pies as there are categories in the cluster variable.

The size of a slice represents the count or percentage in a category of the slice variable, or a summary function of a scale variable. You can display a key to identify the built-in or summary function. The size of slices in different pies can be compared by observing their respective angles.

3-D Effect. Selecting this effect from the drop-down list gives the pie depth.

▶ From the menus choose:

Graphs
 Interactive
  Pie
   Clustered...

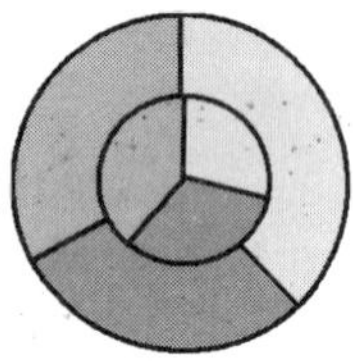

▶ Drag a categorical variable to Slice By.

▶ Drag a categorical variable to Cluster By.

▶ Drag *Count*, *Percent*, or a scale variable to Slice Summary (if it is not there by default).

Optionally, you can:

- Switch between Color and Style.
- Change the Slices Represent summary function for a scale variable.
- Display a key to identify the built-in or summary function.
- Create clustered pies for separate categories by assigning one or more categorical Panel Variables.
- Apply a 3-D effect.

Clustered and Plotted Pie Enhancements

Figure 9-4
Create Clustered Pie Chart: Pies tab

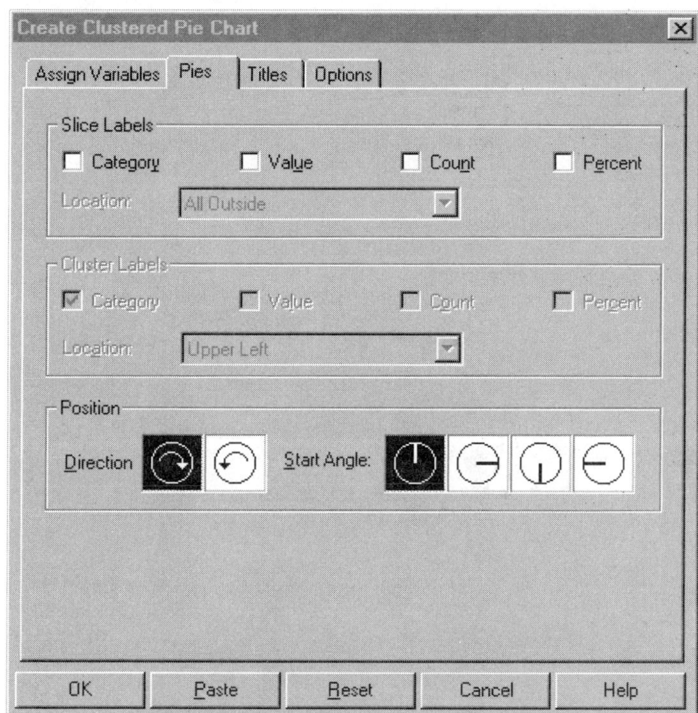

Slice Labels. Slices can have up to four types of labels. The initial appearance of labels is controlled in the ChartLook.

Cluster Labels. Labels available for each pie in a cluster include category labels, category percentage, number of cases, and category value.

Position. Slices start at a position specified by a clock position: 12:00, 3:00, 6:00, or 9:00. After the first slice, the direction the slices follow is either clockwise or counterclockwise.

Create Plotted Pie Chart: Assign Variables

Figure 9-5
Create Plotted Pie Chart: Assign Variables tab

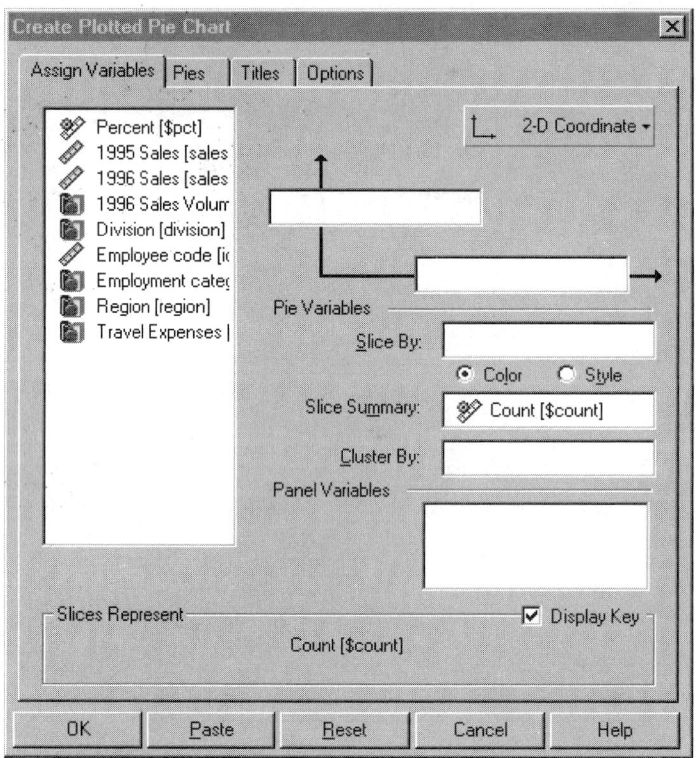

A plotted pie chart contains a set of pies placed at the points defined by rectangular coordinates. It is similar to a scatterplot with pie markers. The pies are all sliced by the same categorical variable.

The size of a slice represents the count or percentage in a category of the slice variable, or a summary function of a scale variable. You can display a key to identify the built-in or summary function.

Scale variables on one or both axes can produce a large number of very small pies.

Number of dimensions. Selecting 2-D Coordinate or 3-D coordinate changes the number of axis targets for variable selection. Selecting 3-D Effect specifies that the pies are three-dimensional objects.

For Plotted Pie Options, see "Clustered and Plotted Pie Enhancements" on p. 137.

To Create a Plotted Pie Chart

▶ From the menus choose:

Graphs
 Interactive
  Pie
   Plotted...

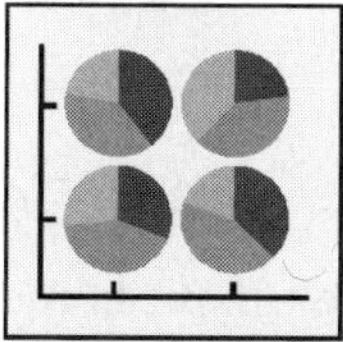

▶ Select 2-D Coordinate for a two-dimensional chart.

▶ To define the pie slices for all pies, drag a categorical variable to Slice By.

▶ To define the subgroups of the pies, drag variables (usually categorical) to the *x1* and *y* axes.

▶ Drag *Count*, *Percent*, or a scale variable to Slice Summary (if it is not there by default).

Optionally, you can:

- Switch between Color and Style.
- Change the Slices Represent summary function for a scale variable.
- Display a key to identify the built-in or summary function.
- Assign a categorical variable for clustering pies.
- Create plotted pie charts for separate categories by assigning one or more categorical Panel Variables.
- Select 3-D Coordinate for a three-dimensional chart.
- Select 3-D Effect to give depth to the pies.

Modifying Pies

To modify the pie elements (all pies) in an existing chart:

▶ From the menus choose:

Format
  Graph Elements
    Pies

or

▶ Right-click a pie and from the context menu choose:

Pies...

▶ Select the desired changes in Pie Options, Summary Function, Labels, or Pie Size.

In the Pies dialog box, you can choose a tab to modify the pie fill, pie border, position, and summary function. You can also change the labels and the size of pies.

Pies: Pie Options

Figure 9-6
Pies: Pie Options tab

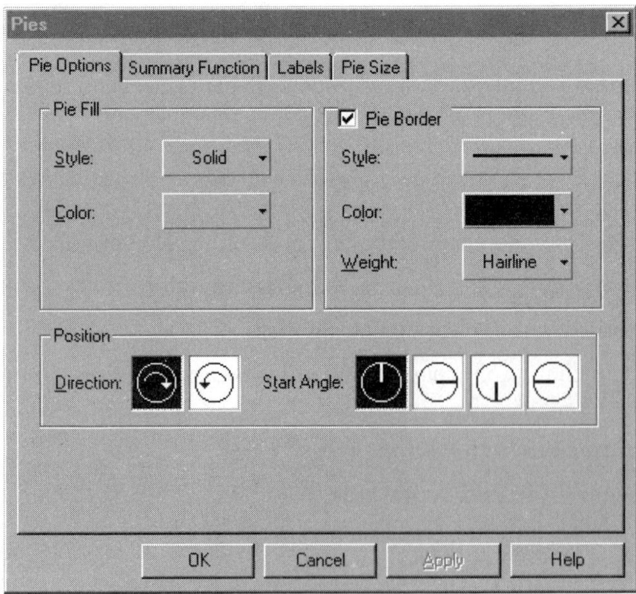

After pies are created, you can change their appearance. These options affect all pies in the chart.

Pie Fill. Color or style not controlled by data can be changed.

Pie Border. Style, color, and weight of the pie border can be changed. This applies to the border of the whole pie in 2-D. In a 3-D pie, there are no borders.

Position. Slices start at a position specified by a clock position: 12:00, 3:00, 6:00, or 9:00. After the first slice, the direction the slices follow is either clockwise or counterclockwise.

Pies: Summary Function

Figure 9-7
Pies: Summary Function tab

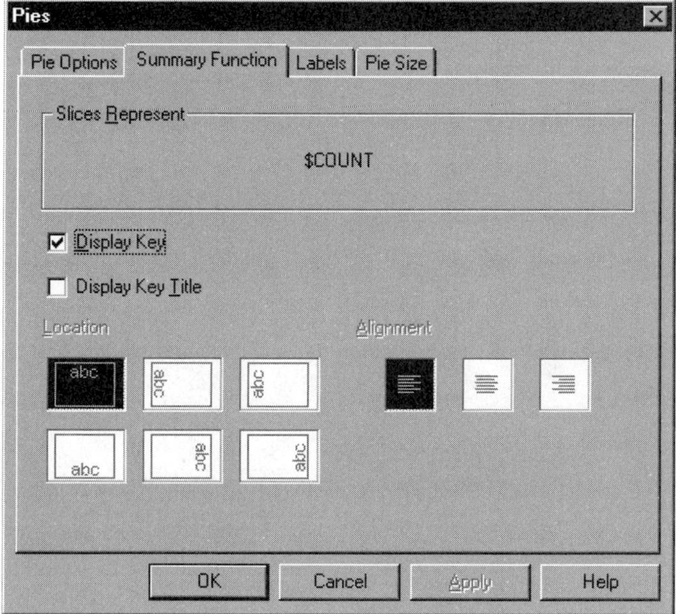

Slices Represent. For an existing chart that was created using a summary function of a data variable, you can change the summary function. For example, if the original slices represent the *sum* of a variable, you can change to the *sums of squares* of the same variable. If *Count* or *Percent* is assigned, it is listed here.

Display key options. These selections change the way summary information is displayed in the chart. You can display the key and determine the alignment and location of the key title.

To Change Pie Chart Summary Function

- Click the Summary Function tab.
- Select the desired options for summary function and key display.

Pies: Labels

Figure 9-8
Pies: Labels tab

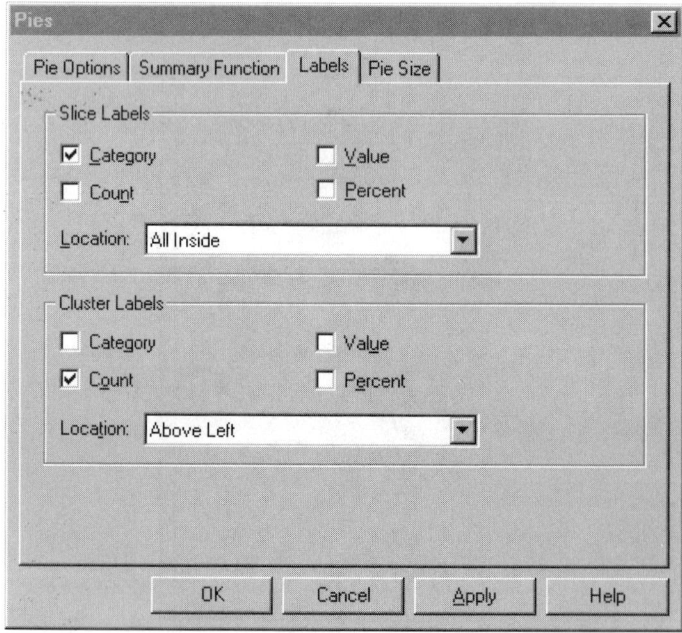

Value labels can have a numeric format. The location of the labels and lines connecting them to the slices or pies can be specified.

Slice Labels. Several text and numeric labels are available for slices derived from a categorical variable assigned to Color or Style. You can also specify the location of the labels in relation to the pie.

Cluster Labels. Labels can be applied to individual pies when the pies are stacked in a cluster. You can also specify the location of the labels outside the pies.

To Change the Labels for a Pie Chart

- Click the Labels tab.
- Enter changes.

Pies: Pie Size

Figure 9-9
Pies: Pie Size tab

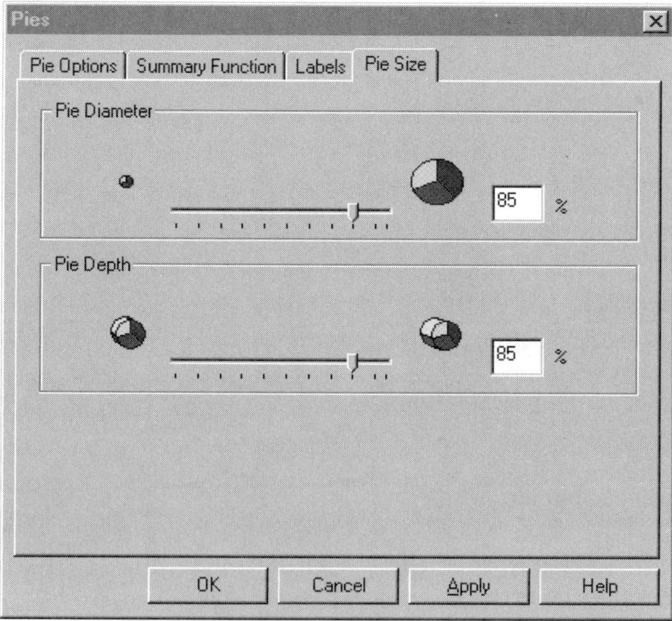

After pie charts are created, you can make the pie smaller or larger, up to a maximum determined by the size of the data region.

If the 3-D effect is turned on, you can specify a depth for the thickness of the pies.

To Change the Size of Pies

- ▶ Click the Pie Size tab.
- ▶ Drag the slider or enter a percentage.

Changing Pie Slice Properties

Individual slices or a selection of several slices have the properties Fill and Border that can be changed as long as the property is not controlled by the data. Individual labels can be turned on or off, and slices can be exploded out from the center.

To Change Pie Slice Properties

- ▶ Select one or more slices in a pie chart.
- ▶ From the menus choose:

  Edit
  Pie Properties

  or

- ▶ Right-click a slice or selected group of slices, and from the context menu choose Properties.

Optionally, you can:

- ■ Change the labels, border, or fill.
- ■ Explode the slice.

Slice Properties

Figure 9-10
Slice Properties dialog box

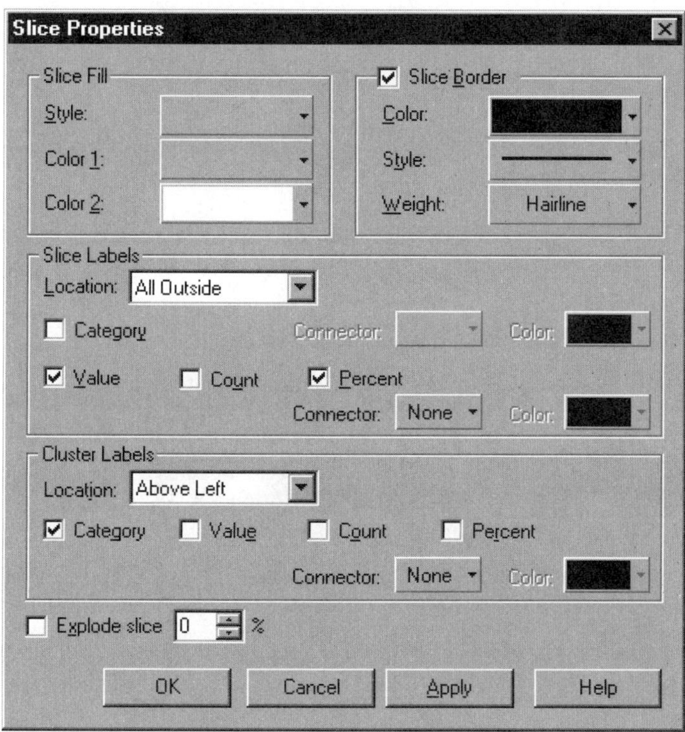

These properties apply only to the selected slice or slices.

Slice Fill and **Slice Border.** The attributes of the fill can be changed if they are not controlled by data. The border color, style, and weight can be changed.

Labels. The labels for the selected slice can be turned on or off, as can the labels for a pie in a clustered pie chart.

Explode slice. The selected slice can be exploded (moved out along a radius) by the percentage entered.

Chapter

10

Scatterplots

In a scatterplot, the actual values of two or three variables are plotted along two or three axes. The resulting cloud of points helps you visualize the relationship between the variables. You can observe whether the points fall near a line or a well-defined curve. In three dimensions, the points may fall near a surface. If a legend variable is used, the characteristics of subgroups become evident.

Study of the plot can help you develop a mathematical model of the relationship. Points that do not fit the relationship stand out in the plot and signal that you should investigate them further.

Sample Output

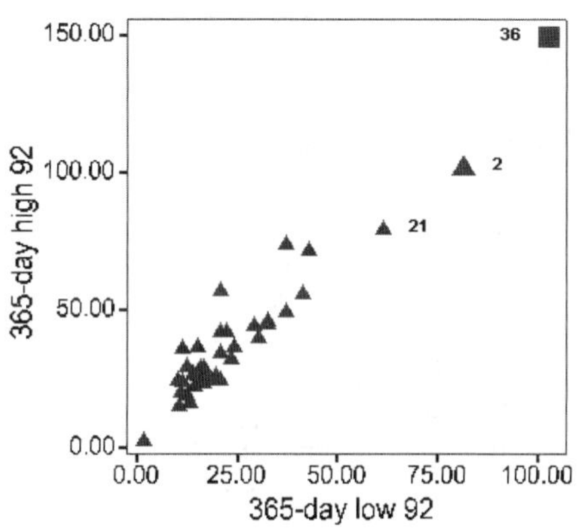

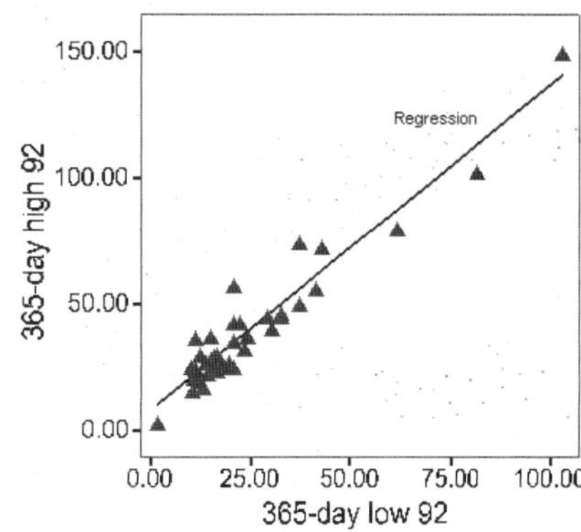

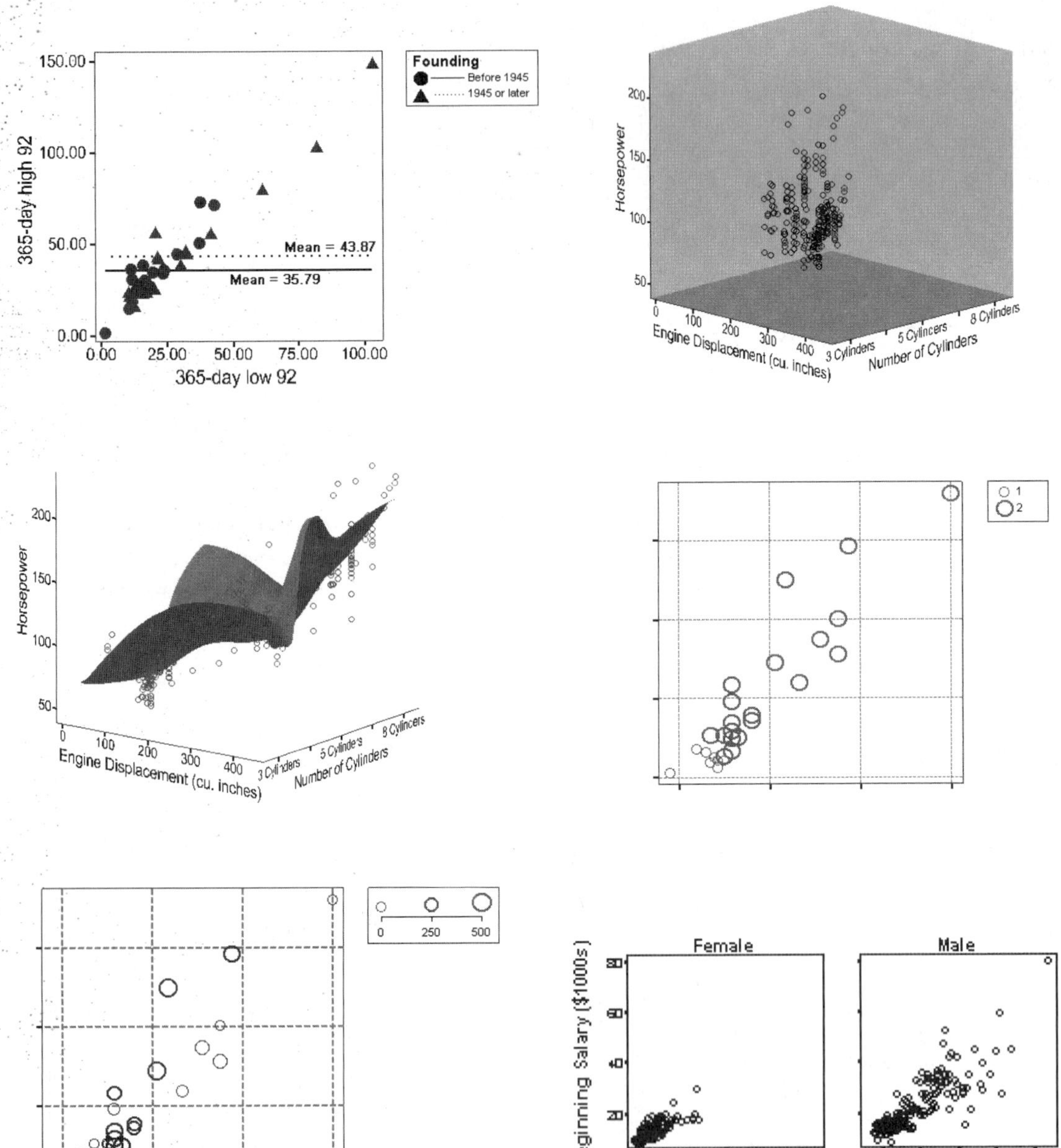
Founding
Before 1945
1945 or later
365-day high 92
365-day low 92
Mean = 43.87
Mean = 35.79
Horsepower
Engine Displacement (cu. inches)
Number of Cylinders
3 Cylinders
5 Cylinders
8 Cylinders
Female
Male
Beginning Salary ($1000s)
Current Salary ($1000s)

To Create a Scatterplot

▶ From the menus choose:

Graphs
  Interactive
    Scatterplot...

Create Scatterplot: Assign Variables

Figure 10-1
Create Scatterplot: Assign Variables tab

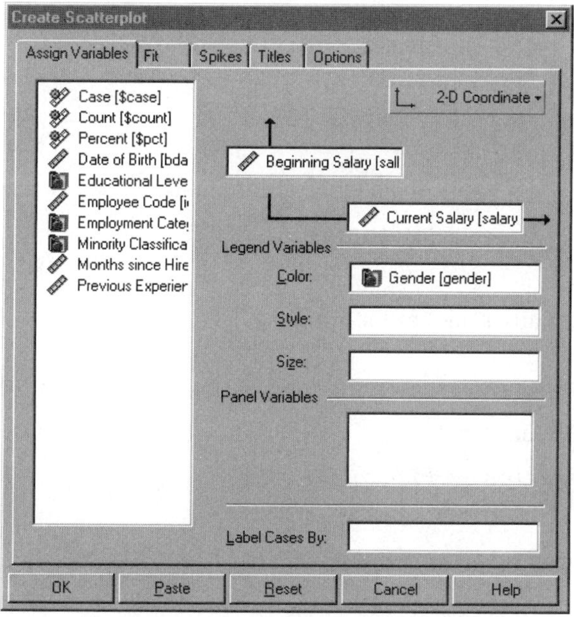

Scatterplots highlight the relationship between two or three quantitative variables by plotting the actual values along two or three axes. They often allow you to see relationships, such as a curvilinear pattern, that descriptive statistics do not reveal, and they can uncover bivariate outliers (for example, a low-priced house with 47 rooms).

Characteristics of subgroups can be studied if you assign a legend variable.

Number of dimensions. Selecting 2-D Coordinate or 3-D Coordinate changes the number of axis targets for variable selection.

Label Cases By. The values of a variable can be used to label points. If no variable is specified, case numbers will be used when labels are displayed.

To Create a Simple Scatterplot

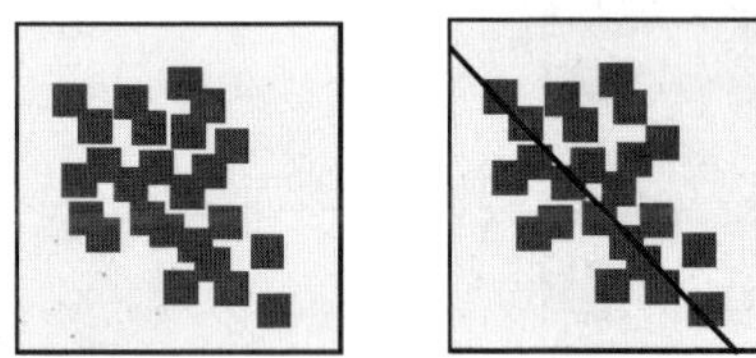

▶ Drag a variable (usually scale) to the *x1* axis.

▶ Drag another variable (usually scale) to the *y* axis.

Optionally, you can:

- Assign a variable for point labels.
- Add fit lines or surfaces (on the Fit tab).

To Create a Scatterplot Ordered by Case Number

▶ Drag a scale variable to the *y* axis.

▶ Drag the built-in variable *Case* to the *x1* axis.

To label the cases with the values of another variable, drag a variable to Label Cases By.

To Create a Scatterplot Split by Categories

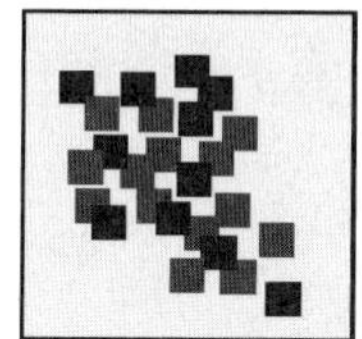
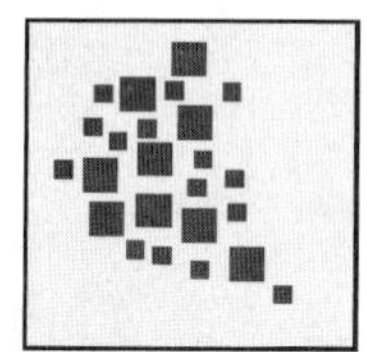
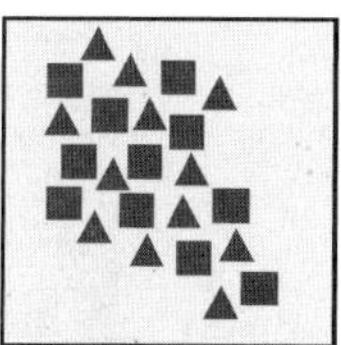

- ▶ Drag a scale variable to the *y* axis.
- ▶ Drag a variable (usually scale) to the *x1* axis.
- ▶ Drag a categorical variable to Color, Style, or Size.

  Optionally, you can drag variables to more than one of the legend targets.

To Create a Scatterplot with Colors or Sizes Assigned by a Summary of a Scale Variable

- ▶ Drag a variable to the *x1* axis.
- ▶ Drag a scale variable to the *y* axis.
- ▶ Drag a scale variable to Color or Size.

  The color or size of each symbol indicates its value in relation to the color or size scale in the legend.

To Create a 3-D Scatterplot

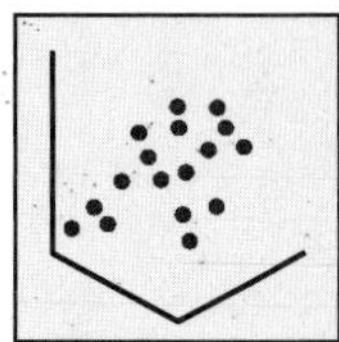

- Select 3-D Coordinate from the drop-down list.

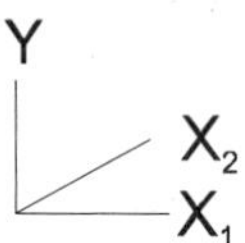

- Drag a scale or built-in variable to the *y* axis (dependent axis).
- Drag variables to the *x1* and *x2* axes.

To Create Scatterplot Panels for Categories

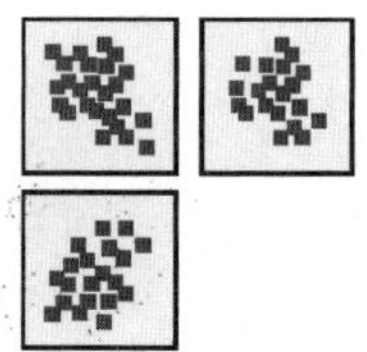

- Drag a variable to the *x1* axis.
- Drag a scale variable or a built-in variable to the *y* axis.
- Drag one or more categorical variables to Panel Variables.

Optionally, you can drag variables to the legend targets.

Create Scatterplot: Fit

Figure 10-2
Create Scatterplot: Fit tab

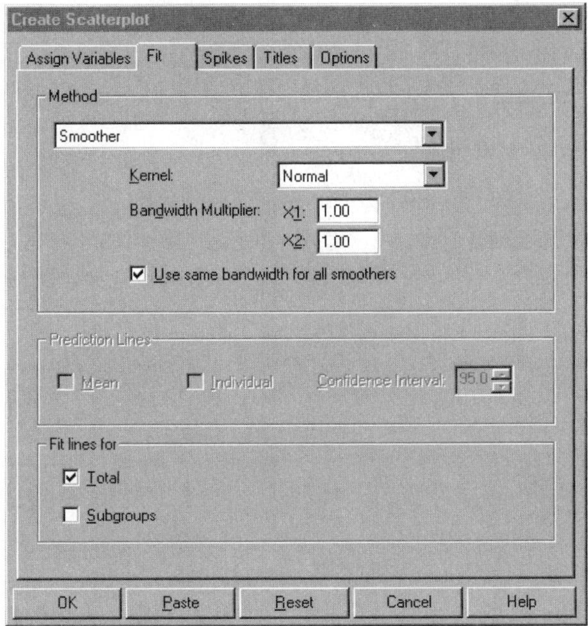

Several methods are available to fit lines to the points in a scatterplot.

Method. Fit lines show the best fit according to the method selected. Available methods for scatterplots are None, Regression, Mean, and Smoother. When Regression is selected, you can specify whether or not to have a constant in the equation. With no constant, the line goes through the origin.

When Smoother (local linear regression) is selected, you can specify the type of kernel, the bandwidth multipliers, and whether to use the same bandwidth for all smoothers. The same bandwidth can be useful for subgroups or panels.

Prediction Lines. When a mean or regression method is used, a mean prediction line or individual prediction lines are available that illustrate a specified confidence level.

Fit lines for. In addition to a fit line for the total cloud, if there is a categorical split, you can select fit lines for subgroups. If you add a fit line, be sure that at least one of these options is selected.

Create Scatterplot: Spikes

Figure 10-3
Create Scatterplot: Spikes tab

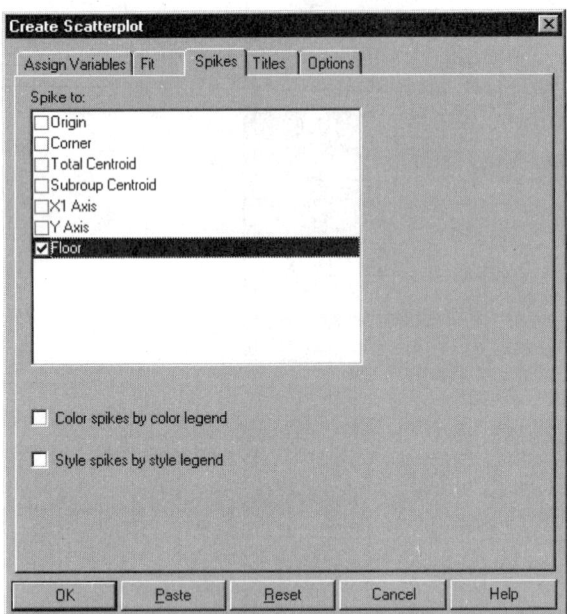

Spikes are lines drawn from cloud symbols to a point, axis, line, or surface. Spikes can help you read values from the axis or compare distances using line length. When drawn to the horizontal axis, spikes are sometimes called drop lines.

Spike to. Spike lines can be drawn to axes, reference lines, mean fit lines, and regression fit lines.

Color spikes by color legend. Matches spike color to the color legend for categorical variables.

Style spikes by style legend. Matches spike style to the style legend for categorical variables.

Modifying a Cloud

To modify a cloud of symbols in an existing scatterplot:

▶ From the menus choose:

Format
  Graph Elements
    Cloud...

or

▶ Right-click a symbol and from the context menu choose:

Cloud...

In the Cloud dialog box, you can choose tabs to modify symbols, labels, or the jittering of points. You can also change the attributes of the whole cloud of symbols.

Cloud: Symbols

Figure 10-4
Cloud: Symbols tab

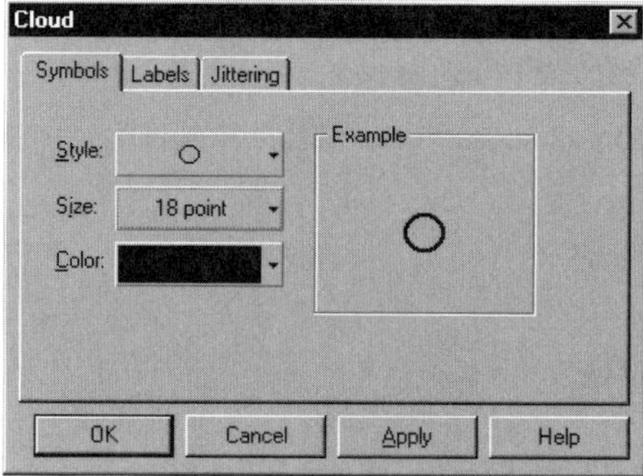

The style, size, and color of the cloud of symbols can be changed, if these attributes are not locked by the data. For example, suppose a variable *Group* is assigned to the color legend, making Group 1 red and Group 2 green. The Color option for the cloud on the Symbols tab is locked in this case, but you can change size and style.

Cloud: Labels

Figure 10-5
Cloud: Labels tab

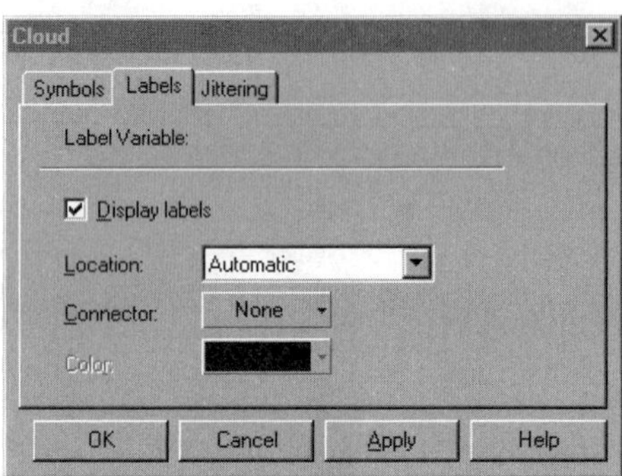

Label Variable. Indicates whether a label variable has been selected. If not, case numbers are used as labels. A label variable can be assigned in the Assign Graph Variables dialog box.

Display labels. Turns all labels on or off.

Location. Labels can be located at various positions around a circle, as times on a clock, or each label can be centered on the symbol.

Connector. Specifies the type of connector between the label and its corresponding symbol.

Color. Changes the color of connectors.

Cloud: Jittering

Figure 10-6
Cloud: Jittering tab

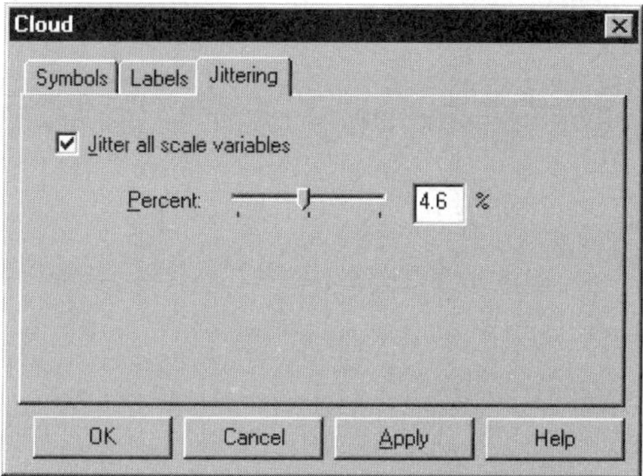

Jittering adjusts the display of points that would fall exactly on top of one another if no adjustment were made.

Jitter all scale variables. Adds a small amount of random noise to any scale data, whether or not the points are coincident. Categorical data are not jittered.

Changing Selected Symbol Properties

You can set the style, size, color, and label of individual symbols or a selection of several symbols.

To Change Individual Symbols in a Scatterplot

- Activate the chart by clicking it.
- Select one or more symbols in the chart.
- Right-click a symbol and from the menus choose:
  Properties

Optionally, you can change the appearance or labels of the selected symbols.

Symbol Properties: Appearance

Figure 10-7
Symbol properties: Appearance tab

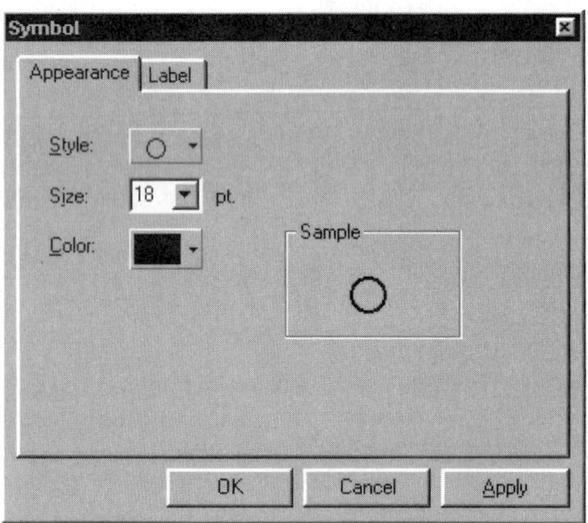

Individual symbols or a selected group of symbols can be changed if they are not controlled by the data. Choices are reflected in the Sample box.

Style. You can use symbols from the software's built-in symbol font or from other fonts installed on your system.

Size. Symbols can vary in size. A particular symbol or group of symbols could be larger for emphasis.

Color. Symbols can vary in color. A group of symbols might be a bright color to call attention to them.

Symbol Properties: Label

Figure 10-8
Symbol properties: Label tab

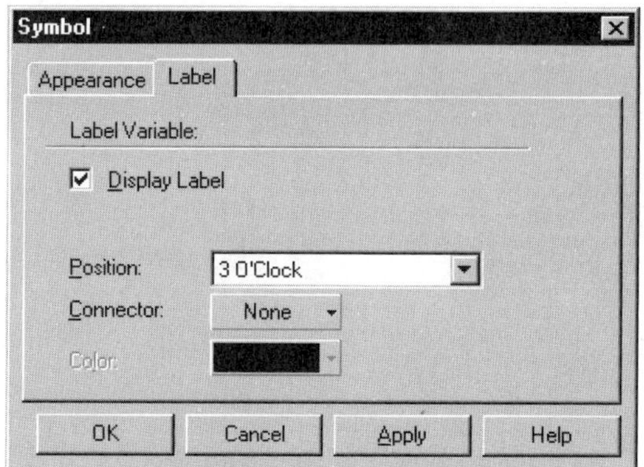

Case labels can be displayed for individual symbols or a selected group of symbols. You can change the format, position, or connector.

Chapter

11

Fit Lines, Surfaces, and Spikes

A fit line or surface can be added to a scatterplot to help you discern the relationship shown in the plot. The following are available for scatterplots:

Mean. For a 2-D chart, a line is drawn at the mean of the dependent (*y*) variable. For a 3-D chart, a plane is displayed.

Regression. Ordinary least squares are used to calculate the regression line or surface.

Smoother. A local linear regression (LLR) curve (or a surface for 3-D) is added to the plot. If the data appear to have many fluctuations, a smoother can help you see underlying patterns.

Groups. When the cloud is split into more than one group, you can show a fit line for all of the points in the cloud or lines for each subgroup.

Spikes. A line is drawn from the cloud symbols to a point, axis, line, or surface. Spikes can help you read values from the axis or compare distances using line length. When drawn to a horizontal axis, spikes are sometimes called **drop lines**.

To Add a Mean Fit Line to an Existing Scatterplot

- ▶ Create a scatterplot (cloud).
- ▶ Activate the chart (double-click it).
- ▶ From the menus choose:

Insert
  Fit Line
    Mean

To Add a Regression Fit Line to an Existing Scatterplot

- Create a scatterplot (cloud).
- Activate the chart (double-click it).
- From the menus choose:

  Insert
  Fit Line
  Regression

To Add a Smoother to an Existing Scatterplot

- Create a scatterplot (cloud).
- Activate the chart (double-click it).
- From the menus choose:

  Insert
  Fit Line
  Smoother

To Adjust a Fit Line or Surface

- Activate the chart (double-click it).
- Select a fit line.
- From the menus choose:

  Edit
  Parameters

  or

- Right-click the fit line and from the context menu choose Parameters.
- Adjust the desired parameters.

Mean Parameters

Figure 11-1
Mean Parameters palette

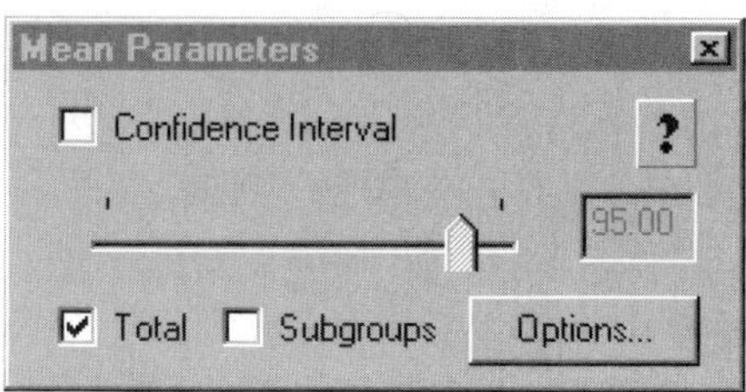

This palette controls the parameters for a mean fit line. You can display a confidence interval around the fit line at a level between 50% and 100%, and this percentage level can be changed.

Total. Display a line for the complete set of points.

Subgroups. If the data points are split into subgroups by a legend variable, you can display a line for each subgroup.

Regression Parameters

Figure 11-2
Regression Parameters palette

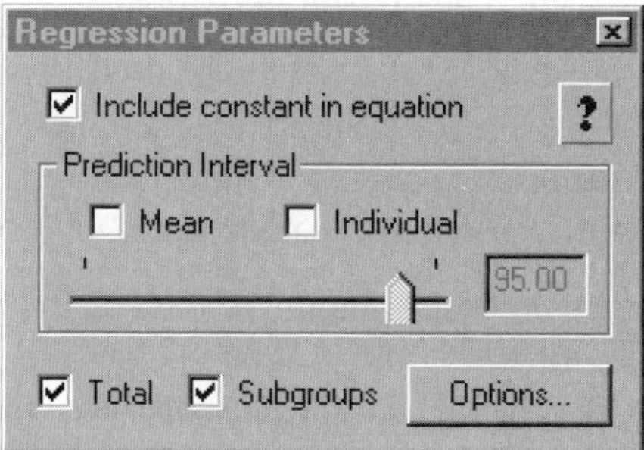

This palette controls the parameters for a regression fit line.

Include constant in equation. Deselect this item to display a regression line through the origin.

Prediction Interval. You can display a confidence interval around the fit line at a level between 50% and 100%. Both Mean and Individual prediction lines are available.

Total. Display a line for the complete set of points.

Subgroups. If the data points are split into subgroups by a legend variable, you can display a line for each subgroup.

Smoother Parameters

Figure 11-3
Smoother Parameters palette

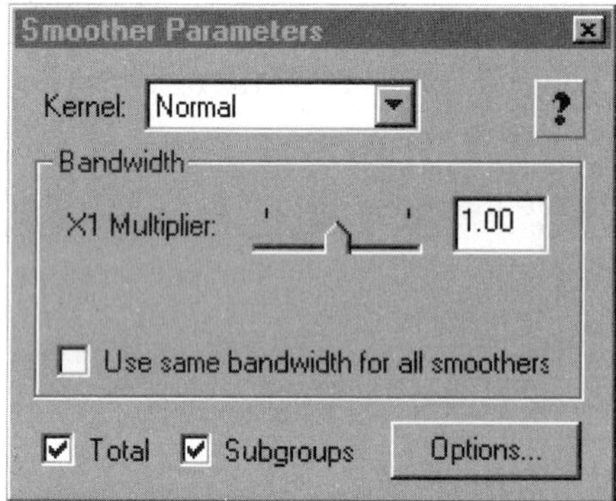

This palette controls the parameters for a smoother (local linear regression). If you change the parameters, you will see the chart change on the screen.

Kernel. From the drop-down list, you can choose the kernel to be used. A normal kernel is the default. With an Epanechnikov kernel, the curve is not as smooth as with a normal kernel but is smoother than with a uniform kernel. (For more information, see Simonoff, Jeffrey S., *Smoothing Methods in Statistics*, 1996, New York: Springer-Verlag.)

Bandwidth. The bandwidth multiplier changes the amount of data that is included in each calculation of a small part of the smoother. The program determines the default size of the bandwidth that is designated as having a multiplier of 1. The multiplier can be adjusted to emphasize specific features of the plot that are of interest. Any positive multiplier (including fractions) is allowed. The larger the multiplier, the smoother the curve. The range between 0 and 10 should suffice in most applications. For 3-D plots, you can specify a multiplier for each independent axis, ($x1$ and $x2$).

You can select Use same bandwidth for all smoothers when you want the same bandwidth for different subgroups or panels.

Total. Displays a line for the complete set of points.

Subgroups. If the data points are split into subgroups by a legend variable, you can display a line for each subgroup.

For more information on local linear regression, see Fan and Marron, Fast Implementations of Nonparametric Curve Estimators, *Journal of Computational and Graphical Statistics*, 3: 35–56, 1994.

Changing Fit Line Properties

Fit line appearance and labels can be changed from the Options dialog boxes.

Mean and Regression Properties

Figure 11-4
Mean Options dialog box

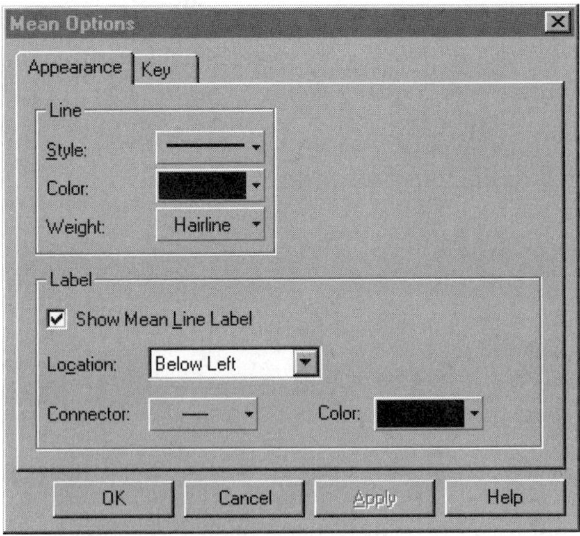

Figure 11-5
Regression Options dialog box

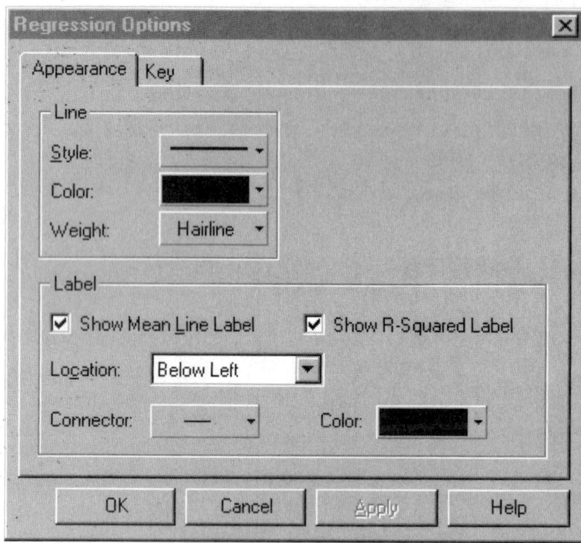

For a selected mean or regression fit line, you can change the style, color, weight, and label. For a regression fit line, you can also choose Show R-Squared Label.

To Change Mean and Regression Fit Line Properties

- Activate the chart (double-click it).
- Select a fit line.
- From the menus choose:

  Edit
  Properties...

  or

- Right-click the fit line and from the context menu choose Options.

Optionally, you can change the style, weight, color, and labels.

Smoother Properties

Figure 11-6
Smoother Options dialog box

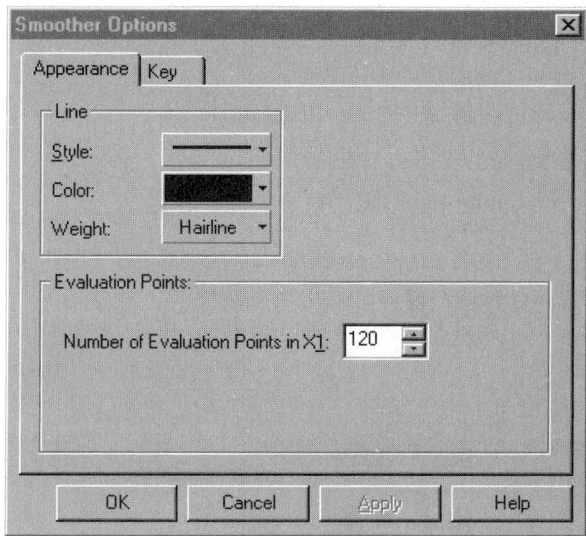

For a selected mean fit line, you can change the style, color, weight, and label.

Evaluation Points govern the number of points used in the evenly spaced grid on which the smoother will be evaluated. The default for a 2-D smoother is 120, while for the 3-D smoother, it is 30 by 30. The larger the number of evaluation points, the finer will be the rendering of the smoother; however, it is also more expensive computationally. Particularly in the three-dimensional case, the evaluation time for smoothers increases rapidly with the number of evaluation points. If you change the number of evaluation points, you should try to choose a number slightly less than the nearest power of 2 because the convolution algorithm is used. For example, it is better to choose 15 (which is 2 to the 4th power minus 1) rather than to choose 17.

To Change Smoother Properties

- ▶ Activate the chart (double-click it).
- ▶ Select a mean fit line.

▶ From the menus choose:

Edit
  Properties...

or

▶ Right-click the fit line and from the context menu choose Options.

Optionally, you can:

- Change the style, weight, color, and labels.
- Change the number of evaluation points for the *x1* and *x2* axes.

Adding Spikes to a Scatterplot

Figure 11-7
Spikes dialog box

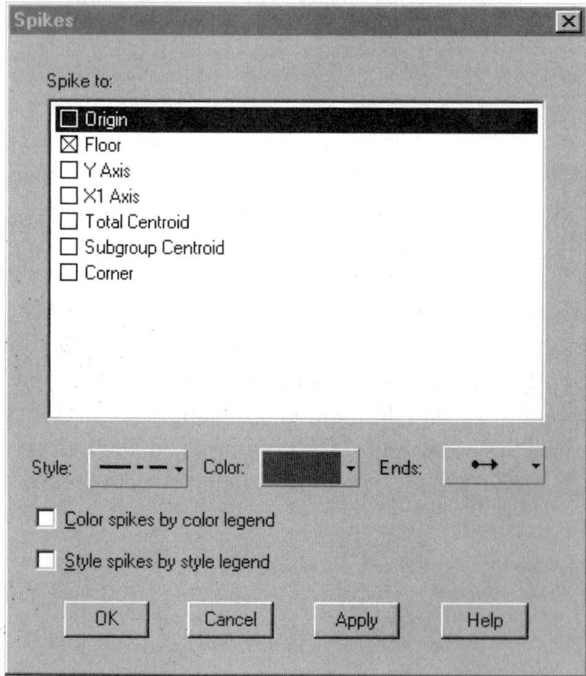

Spikes are lines drawn from cloud symbols to a point, axis, line, or surface. Spikes can help you read values from the axis or compare distances using line length. When drawn to a horizontal axis, spikes are sometimes called **drop lines**.

Spike to. Spike lines can be drawn to origins, the floor, axes, reference lines, and mean or regression fit lines. You can choose style, color, and ends options for spike lines.

Color spikes by color legend. Matches spike color to the color legend for categorical variables.

Style spikes by style legend. Matches spike style to the style legend for categorical variables.

To Add Spikes to an Existing Scatterplot

- Create a scatterplot (cloud).
- Activate the chart (double-click it).
- From the menus choose:

  Insert
    Spikes...

- Spike to floor, axes, origins, reference lines, and mean or regression fit lines.
- Choose color and style options.

Changing Spike Properties

Spikes can be changed from the Properties dialog boxes.

Spike Properties

Figure 11-8
Spike Properties dialog box

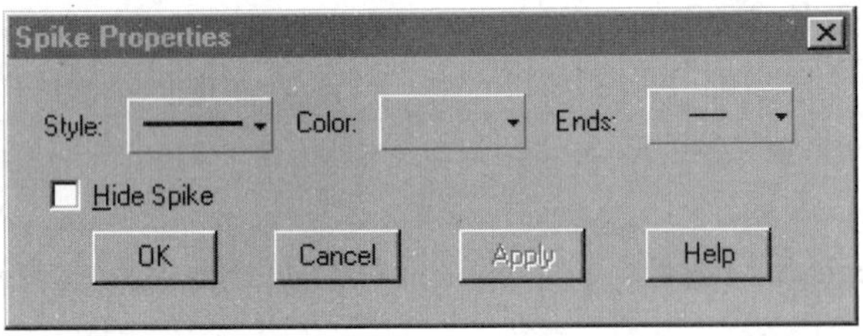

For a selected spike line, you can change the style, color, and ends. Selected spikes can also be hidden.

To Change Spike Properties

- ▶ Activate the chart (double-click it).
- ▶ Select a spike line.
- ▶ From the menus choose:

  Edit
  Properties...

  or

- ▶ Right-click the spike line and from the context menu choose Properties.

Optionally, you can:

- Change the style, color, and ends for spike lines.
- Hide the selected spike lines.

Chapter

12

Modifying Interactive Charts

After creating a chart, you may wish to modify it, either to obtain more information about the data or to enhance the chart for presentation. Dynamic chart modification capabilities described in this chapter allow you to:

- Change labeling.
- Adjust each axis.
- Modify panels.
- Change legends and keys.
- Change the size and fill of the data region.
- Use the Chart Manager to edit or delete chart objects.
- Rearrange chart objects.
- Edit and apply ChartLooks.
- Change colors and styles of chart objects.

In addition, you can make the following modifications by using information in previous chapters:

- Change variable assignments.
- Add or delete graphic elements.
- Change summary functions.
- Add fit lines, reference lines, or surfaces.

To Activate a Chart in the Viewer

▶ Double-click anywhere in the chart.

or

▶ Select the chart and from the menus choose:

Edit
  SPSS Interactive Graph Object
    Edit *or* Open

The menus change to Interactive Graphics Editor menus, and the chart has its own movable toolbars.

Selection of Chart Objects to Modify

Objects in the chart can be selected separately or in groups and then modified.

Examples:

- Select one bar in a simple bar chart and change its color.
- Select the set of red bars and apply a texture.
- Select two pie slices and explode them.
- Select an axis and change the scale and the line style.

Context menu. A right-click on most objects displays a context menu. At the bottom of the context menu for a chart element (bars, cloud, pie, etc.) are two items: the name of the element and Properties (for example, Bars and Properties).

- To modify the whole element (for example, all the bars in a chart), choose the name of the element.
- To modify only the selected object or objects, choose Properties.

Figure 12-1
Context menu

Example:

Right-click one bar in a simple bar chart with no legend. To change the color of only the selected bar, choose Properties from the context menu. To change the color of all the bars simultaneously (the bar element), choose Bars from the context menu.

Changing a whole category. If you want to apply properties to a category of objects, you should select the category in the legend, not the set of individual objects within the category.

To Select and Modify a Chart Object

- Activate the chart (double-click it).
- Right-click the object to be modified.

  The object is selected and a context menu is displayed. You can choose an action or a dialog box from the context menu.

  or

- Click the object to be modified.

▶ Select a command from the menus at the top of the Viewer.

or

▶ Double-click the object to be modified.

This displays a dialog box for editing the object you clicked. Double-clicking a graphical element displays the dialog box for that element. For example, double-clicking a bar displays the Bars dialog box.

To Select a Category of Objects

▶ Click the category swatch in the legend. For example, to select the red bars in a chart, click the red swatch in the legend.

To Move a Chart Object

▶ Activate the chart (double-click it).

▶ Drag an object (such as a legend or title) to a new position.

Titles, captions, legends, keys, and axis titles can be moved. As you make other changes, the object retains its position relative to the data region.

Interactive, Interactive (Detached), and Static Charts

An interactive chart has access to the variables used to create it. Using the Assign Graph Variables dialog box, you can change variable assignments whenever the chart is activated.

- If the data file that was used to create the chart is still open and nothing has changed in the Data Editor since the chart was created, the chart is labeled **Interactive** in the status bar of the Viewer. You can change any of the variable assignments for interactive charts, using all of the variables available in the active data file. These charts use the Interactive Chart Editor.
- If Save data with the chart is selected on the Interactive tab of Options and the data file has been changed or a new data file has been opened, the chart is detached from the data file and is labeled **Interactive (detached)** in the status bar of the Viewer. For a detached chart, you can still change variable assignments; however, only

variables used while the chart was actively connected to the open data file are now available. The Assign Graph Variables dialog box contains a message about available variables.

- All interactive charts become static charts if Save only summarized data is selected on the Interactive tab of Options (Edit menu of the Viewer). In a **static** chart, only the summarized data is saved, and you cannot change variable assignments, although you can change attributes such as color, fill, and symbol size. You can turn an interactive chart into a static chart by right-clicking and choosing Save only summarized data from the context menu. A static chart cannot be changed to an interactive chart.
- Non-interactive charts and charts created in previous versions of the software are not interactive. The chart objects can be edited for attributes such as color, but the variable assignments cannot be changed. These charts use the Chart Editor window.

Note: In the SmartViewer, all charts are either Interactive (detached) or Static charts.

Figure 12-2
Assign Graph Variables dialog boxes for an Interactive chart and an Interactive (detached) chart

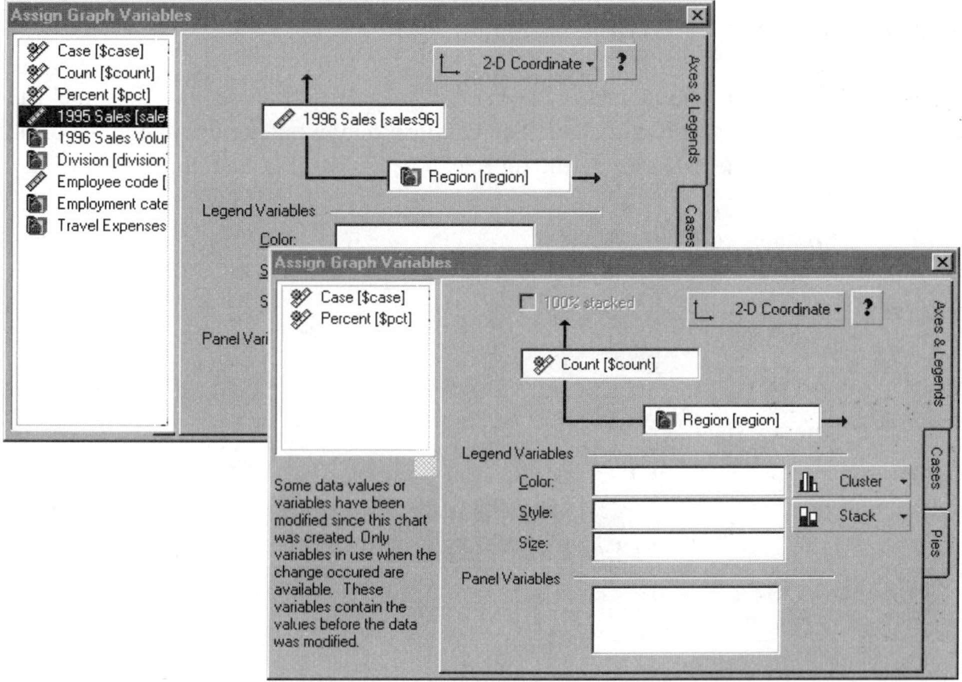

To Change the Assignments of Variables

- ▶ Activate the chart (double-click it).
- ▶ From the menus choose:

  Edit
    Assign Variables

  or

- ▶ Click the Assign Variables tool on the chart toolbar.
- ▶ Drag the desired variables to their new targets.

  The chart changes immediately.

There is no need to drag the previous variables out of a variable target before dragging another variable to the target. The variables pivot (exchange positions) when you drag and drop one variable on top of another.

Modifying 3-D Charts

Three-dimensional charts have some special controls displayed on the 3-D palette when the chart is activated. You can turn on the palette or change the lighting by clicking the 3-D tool on the toolbar. The 3-D tool is available only in 3-D charts.

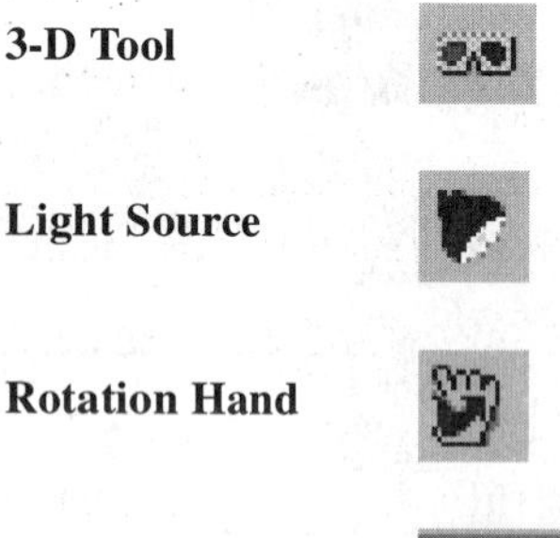

Rotation Dial

Light Source. The position of the light source can be changed. This changes the shading of various surfaces and helps the objects appear more realistic. The position of the light source can direct the observer's attention to important features of the chart.

Rotation. Three-dimensional charts can be rotated both horizontally and vertically. Rotation facilitates seeing what is behind the objects that are in the front area of the chart. It is also useful for visually spotting patterns in the data. Two types of tools are available for rotating the chart: the rotation hand and the dials.

To Rotate a 3-D Chart

▶ If the 3-D palette is not displayed, click the 3-D tool on the toolbar and select 3-D Palette.

There are two dials in the 3-D tool palette, one horizontal and one vertical.

▶ Drag either dial with the mouse.

The chart rotates when the dial is turned by the mouse. The number of degrees of rotation is indicated in a text box. Another way to set the rotation amount is to enter the number of degrees in the text box.

▶ To reset the rotation in either direction to its default value, click the Vertical Reset tool or the Horizontal Reset tool (the rotating arrow icons next to the text boxes).

Optionally, you can click the rotation hand and then drag within the chart itself.

To Display the 3-D Palette

▶ Activate a 3-D chart (double-click it).

▶ If the 3-D palette is not displayed, click the 3-D tool on the toolbar and select 3-D Palette.

or

▶ From the menus choose:

View
 3-D Palette

To Change the Direction of Light

- Activate a 3-D chart (double-click it).
- On the 3-D palette, click the Light Source tool.
- Select the direction of the light source.

or

- Click the 3-D tool on the toolbar to change the lighting or activate the palette.

Chart Manager

Figure 12-3
Chart Manager dialog box

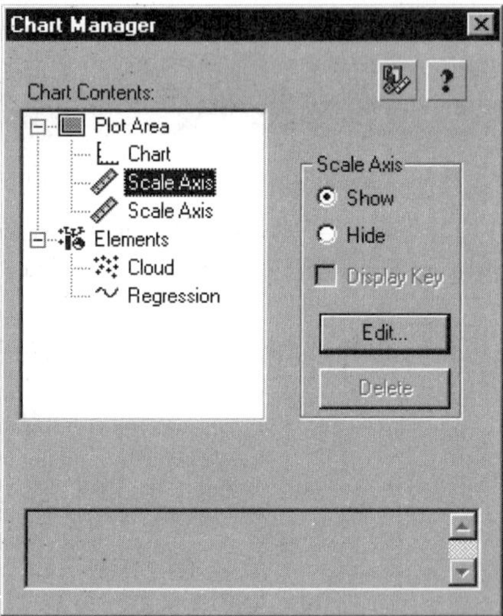

The Chart Manager gives easy access to all of the separate components that make up a chart. They can be selected individually on the list, and then edited, deleted, or hidden. Keys can be displayed for chart elements such as clouds and fit lines.

The Chart Manager also gives information or warnings about individual components of the chart. For example, if the selected component is Bar, the Chart Manager displays the summary function currently in use for bars in the chart. Warnings are preceded by an exclamation point.

To Use the Chart Manager

- ▶ Activate the chart (double-click it).
- ▶ From the menus choose:

  Edit
   Chart Manager...

  or

- ▶ Click the Chart Manager tool.

- ▶ Select an item in the Chart Contents list.
- ▶ Read any information about the item that appears under the list.

  Optionally, you can:

  - Show or hide the selected item.
  - Display a key associated with the selected item, if available.
  - Edit the selected item, if available.
  - Delete the selected item from the chart.
  - Click the Assign Graph Variables tool to open the Assign Graph Variables dialog box.

Inserting Additional Elements

You can add elements to an interactive chart to convey additional information. For example:

- Add scatterplot clouds or error bars to a bar chart of means to show the distribution of data.
- Add error bars to bar or line charts of means to show confidence intervals for the mean values.
- Add additional lines to a line chart to display lines for different summary functions (for example, mean and median).
- Add fit lines to scatterplots to show trends and patterns.

Inserted elements often require additional modification for adequate display. The default color of many inserted elements is often the same as the color of existing elements in the chart, making it difficult to distinguish separate elements (for example, a red line displayed on a red bar is essentially invisible). Also, when inserting an element of the same type as an element that already exists in the chart, it may appear as if nothing has happened because the new element is exactly the same as the original element. For example, if you want to insert a line that displays median values in a line chart that displays mean values, the default inserted line also shows means, making the two lines indistinguishable.

The easiest way to change the attributes of an inserted element that is difficult to see or select is to select the element in the Chart Manager.

To Insert Additional Elements in a Chart

▶ Activate the chart (double-click it).

▶ From the menus choose:

Insert
  [element type]

or

▶ Click the Insert Element tool on the chart toolbar.

▶ Select an element type from the list.

Any element you select is inserted in the chart. However, only elements that are compatible with the information already displayed in the chart are displayed. For example, error bars will be displayed on a bar chart that displays mean values of a scale variable but not on a bar chart of simple counts. In many cases, the Chart Manager contains information that explains why an element is not displayed.

Figure 12-4
Element information in the Chart Manager

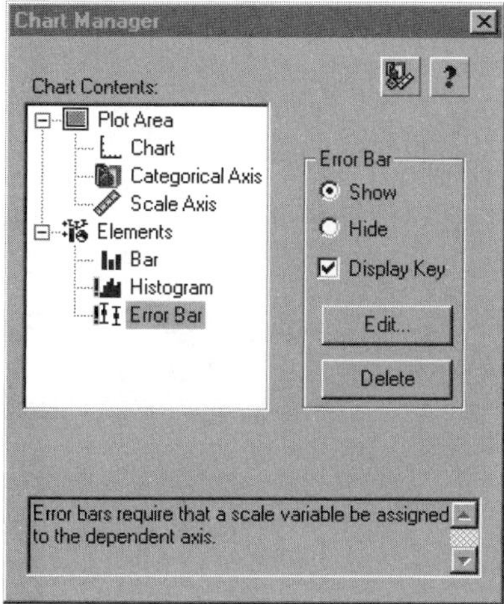

Keys

Each element in a chart can have a key. The key shows summary information about the element. You cannot edit the text of a key, but you can change the key display properties in the chart modifications dialog box. If you change the summary function for an element, the key changes accordingly.

Dragging. A key can be dragged with the mouse to a new position in the chart.

To Show or Hide a Key

- Activate the chart (double-click it).
- From the menus choose:

  Edit
    Chart Manager...

- Select an element in the list.
- Select or deselect Display Key.

  or

- If the key is displayed, right-click the key and choose Hide Key.

Key Properties

Figure 12-5
Key display properties on the Summary Function tab

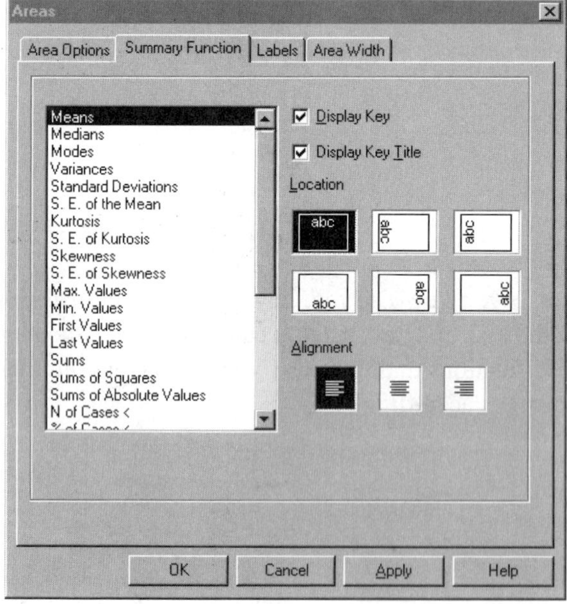

A key shows summary information about a chart element. For all chart elements, the following options can be changed:

Display Key. Deselect this item to hide the key.

Display Key Title. The title for a key can be on or off.

Location. The title can be in various positions with respect to the text of the key.

Alignment. The title can be at either edge or centered.

To Change Key Properties

- Activate the chart (double-click it).

- From the menus choose:

  Format
    Key
      [element name]

  or

- Right-click the key, and from the context menu choose Properties.

- Select the desired options.

Data Region

Figure 12-6
2-D and 3-D Data Region dialog boxes

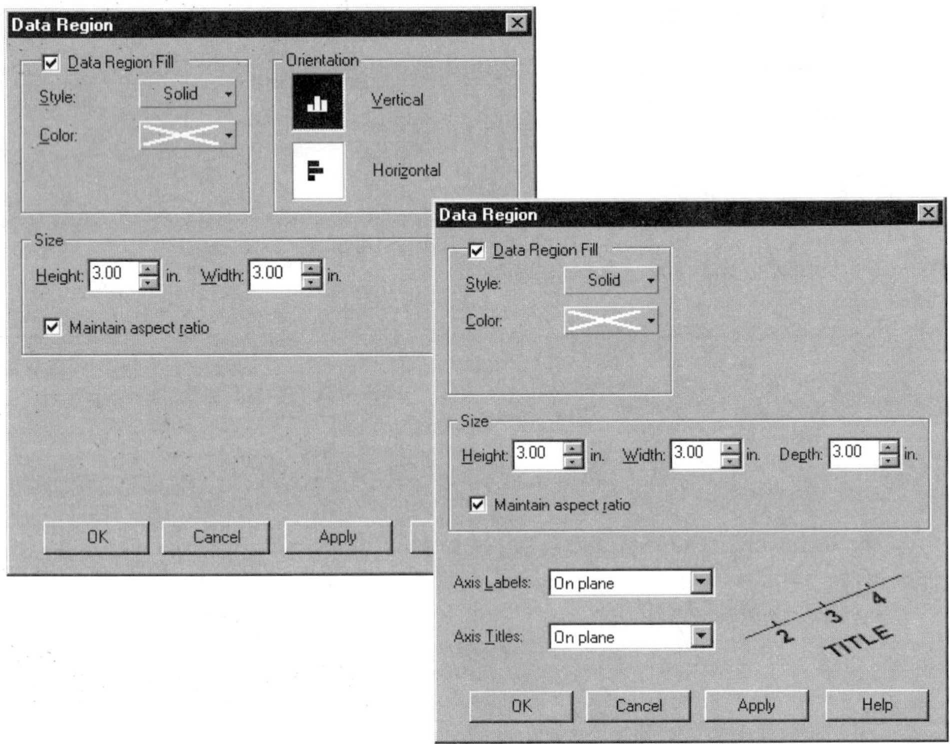

A 2-D data region is the area where the data are plotted, initially defined by the position of the axes. A 3-D data region is the volume where the data are plotted, initially defined by the position of the axes. Other objects in the chart are located with respect to the data region.

Data Region Fill. The background of the data region can have a fill or be turned off. In a 3-D chart, the fill is shaded according to the location of the light source.

Orientation (2-D only). The dependent (*y*) axis can be either vertical or horizontal. Changing orientation swaps the axes, along with their assigned variables.

Size. The size of the data region can be specified. This area or volume does not include axis labels or axis titles. If Maintain aspect ratio is selected, entering a height, width, or depth automatically changes the other two so that the ratio is maintained. Units are determined from the Interactive tab of the Options dialog box (Edit menu in the Viewer).

Axis Labels (3-D only). Labels can face the front of the chart or lie on the plane formed by two intersecting axes.

Axis Titles (3-D only). Titles can face the front of the chart or lie on the plane formed by two intersecting axes. Labels and titles can have different orientations.

To Change the Appearance of the 2-D Data Region

▶ Activate a 2-D chart.

▶ From the menus choose:

Format
  Data Region...

or

▶ Click the Chart Manager tool, select Chart, and click Edit.

▶ Select the desired characteristics.

Optionally, you can:

- Change the fill.
- Change the size.
- Change the orientation.

To Change the Appearance of the 3-D Data Region

▶ Activate a 3-D chart.

▶ From the menus choose:

Format
  Data Region...

or

▶ Click the Chart Manager tool, select Chart, and click Edit.

▶ Select the desired characteristics.

Optionally, you can:

- Change the fill.
- Change the size.
- Change label and title orientation.

Panels

Panels are a means of incorporating more data dimensions in a chart. Each panel contains a chart for a different set of cases, determined by categories of a variable or a combination of categories.

To Change a Panel Data Region

▶ Activate a paneled chart (double-click it).

▶ From the menus choose:

Format
  Data Region...

▶ Click a tab (Size, Categories, Appearance, Arrangement, or Titles).

▶ Select the desired options.

▶ Click OK to apply the new options and close the dialog box, or click Apply to apply the new options and leave the dialog box open.

Panel Data Region: Size

Figure 12-7
Panel Data Region: Size tab

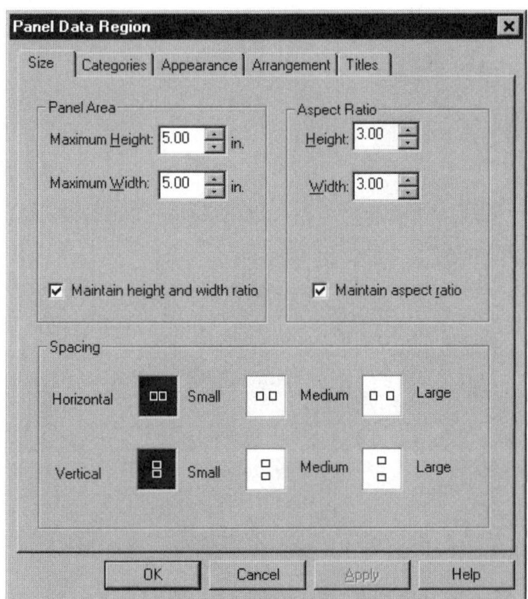

Panel Area. Specifies the size, in inches, of the panel area. The default size is 5×5. The height and width ratio is maintained by default.

Aspect Ratio. Changes the ratio of lengths for panels. Values for height, width, and depth (3-D chart only) represent a ratio, not actual lengths. To make panels larger or smaller, change the panel area values. The aspect ratio is maintained by default.

Spacing. Allows you to customize the orientation and spacing of panels in the panel area.

To Change Panel Data Region Size

- Click the Size tab.
- Deselect Maintain height and width ratio and Maintain aspect ratio to change panel size ratios.
- Select the desired options.

Panel Data Region: Appearance

Figure 12-8
Panel Data Region: Appearance tab for 2-D and 3-D

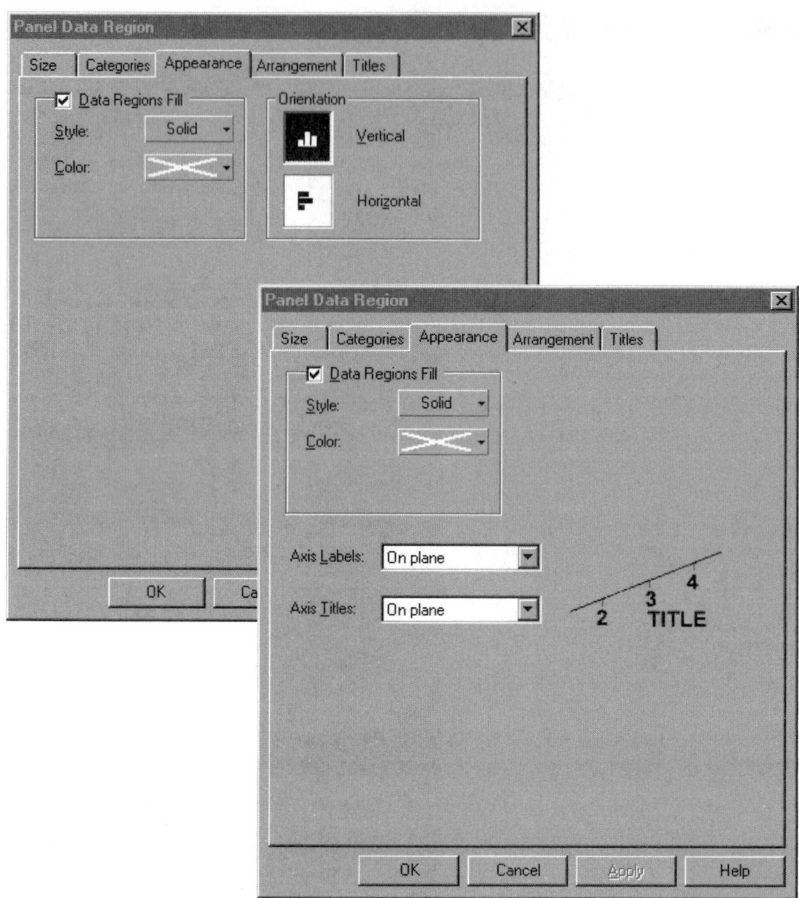

Data Region Fill. The fill of the data region is the background behind the elements. Style and color of the data region can be changed.

Orientation (2-D only). Changing the orientation of the data region here has the same effect as changing the orientation on the Assign Variables dialog box. The variables are switched, along with the axes.

Axis Labels (3-D only). Labels can face the front of the chart or lie on the plane formed by two intersecting axes.

Axis Titles (3-D only). Titles can face the front of the chart or lie on the plane formed by two intersecting axes. Labels and titles can have different orientations.

To Modify Panel Data Region Appearance

- Click the Appearance tab.
- Select the desired options.

Panel Data Region: Arrangement

If panels are based on only one variable, you can adjust the arrangement of panels.

Figure 12-9
Panel Data Region: Arrangement tab

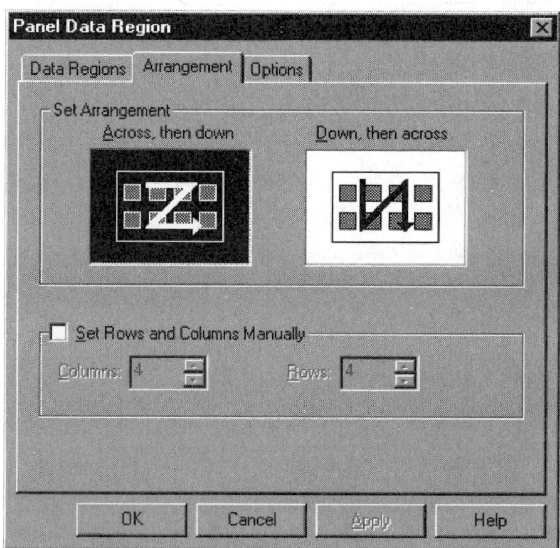

Set Arrangement. Across, then down means that the first row is filled by categories, then the second row, and so on. The other choice, Down, then across, means that the first column is filled, then the second column, the third, and so on.

Set Rows and Columns Manually. If you have both rows and columns, they can be arranged automatically, or you can select this item and specify either the number of rows or the number of columns, depending on which arrangement is selected.

To Change the Arrangement of Panels

- ▶ Click the Arrangement tab.
- ▶ Select the desired options.

Panel Data Region: Titles

Figure 12-10
Panel Data Region: Titles tab

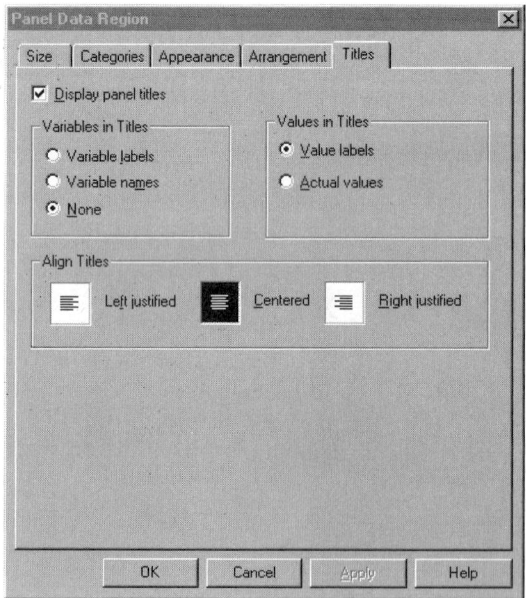

Display Panel Titles. Titles for each panel can be displayed or hidden.

Variables in Titles. Specifies whether panel titles will feature variable labels such as *Employment Category* or variable names such as *jobcat*.

Values in Titles. Specifies whether panel titles will feature value labels, such as *Managerial,* or actual values, such as *jobcat 3.*

Align Titles. Positions panel titles as centered or left- or right-justified.

To Change Panel Data Region Titles

- Click the Titles tab.
- Select the desired options.

Layout

Objects in a chart can have various arrangements in and around the data region. These objects include the title, subtitle, caption, legend, and key.

Figure 12-11
Default layout

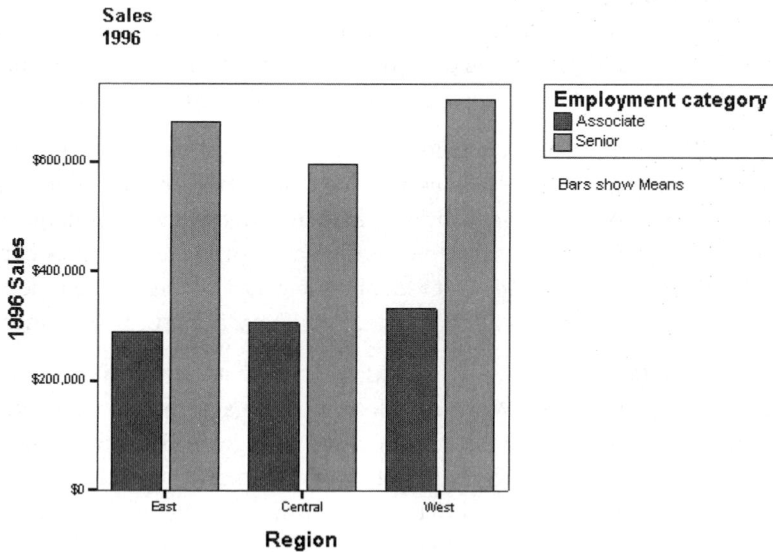

After the chart is made, you can drag the chart objects to new positions.

To Arrange Chart Objects

- ▶ Activate the chart.
- ▶ From the menus choose:

Format
  Arrange All

The title, subtitle, caption, legends, and keys are arranged around the data region of the chart in default positions. You can drag them to new positions.

Legend Modification

Color, size, and style are often used to encode independent data dimensions visually in a chart. For example, red bars or lines could represent domestic sales, while green bars or lines might represent international sales. Similarly, small symbols and large symbols can be used to distinguish categories, as can different styles of symbols or different styles of fill. You can make distinctions in color or size on a continuous scale as well as on discrete categories.

A legend shows how to decode color, size, or style in a chart. You can assign variables to a legend on the Assign Variables tab when creating a chart or later when modifying a chart. A legend has many properties that are subject to change.

Categorical legends. When a categorical variable is assigned to a legend target, each category in the legend variable is assigned a color, style, or size as determined by the ChartLook. When a categorical variable is assigned, the elements in the chart are split or divided into groups. The assignment is displayed in a legend on the chart. Up to three legend variables can be assigned at the same time, depending on the type of chart. Each of these assignments creates a separate legend. Thus, a chart can have multiple legends.

Scale legends. In the legend, a scale variable can be assigned to Color or Size, when those targets are available. When a scale variable is assigned to a legend, the existing elements take on the color or size defined by the legend. By default, the scale for categories is determined according to the mean of the variable. For example, suppose that the variable *age* is assigned to color and (on a continuous scale) the mean age ranges from light red (20 years) to dark red (95 years). An object in the chart that represents a summary of values for 25 cases would be colored according to the mean age of those 25 cases.

Position and display. A legend can be dragged to a new position. It can also be hidden.

To Change Legend Properties

- Activate the chart (double-click it).
- From the menus choose:

  Format
  Legend

- Choose Color Legend, Style Legend, or Size Legend.

  or

- Double-click the legend to be modified.

  or

- Open the Chart Manager, select the legend, and click Edit.
- Click a tab.
- Select the desired options.

  If you click Apply, the new properties are applied to the selected legend and the dialog box remains open. If you click OK, the properties are applied to the legend and the dialog box closes.

To Change the Position of a Legend

- Activate the chart (double-click it).
- Use the mouse to drag the legend to a new position.

To Show or Hide a Legend

- Activate the chart (double-click it).

- From the menus choose:

  Edit
  Chart Manager...

  or

- Click the Chart Manager icon.

- Select the legend of interest in the Chart Contents. This enables the Show and Hide radio buttons.

- Select Show or Hide.

  or

  If the legend is displayed, right-click the legend and choose Hide Legend from the context menu.

Legend: Title

Figure 12-12
Legend: Title tab

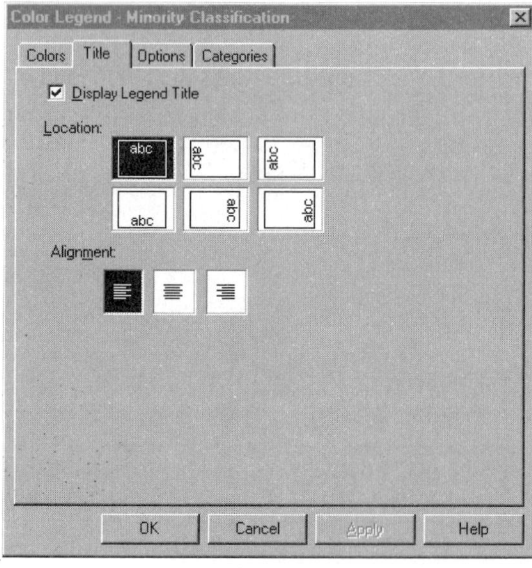

Legend titles can be displayed or turned off.

Location. The title can be located with respect to the edges of the legend. When the title is vertical on either side of the legend box, the title orientation can be either up or down.

Alignment. Alignment places the title at either edge or in the center of the legend box.

To Change a Legend Title

▶ Click the Title tab.

Optionally, you can:

- Turn the legend title on or off.
- Change the alignment and location of the legend title.

To change text in the legend, double-click the text to be changed or use the Text tool.

Categorical Legend: Options

Figure 12-13
Categorical Legend: Options tab

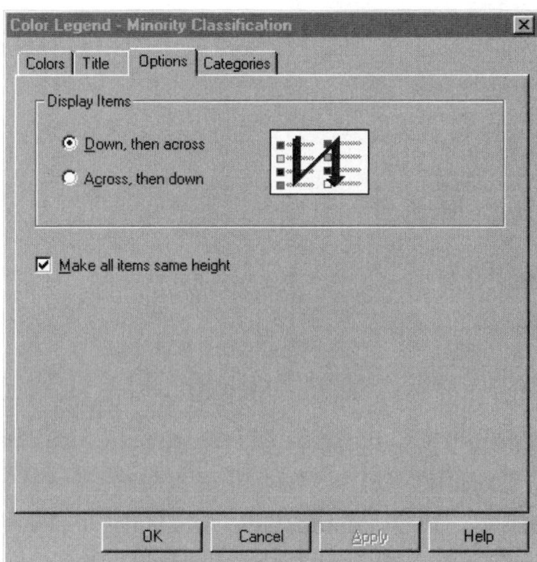

For a categorical legend having more than one column, items can be ordered in rows (across, then down) or columns (down, then across). Also, all items can be assigned the height of the tallest item. This feature is useful for a legend that has more than one column.

To Change the Display Arrangement of a Categorical Legend

- Click the Options tab.
- Select the desired display formats.

Categorical Legend: Categories

Figure 12-14
Color or Size Legend (Categorical): Categories tab

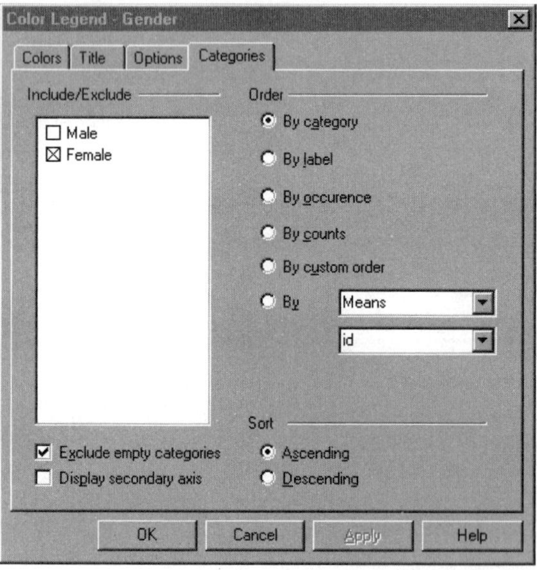

Through the Categorical Legend dialog box, you can reorder categories for display in your chart. You can change the order, sort and type of categories included.

Panel Variable. Selects which variable to reorder for charts with panel variables.

Include/Exclude. Controls which categories are displayed in the chart.

Exclude empty categories. Hides categories with no data.

Order. Reorders categories manually by drag and drop. Standard order uses properties such as Label, Occurrence, and Counts.

Sort. Displays categories in ascending or descending order.

Display secondary axis. Displays a second axis in the chart that mirrors the primary axis. (*Note:* Secondary axes are not displayed for 3-D or paneled charts.)

To Modify Legend Categories

▶ Click the Categories tab.

▶ Reorder categories for display in your chart.

Optionally, you can:

- Reorder the variables in the list by dragging and dropping them.
- Exclude empty categories.
- Display a secondary axis.
- Sort categories by ascending or descending order.

Color Legends

In color legends, if a categorical variable is assigned, each category is assigned a distinct color. If a scale variable is assigned to a color legend, a continuous color gradient is used to indicate the values along a scale. For summary elements, the scale is determined by a summary function.

Color Legend (Categorical): Colors

Figure 12-15
Color Legend (Categorical): Colors tab

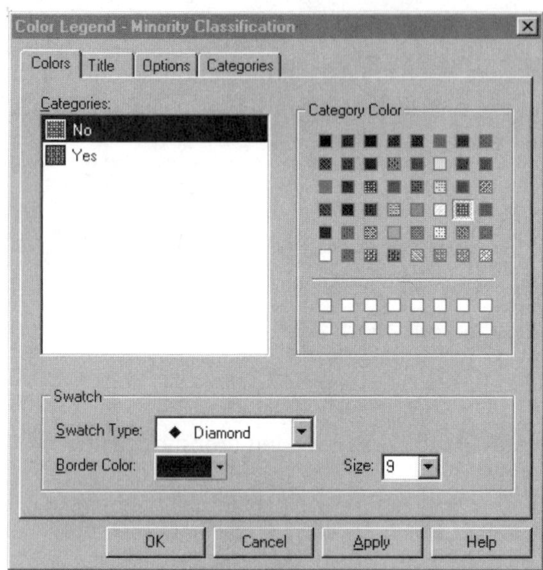

You can select categories individually to change colors. You can also change the swatch in the legend, as well as the size and the color of the border around the swatch.

To Change Colors in a Category Legend

- ▶ Click the Colors tab.
- ▶ Select a category.
- ▶ Select the desired color for that category.

Optionally, you can modify the swatch in the legend.

To Add Custom Colors to a Color Legend

- Click the Colors tab.
- Double-click one of the 16 custom color swatches at the bottom of the palette.
- Define a custom color.

  You can assign the custom color to any category in the list.

Color Legend (Scale): Colors

Figure 12-16
Color Legend (Scale): Colors tab

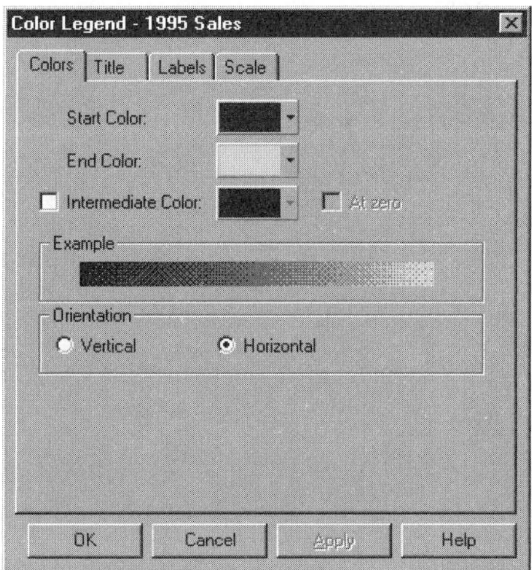

When a scale variable has been assigned to the Color target on the Assign Variables dialog box, colors are assigned to categories according to the value of a summary function. Colors are assigned to symbols by their values along the scale. For example, in a bar chart, the color of each bar can indicate the mean age of persons in a category. In a scatterplot, the color of a symbol can indicate the age for each case, if the scale variable *age* is assigned to Color. In this dialog box, you can customize the color gradient.

Start Color. Assigned to the smallest value in the data range.

End Color. Assigned to the largest value in the data range.

Intermediate Color. If you want a three-color gradient, an intermediate color can be selected. It will be placed halfway between the smallest and largest values in the data range.

Intermediate Color At zero. If a three-color gradient is selected, the intermediate color value can be assigned to the location of the value 0 in the data range. If there is no 0 in the data range, the intermediate color is not used.

Orientation. The gradient can be displayed in the legend either horizontally or vertically.

To Modify Colors in a Scale Legend

- ▶ Click the Colors tab.
- ▶ Select starting and ending colors.

Optionally, you can:

- ■ Change the orientation of the gradient in the legend.
- ■ Select an intermediate color.

Color or Size Legend (Scale): Scale

Figure 12-17
Color or Size Legend (Scale): Scale tab

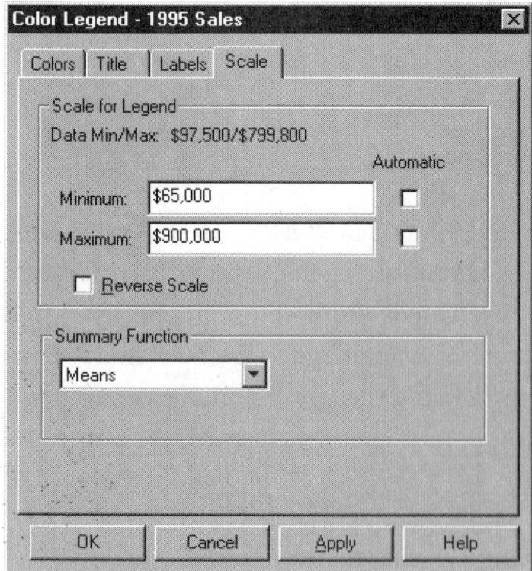

In a color scale legend, you can specify the minimum and maximum values to be associated with the colors at the ends of the scale. For example, suppose a scale represents mean ages with a gradient from red (minimum) to blue (maximum). Assuming that the cases represent adults, you could associate red with age 20 and blue with age 95. The colors in the spectrum between red and blue represent the ages between 20 and 95. Similarly, in a size scale legend, you can specify the minimum and maximum values for symbol sizes at either end of the scale.

By default, the minimum and maximum data points are used at the ends of the scale. You can specify other values for the minimum and maximum. You can also reverse the scale.

Summary Function. The values of the summary function of the scale variable are represented by colors in the strip. The default summary function is Means.

To Modify a Legend Scale

▶ Click the Scale tab.

▶ To specify minimum and maximum values, deselect Automatic and enter values.

Optionally, you can:

- Reverse the scale.
- Change the summary function.

Color or Style Legend (Scale): Labels

Figure 12-18
Color or Style Scale Legend: Labels tab

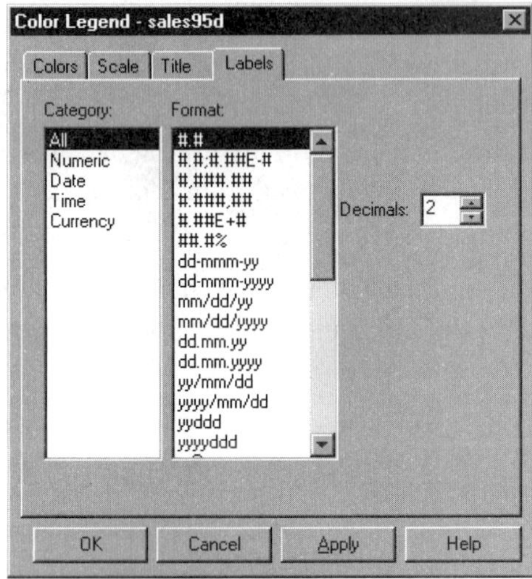

You can change the print format of the scale value labels on legends.

Category. The categories define various groups of formats listed in the next column.

Format. You can use formats to suppress or add percentage signs and dollar signs and to switch between scientific notation and regular numeric display.

Decimals. This sets the number of decimals displayed in the legend labels.

To Change Labels on a Scale Legend

- Click the Labels tab.
- Select the desired options.

Style Legends

Style is interpreted differently by various chart elements. A bar has a fill style, a line can be made up of dashes or dots, and a symbol in a scatterplot or other chart can have a shape.

Style Legend (Categorical): Symbol

Figure 12-19
Style Legend (Categorical): Symbol tab

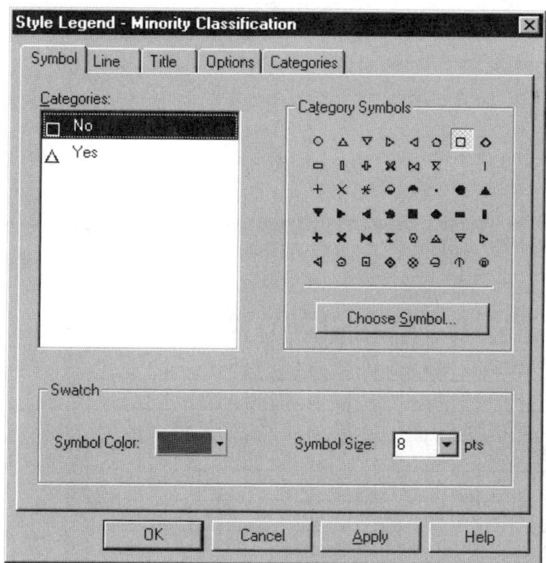

Symbols can be assigned to represent categories in a cloud of points or in a dot chart. The list of currently available symbols is displayed in this dialog box. To use a symbol from a font that is not displayed here, click Choose Symbol.

The color and size of the symbol can be changed if they are not assigned in other legends.

To Change the Symbol for a Category

- ▶ Click the Symbol tab.
- ▶ Select a category in the list.
- ▶ Choose the desired symbol for the selected category.

Optionally, you can:

- Click Choose Symbol and select a different font for symbols.
- Change color and size if they are not controlled by the data.

Symbol

Figure 12-20
Choose Symbol dialog box

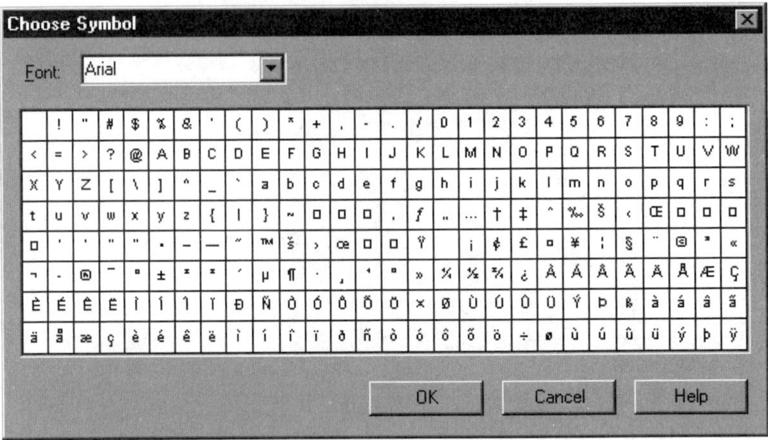

For interactive charts, you can select a symbol from any font stored on your system.

To Select a Legend Symbol from a Font

- ▶ Click the Symbol tab.
- ▶ Click Choose Symbol.

- Select a font for symbols.
- Double-click a symbol.

Style Legend (Categorical): Fill

Figure 12-21
Style Legend (Categorical): Fill tab

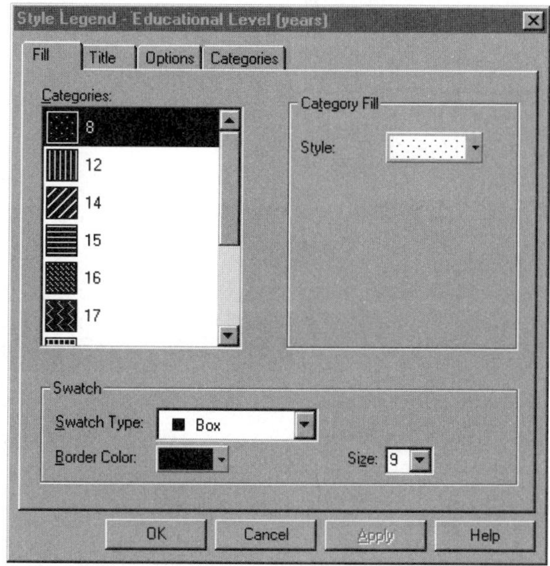

Fill styles can be assigned to distinguish categories in some chart elements. For example, one category might use cross-hatching and another might use vertical lines.

To Change Category Fill Styles

- Click the Fill tab.
- Select a category in the list.
- Select the desired fill style and color for the selected category.

Optionally, you can change the shape, color, and size of the swatch if these characteristics are not controlled by the data.

Style Legend (Categorical): Line

Figure 12-22
Style Legend (Categorical): Line tab

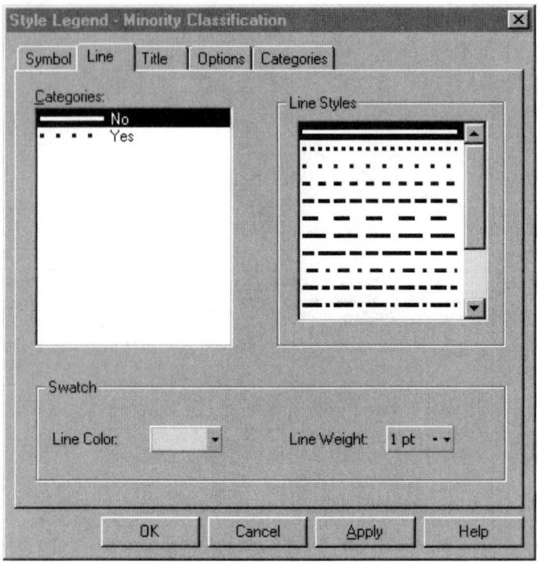

Line styles can be assigned to distinguish categories in some chart elements. For example, one category might use a solid line, and another, a dashed line.

To Change Line Styles for Categories

- Click the Line tab.
- Select a category in the list.
- Select the desired line style for the selected category.

Optionally, you can change the color and weight of the swatch line if these characteristics are not controlled by the data.

Size Legends

Size is interpreted according to the type of element. For symbols, the height is measured; for lines, the weight of the line is measured.

Size Legend (Categorical): Symbol

Figure 12-23
Size Legend (Categorical): Symbol tab

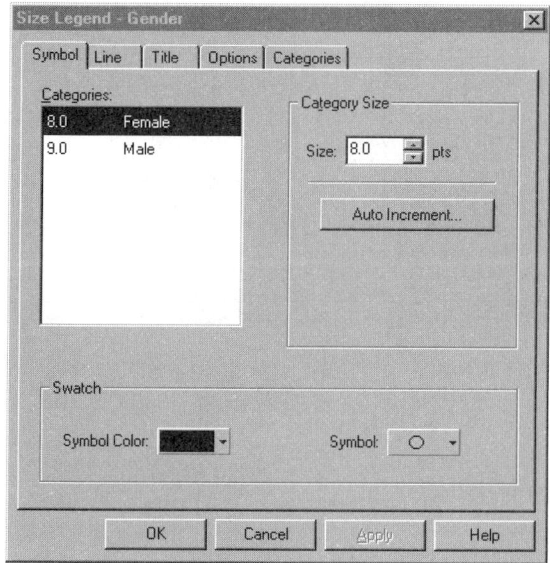

Each category can have an individual size assigned. Sizes can be assigned automatically with a specified starting size and an increment.

To Change the Sizes for Categories

- Click the Symbol tab.
- Select a category in the list.
- Enter the desired size for the selected category.

Optionally, you can:

- Assign automatic increments in size, with a specified starting size and an increment (percentage or fixed amount).
- Change the color and shape of the swatch if these characteristics are not controlled by the data.

Auto Increment

Figure 12-24
Auto Increment dialog box

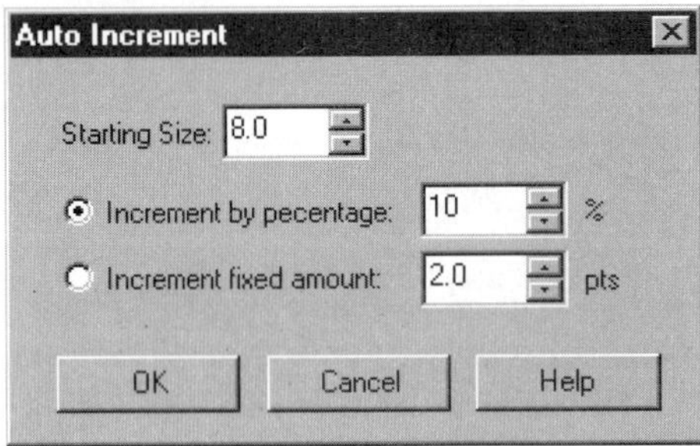

You can specify increments in the size of symbols as a percentage or a fixed amount. The starting size for the smallest symbol can be specified.

To Set Automatic Increments for Symbols

- ▶ Click the Symbol tab and click Auto Increment.
- ▶ Select a starting size.
- ▶ Select increments.

Size Legend (Categorical): Line

Figure 12-25
Size Legend: Line tab

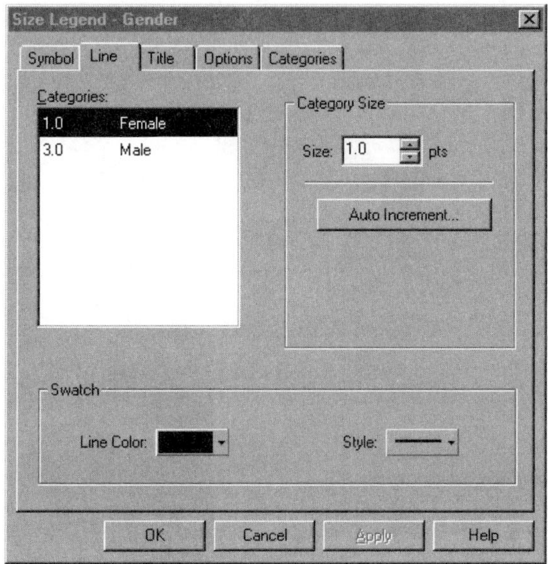

If a categorical variable is assigned to a size legend, lines corresponding to the categories can have different weights.

Weight. Weights can be specified for each category (to one decimal place).

Auto Increment. To resize all lines at once, click Auto Increment.

Swatch. The swatch in the legend can have a color and style if these characteristics are not controlled by the variable assignments.

To Change Line Weights Assigned to Categories

- ▶ Click the Line tab.
- ▶ Select a category.
- ▶ Enter a size.

Optionally, you can assign automatic increments.

Size Legend (Scale): Symbol

Figure 12-26
Size Legend: Symbol tab

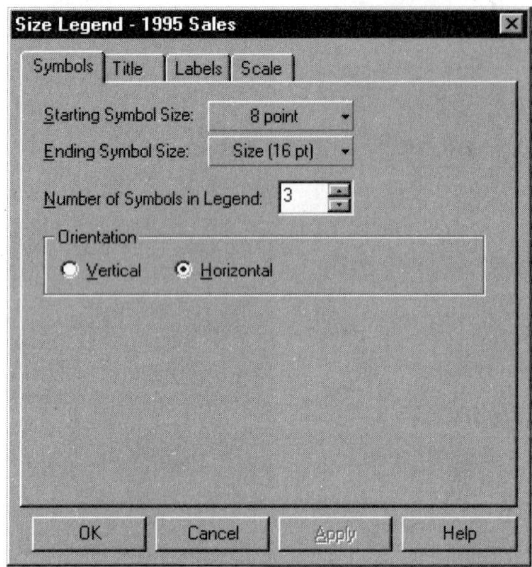

If a scale variable is assigned to a size legend, you can adjust the size range of the symbols and the type of display in the legend.

This feature is commonly used to make a bubble plot (with empty symbols such as circles), where a scale variable is assigned to the size legend. The plot is examined to see if the large and small bubbles form a pattern within any other patterns. Another use for a scale size legend is to create an influence plot, assigning DfBeta values or covariance ratios (from regression calculations) to the size legend.

To Change a Scale Size Legend

- ▶ Click the Symbol tab.
- ▶ Specify starting and ending sizes.
- ▶ Select the type of legend display.

Optionally, you can:

- Select the type of legend display.
- Select the orientation.

Frame Properties

Legends and keys can have frames. For these frames, you can select properties for the border, margins, and fill.

Figure 12-27
Frame properties dialog box

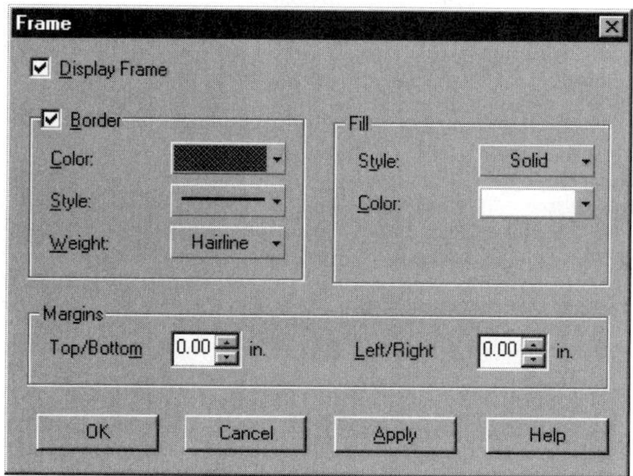

For margins, the units are determined from settings defined on the Interactive tab of Options (Edit menu).

To Change Frame Properties

- ▶ Activate the chart (double-click it).
- ▶ Select a legend or a key.

▶ From the menus choose:

Format
  Frame...

or

▶ Right-click the legend or key and choose Frame.

▶ Select the desired frame options.

Optionally, you can:

- Display a frame for the object.
- Change the border.
- Change the fill style and colors.
- Set margins.

Axis Modification

The axis properties of interactive graphs can be changed in the Scale Axis or Category Axis dialog box. Using the tabs on one of these dialog boxes, you can:

- Change the tick format and range.
- Control the appearance of major ticks, minor ticks, and the axis line.
- Determine the frequency, placement, and formatting of axis labels.
- Specify text and alignment of axis titles.
- Determine placement and appearance of grid lines.
- Determine placement and appearance of reference lines.
- Display a secondary axis for 2-D charts (not available for paneled charts).

To Change Axis Properties

▶ Activate the chart by clicking it.

▶ Double-click an axis or its labels.

or

- From the menus choose:

  Format
  Axis
  [axis name]

  or

- Open the Chart Manager, select an axis, and click Edit.
- Click a tab (Scale, Appearance, Labels, Title, Grid Lines, or Reference Lines).
- Select the desired options.
- Click OK (which closes the dialog box) or Apply (which leaves the dialog box open).

Scale Axis: Title

Figure 12-28
Scale Axis: Title tab

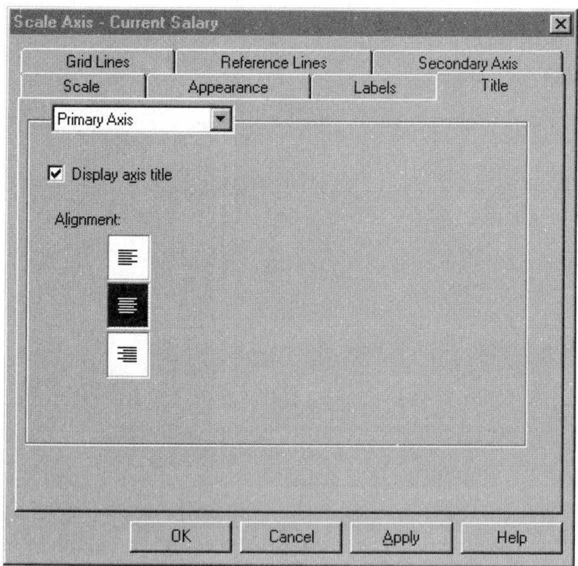

You can change titles for both the primary and secondary axes.

Display axis title. To suppress the axis title, deselect Display axis title.

Alignment. The text can be aligned with either end of the axis or in the middle. You can also drag it to a new position.

To Modify an Axis Title

- ▶ Click the Title tab.
- ▶ Select the desired options.

To edit the axis title, double-click it or use the Text tool.

Scale Axis: Scale

Figure 12-29
Scale Axis: Scale tab

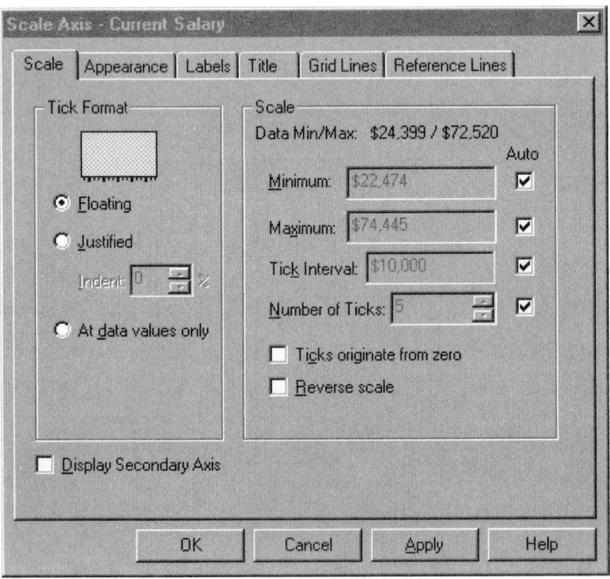

Tick Format. Determines how major ticks are positioned on the axis. The illustration at the top of this group changes as you make a new selection. To place ticks only at the ends of the axis, select Justified and specify Number of ticks = 2.

Scale. Adjustments to the scale can help you emphasize specific characteristics of a chart.

Minimum. With Auto selected, the program chooses the minimum value of the scale. You can deselect Auto and enter a value.

Maximum. With Auto selected, the program chooses the maximum value of the scale. You can deselect Auto and enter a value.

Tick Interval. The distance between ticks. You can deselect Auto and enter a value. This item is linked to the number of ticks.

Number of Ticks. You can choose Auto or enter a number. This item is linked to the tick interval.

Ticks originate from zero. The first tick is at the 0 point.

Reverse scale. The scale is switched between ascending and descending.

Display Secondary Axis. Creates a secondary axis. Click the Secondary Axis tab to specify options. *Note:* Secondary axes are not displayed for 3-D or paneled charts.

To Modify the Scale on a Scale Axis

▶ Click the Scale tab.

▶ Select a tick format.

Optionally, you can:

- Deselect Auto and enter a value for Minimum, Maximum, or Tick Interval.
- Deselect Auto and change the Number of Ticks.
- Set the origin for ticks at zero.
- Reverse the scale.
- Select or deselect Display Secondary Axis.

Scale Axis: Appearance

Figure 12-30
Scale Axis: Appearance tab

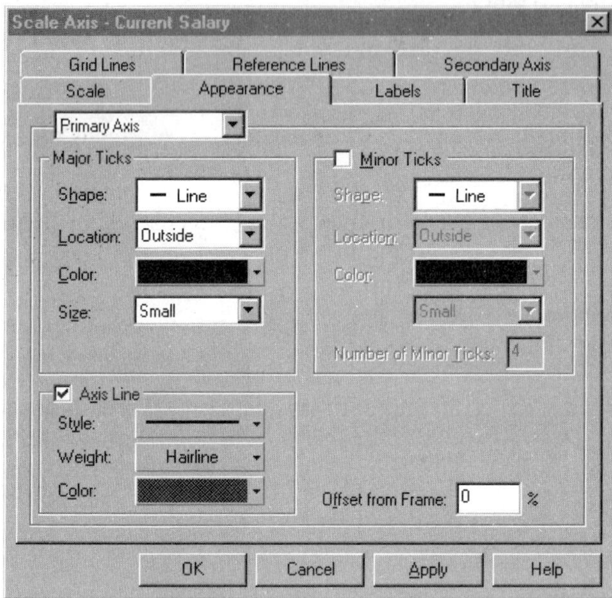

For both the primary and the secondary axes, the appearance of ticks and of the axis line can be changed.

Primary Axis/Secondary Axis. Specifies an axis to modify.

Major Ticks and **Minor Ticks.** You can change the shape, location relative to the axis, color, and size of either kind of ticks. Minor ticks can be turned off, or you can specify the number of minor ticks between adjacent major ticks.

Axis Line. The style, weight, and color of the axis line can be changed, or the line can be turned off.

Jitter. Adds a small amount of random noise to any scale data, whether or not the points are coincident. Categorical data are not jittered.

Offset from Frame. The axis can be moved away from the data region by a percentage of the size of the data region.

To Modify the Appearance of a Scale Axis

- Click the Appearance tab.
- Select the desired options.

Scale Axis: Labels

Figure 12-31
Scale Axis: Labels tab

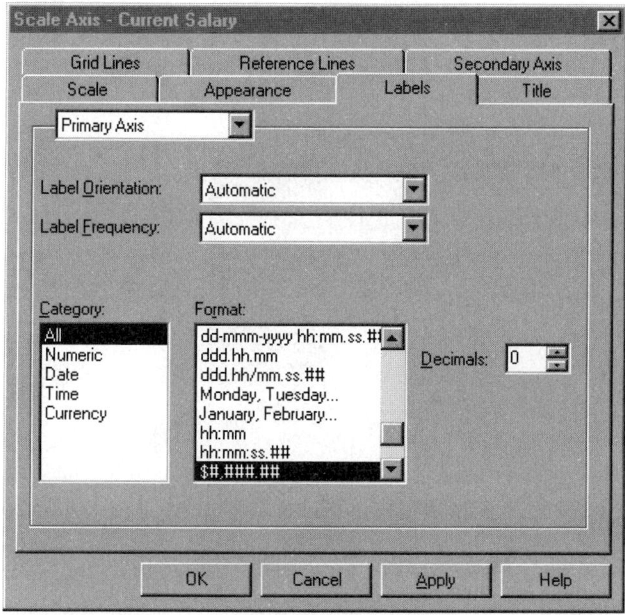

The properties of axis labels include their orientation and frequency. When automatic settings are selected, the program chooses an orientation and frequency that avoid overlap. You can select label properties for both the primary and the secondary axes.

Label Orientation. Controls the orientation of the labels in relation to the axis.

Label Frequency. Determines how many major ticks are labeled.

Format. You can select a label format and the number of decimal places. The Category box lists groups of data formats shown in the Format box. To view all possible formats, select All. To view a smaller group of formats, select one of the categories.

To Modify Scale Axis Labels

- Click the Labels tab.
- Select the desired options.

Scale Axis: Grid Lines

Figure 12-32
Scale Axis: Grid Lines tab

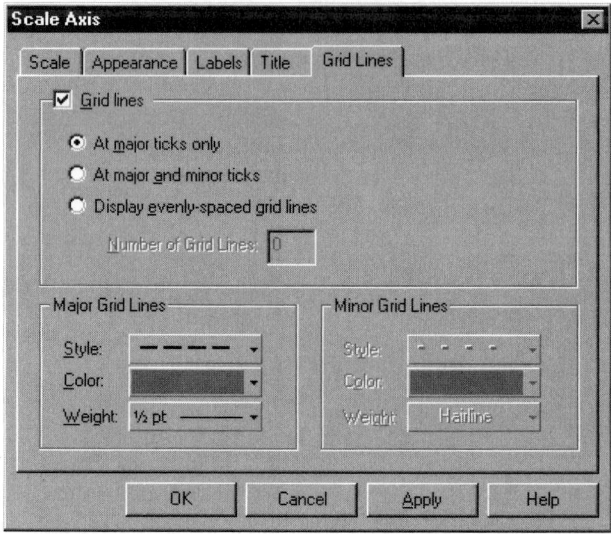

Grid lines, drawn at major and minor ticks along an axis, can be turned on or off. You can also enter a specific number for grid lines spaced evenly along the axis. The style, color, and weight can be specified for both major and minor grid lines.

To Modify Scale Axis Grid Lines

- Click the Grid Lines tab.
- Select the desired options.

Scale Axis: Reference Lines

Figure 12-33
Scale Axis: Reference Lines tab

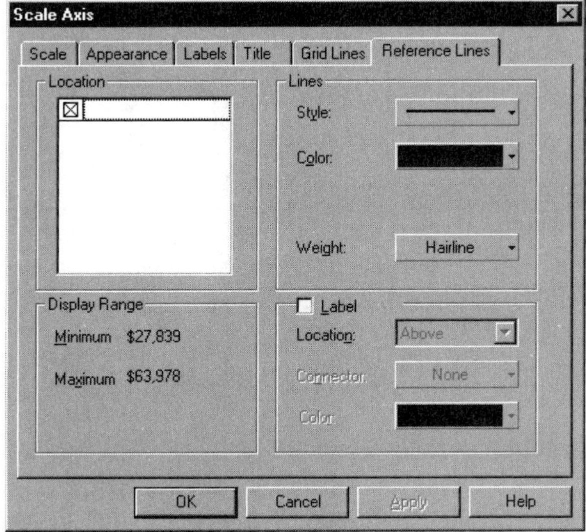

Reference lines are optional lines drawn on a bar chart, line chart, or scatterplot to emphasize a particular value on a scale or category axis.

Reference lines are positioned at values on the scale axis. Labels and connectors can be displayed. The style, color, and weight can be specified for each line.

To Create Scale Axis Reference Lines

- Click the Reference Lines tab.
- Select an item in the Location box and enter a value within the display range.

▶ Select options such as labels, line style, color, and weight.

Scale Axis: Secondary Axis

Figure 12-34
Scale Axis: Secondary Axis tab

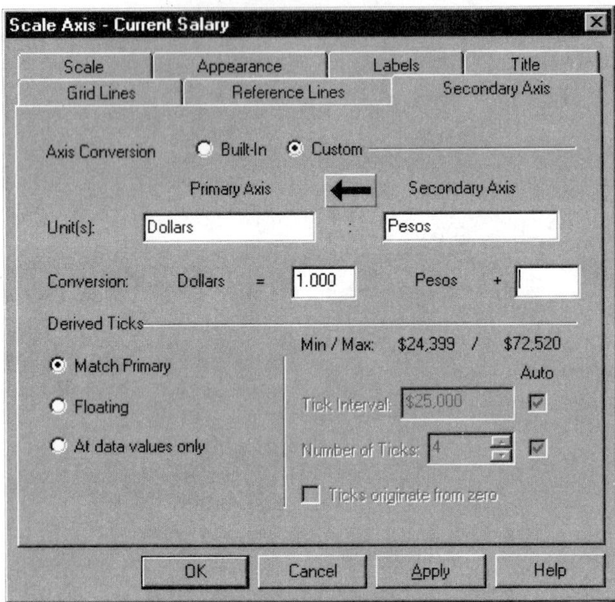

Displaying a secondary axis creates two frames of reference for the same variable. For example, data can be referenced in both dollars and francs. *Note:* Secondary axes are not displayed for 3-D or paneled charts.

Axis Conversion. Options include a standard built-in conversion or a custom conversion.

Units. Provides a unit list for built-in conversions. When custom conversion is selected, you can create new units by typing in the field. The arrow control transforms the direction of the algebraic expression.

Conversion. Illustrates the algebraic expression for a conversion. You can customize a conversion by entering new data values for each unit.

Derived Ticks. Displays options for major ticks on the secondary axis (minor ticks are chosen on the Appearance tab). Ticks can match the primary axis ticks or appear only at data values. Interval and number can be specified for floating ticks.

To Create a Secondary Axis

- Select Display Secondary Axis.
- Click the Secondary Axis tab.
- Select Built-in or Custom.
- Select a unit type. For custom conversions, enter a name for the units on the primary and secondary axes.
- Select options for derived ticks.

  Note: Secondary axes are not displayed for 3-D or paneled charts.

Category Axis: Categories

Figure 12-35
Categorical Axis: Categories tab

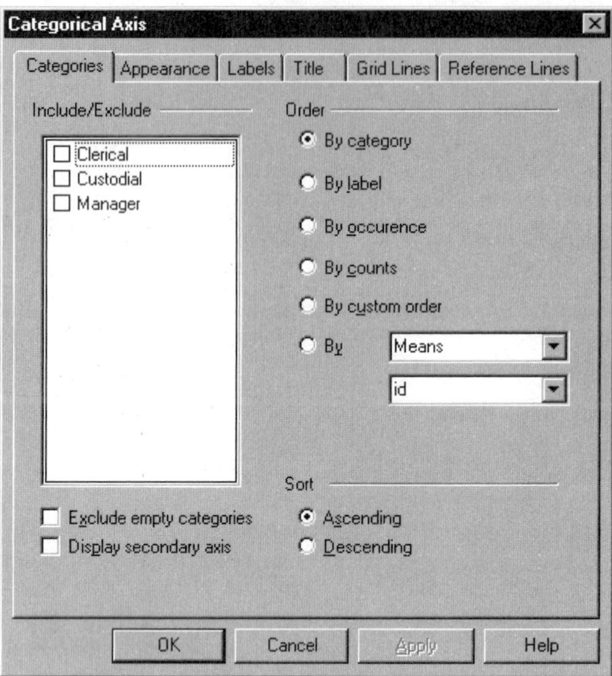

Reordering and excluding categories allows you to create a customized chart. You can change the order, sort, and type of categories.

Panel Variable. Selects which variable to reorder for charts with panel variables.

Include/Exclude. Controls which categories are displayed in the chart.

Exclude empty categories. Hides categories with no data. Empty categories are excluded by default. A category is defined as any value with a defined value label.

Order. Reorders categories manually by drag and drop. Standard order uses properties such as label, occurrence, and counts.

Sort. Displays categories in ascending or descending order.

Display secondary axis. Displays a second axis in the chart that mirrors the primary axis. *Note*: Secondary axes are not displayed for 3-D or paneled charts.

To Modify Categories

- ▶ Click the Categories tab.
- ▶ Select categories to exclude (deselect to include).
- ▶ Select a built-in category order such as Category, Label, Occurrence, or Counts.

or

- ▶ Select Custom Order. You can reorder categories by dragging and dropping them.

or

Order categories by the summary function of another variable:

- ▶ Select a summary function from the drop-down list.
- ▶ Select a variable from the drop-down list.

Optionally, you can:

- Exclude empty categories (default).
- Display a secondary axis (not available for 3-D or paneled charts).
- Sort categories in ascending or descending order.

Changing Category Order

Categories can be reordered or omitted for display in your chart. There are three ways to reorder categories.

Order by Property Type. Each categorical variable can be ordered by properties such as Values, Label, Occurrence, and Counts.

Order by Function of Another Variable. Reorder categories by the summary function of another variable. Certain functions, such as Means, require a scale variable. Properties such as N of Cases or Percentiles require you to define the property value.

Create a Custom Order. Categorical variables can also be reordered manually. Drag and drop the categories to create a new order for the chart display.

Category Axis: Appearance

Figure 12-36
Categorical Axis: Appearance tab

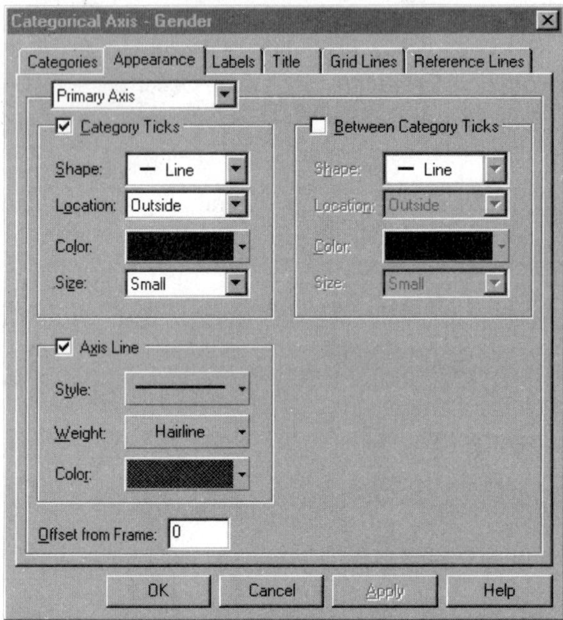

For both the primary and secondary axes, the appearance of ticks and of the axis line can be changed.

Category Ticks and **Between Category Ticks.** Changes the shape, location, color, and size of ticks. Select Between Category Ticks to place ticks halfway between adjacent category ticks.

Axis Line. The style, weight, and appearance of the axis line can be changed.

Offset from Frame. The axis can be moved away from the data region by a percentage of the size of the data region.

To Modify the Appearance of a Category Axis

- Click the Appearance tab.
- Select the desired options.

Category Axis: Labels

Figure 12-37
Categorical Axis: Labels tab

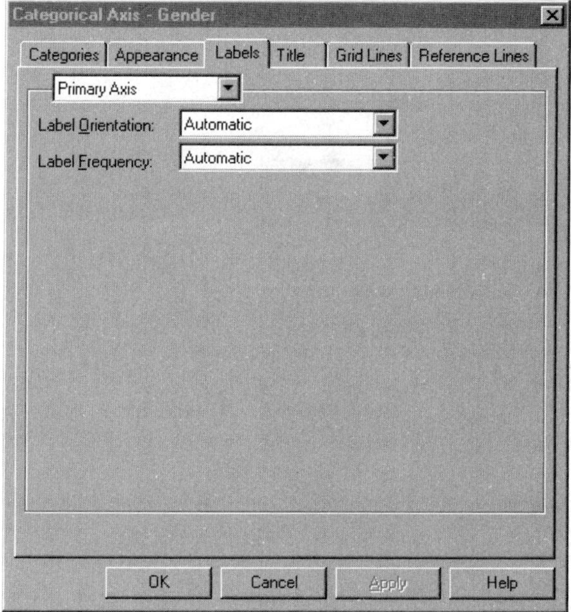

You can select label properties for both the primary and secondary axes.

Label Orientation. Labels are oriented with respect to the axis. Automatic lets the program choose an orientation with minimum overlap for the specified frequency. Other choices include Horizontal, Parallel to axis, Staggered in 2 rows, Staggered in 3 rows, Rotated 90 degrees, and Rotated 270 degrees.

Label Frequency. The number of labels is specified in relation to the category ticks. Choices include Automatic, No labels, All categories, Every other category, and Every third category.

To Modify Category Axis Labels

- Click the Labels tab.
- Select the desired options.

Category Axis: Grid Lines

Figure 12-38
Categorical Axis: Grid Lines tab

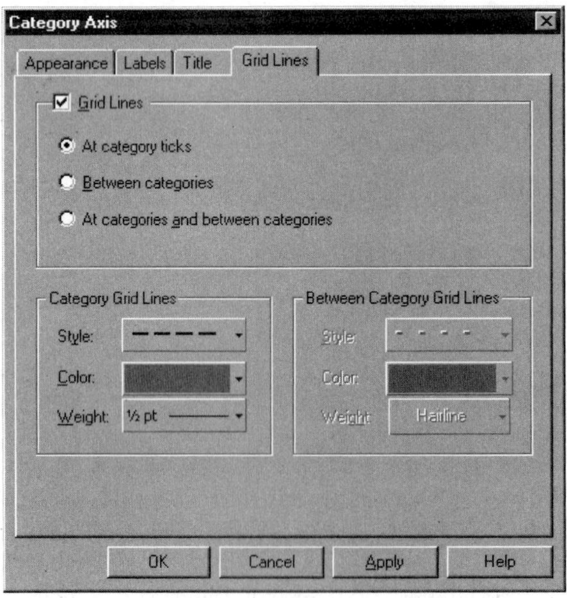

Grid lines, drawn at category ticks and between-category ticks along an axis, can be turned on or off. You can also enter a specific number for grid lines spaced evenly along the axis. The style, color, and weight can be specified for both category and between-category grid lines.

To Modify Category Axis Grid Lines

- Click the Grid Lines tab.
- Select the desired options.

Category Axis: Reference Lines

Reference lines are optional lines drawn on a bar chart, line chart, or scatterplot to emphasize a particular value on a scale or category axis.

For each reference line, determine the position of the line by selecting one or more categories. You can also choose to display labels and connectors. The style, color, and weight can be specified for reference lines.

To Create Category Axis Reference Lines

- Click the Reference Lines tab.
- Select a category to include or exclude reference lines.
- Select options such as labels, line style, color, and weight.

Grid Lines

Grid lines can be displayed or hidden, perpendicular to each axis. You can modify grid lines for each axis by modifying the axis, or you can access a dialog box that shows the features of grid lines for all axes. This dialog box has a tab for each axis.

Figure 12-39
Grid Lines dialog box

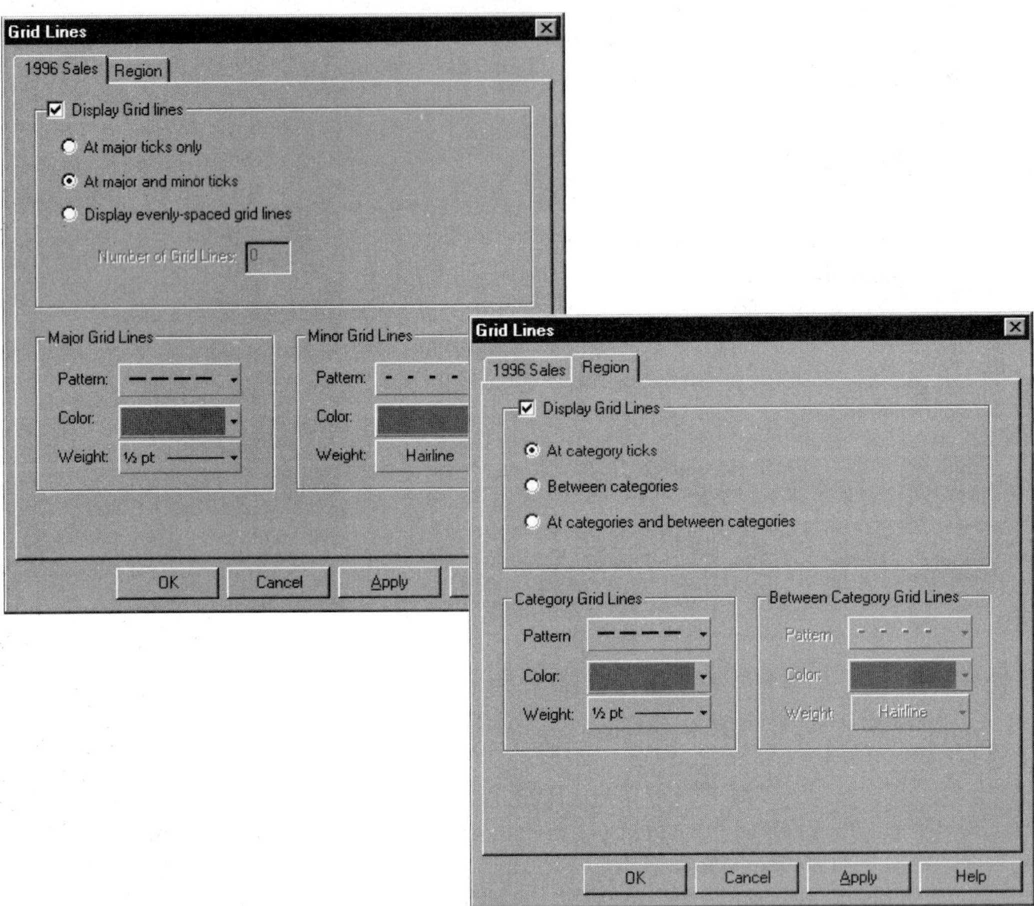

Display Grid lines. If grid lines are turned on for a scale axis, they can be at major ticks (scale axis), at both major and minor ticks, or evenly spaced in the data region. For a category axis, grid lines can be at category ticks, between category ticks, or both.

Major or **Category Grid Lines.** The pattern, color, and weight of major grid lines can be changed.

Minor or **Between Category Grid Lines.** The pattern, color, and weight of minor grid lines can be changed.

To Modify Grid Lines

- ▶ Activate the chart (double-click it).
- ▶ From the menus choose:

  Format
  Grid Lines...

- ▶ Select the features you want for grid lines associated with each axis.

Reference Line Properties

Figure 12-40
Reference Lines dialog box

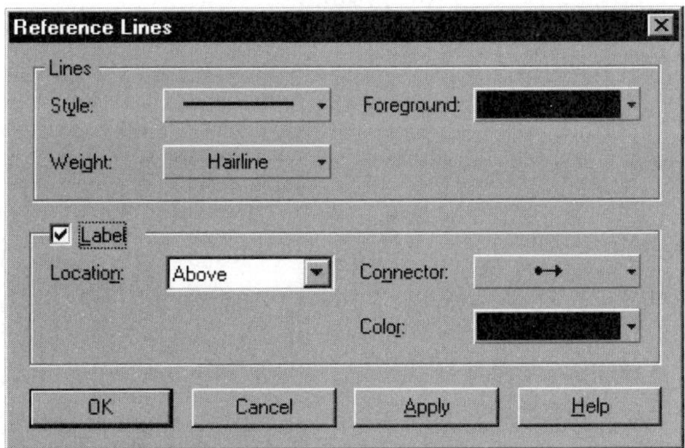

Reference lines are optional lines drawn on a bar chart, line chart, or scatterplot to emphasize a particular value on a scale or category axis. You can change the properties of each reference line in order to customize the appearance of your chart. Line style, weight, color, connectors, and label options can be specified.

To Modify Reference Line Properties

▶ Activate the chart (double-click it).

▶ From the menus choose:

Edit
  Reference Line Properties

or

▶ Right-click over the reference line.

▶ Select Properties from the menu.

Optionally, you can:

- Specify line style, weight, color, and foreground.
- Specify label location, connector, and color.

Changing the Appearance of Charts

You can change the appearance of a chart by editing an individual chart, by changing chart properties, or by applying a ChartLook. ChartLooks are similar to TableLooks. Each ChartLook consists of a collection of chart properties, including specifications for colors, styles, sizes, text objects, filled objects, lines and symbols, and axes. With a ChartLook, you can apply the collection of properties to a chart all at once. You can select from a list of preset ChartLooks, or you can create and save a custom ChartLook.

ChartLook

Figure 12-41
ChartLook dialog box

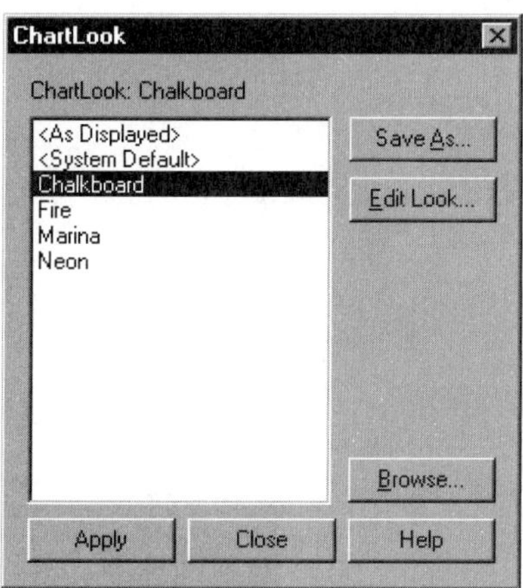

A ChartLook is a set of properties that defines the appearance of an interactive chart. You can select a previously defined ChartLook or create your own. When you create an interactive chart from the Graphs menu, you can choose a ChartLook from the list on the Options tab.

ChartLooks are stored in files with the extension *.clo* (if file extensions are displayed), making it easy to copy the file and give a ChartLook to other members of a group.

Default ChartLook for new interactive charts. You can use any defined ChartLook as the default ChartLook for new interactive charts. The default ChartLook is set on the Interactive tab of the Options dialog box. (You can access this dialog box from the Edit menu of the Viewer.)

To Apply a ChartLook to an Interactive Chart

▶ Activate the chart (double-click it).

▶ From the menus choose:

Format
  ChartLooks...

- Select a ChartLook from the list of files. To select a file from another directory, click Browse.
- Click Apply to apply the ChartLook to the activated chart.

or

- Double-click the ChartLook you want to apply.

All of the properties defined in the ChartLook are applied to the chart, regardless of any previous changes made to the chart.

To Edit or Create a ChartLook

- Activate a chart (double-click it).
- From the menus choose:

Format
  ChartLooks...

- Select a ChartLook that is similar to the look you want to create.
- Click Edit Look.
- Adjust the chart properties for the attributes you want and click OK.
- Click Save As to save it as a new ChartLook.
- Select a directory and enter a filename.

Editing a ChartLook affects only the selected chart. An edited ChartLook is not applied to any other charts that use that ChartLook unless you select those charts and reapply the ChartLook.

To Create a New ChartLook from a Chart

- Activate a chart that has a look you want to save (double-click it).

▶ From the menus choose:

Format
  ChartLook...

▶ Select <As Displayed> from the list.

▶ Click Save As.

▶ Select a directory and enter a filename.

To Delete a ChartLook

The original directory where ChartLooks are stored is *Looks*, a subdirectory of the directory where the program is installed. ChartLooks can be stored in any directory.

▶ Find the directory where the ChartLook is stored.

▶ Delete the ChartLook file (*filename.clo*).

The <System Default> ChartLook cannot be deleted.

Interactive Chart Properties

The Chart Properties dialog box allows you to set various properties of an interactive chart and save a set of those properties as a ChartLook. Using the tabs on this dialog box, you can set:

- The color sequence for a categorical legend or color range for a scale legend
- The fill, symbol, and line sequences for categorical legends
- Sizes of symbols and lines for categorical and scale legends
- Text properties for objects such as titles and labels
- Fill and borders for chart objects such as bars and pie slices
- The look of axes and ticks along the axes
- Properties of lines, symbols, and connectors

To Change Interactive Chart Properties

- Activate the chart (double-click it).
- From the menus choose:

  Format
   Chart Properties...

- Click a tab (Colors, Styles, Sizes, Text, Filled Objects, Lines & Symbols, or Axes).
- Select the options you want.
- Click OK or Apply.

The new properties are applied to the selected chart. To apply new chart properties to a ChartLook instead of just the selected chart, edit the ChartLook (Format menu, ChartLooks).

Chart Properties: Colors

Figure 12-42
Chart Properties: Colors tab

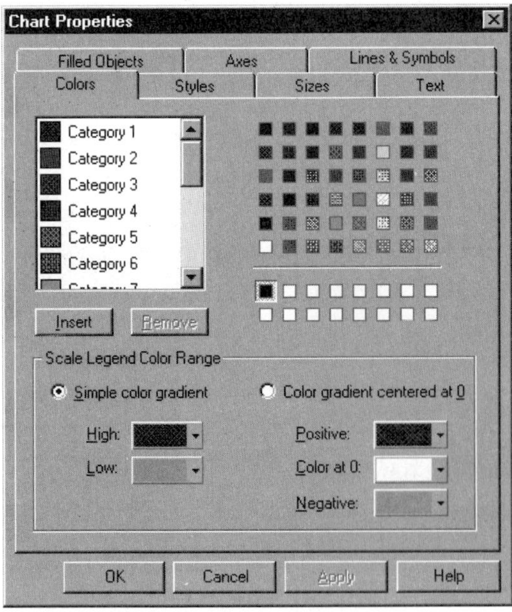

The sequence of colors in a categorical legend or the range of colors in a scale legend can be specified. If a variable has more categories than the list, the sequence is repeated.

Categorical sequence. The list of numbered categories displays the sequence of colors for categories. When the ChartLook is applied to a chart with a color category legend, colors are assigned to the categories in the order listed here. From this dialog box, you can rearrange the list or assign a new color to any category.

Scale Legend Color Range. When the chart properties are applied to a chart with a scale variable assigned to the Legend Color target, the color gradient is used. A simple gradient ranges between two colors for high and low values.

Intermediate Color. If you want a three-color gradient, you can select an intermediate color. This color will be placed halfway between the smallest and largest values in the data range.

Intermediate color at zero. If you select a three-color gradient, the intermediate color value can be assigned to the location of the value 0 in the data range. If there is no 0 in the data range, the intermediate color is not used.

To Change the Color Sequence for Categories

▶ Activate a chart (double-click it).

▶ From the menus choose:

Format
  Chart Properties...

▶ Click the Colors tab.

▶ To change a category color assignment, select a category and then select a color for that category from the palette.

Optionally, you can:

- Insert a new category above the selected category.
- Remove a selected category.

To Change the Scale Legend Color Range

▶ Activate a chart (double-click it).

▶ From the menus choose:

Format
 Chart Properties...

▶ Select Simple color gradient or Color gradient centered at 0.

▶ Select colors for the various positions in the gradient.

To Add Custom Colors to a ChartLook Palette

▶ Activate a chart (double-click it).

▶ From the menus choose:

Format
 Chart Properties...

▶ Double-click one of the 16 custom color swatches at the bottom of the palette.

▶ Define a custom color.

You can assign the custom color to any category in the list.

Chart Properties: Styles

Figure 12-43
Chart Properties: Styles tab

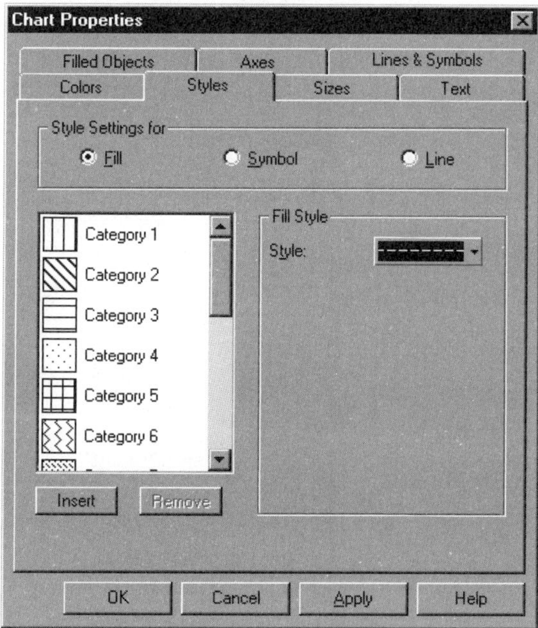

The sequence of styles in a categorical legend can be specified. The list displays the sequence in which styles will be assigned whenever there is a style legend.

Different lists are displayed, depending on whether Fill, Symbol, or Line is selected. A chart uses whichever sequences are applicable. For example, if a chart has both bars and error bars, the Fill sequence is used for the bars and the Line sequence is used for the error bars.

To Change Chart Properties: Styles

- Click Fill, Symbol, or Line.
- Click a category.
- Select a style for that category.

▶ Select each style you want to change and change it.

Optionally, you can:

- Insert a new category below the selected category.
- Remove a selected category.

Chart Properties: Sizes

Figure 12-44
Chart Properties: Sizes tab

Chart Properties
Filled Objects | Axes | Lines & Symbols
Colors | Styles | Sizes | Text

Categorical Legend Symbol Sizes
Starting Size: 8 pts.
Increment by percentage: 0.0 %
Increment fixed amount: 0.1 pts.

Scale Symbol Sizes
Smallest Value: 8 pts. Largest Value: 16 pts.

Categorical Legend Line Weigths
Starting Size: 0.7 pts.
Increment by percentage: 0.0 %
Increment fixed amount: 0.0 pts.

OK | Cancel | Apply | Help

The settings on this tab determine the sequence of symbol sizes or line weight specifications to be applied whenever there is a size legend.

Categorical Legend Symbol Sizes. If a categorical variable is assigned to the Legend Size target, symbols in the chart will be different sizes, according to the starting size (size of the symbol attached to the first category) and the increment for each successive category symbol, by percentage or by a fixed amount.

Scale Symbol Sizes. If a scale variable is assigned to the Legend Size target, this specification controls the size of the smallest and largest symbol used for the scale. The program interpolates for in-between values.

Categorical Legend Line Weights. If a categorical variable is assigned to the Legend Size target, lines that represent the categories will be different weights, according to the starting size and the increment specified.

To Change Chart Properties: Sizes

▶ Click the Sizes tab.

▶ Enter any changes.

Optionally, you can:

- Change the starting size and increment for categorical symbol sequences.
- Change the smallest and largest values for scale symbol sizes.
- Change the starting size and increment for categorical line weight sequences.

Chart Properties: Text

Figure 12-45
Chart Properties: Text tab

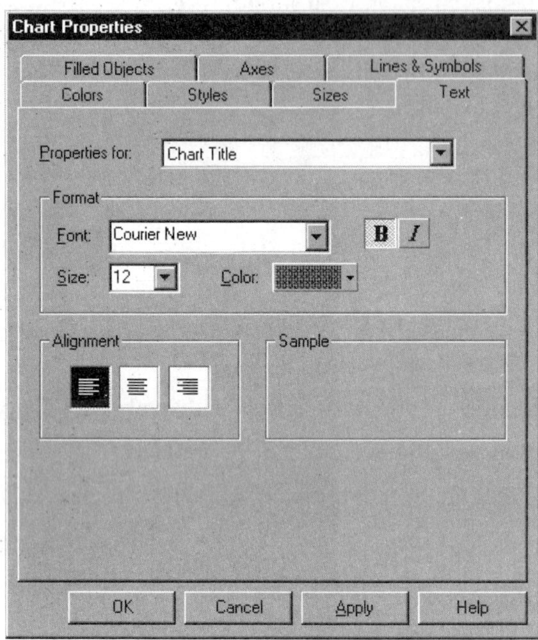

Text properties can be specified for each text object in a chart, including the chart title, chart subtitle, axis title, axis value label, category value label, legend title, legend item, key title, key text, element label text, and caption. When you select a text object from the drop-down list, its characteristics are displayed in the Format and Alignment boxes. The settings apply to the entire text object, even if only part of it is selected.

To Change Chart Properties: Text

- Click the Text tab.
- Select a text object from the drop-down list.
- Select the desired properties for the text object.

Optionally, you can:

- Change the font, point size, and text color.
- Specify bold, italic, and underline.
- Change the text alignment.

Chart Properties: Filled Objects

Figure 12-46
Chart Properties: Filled Objects tab

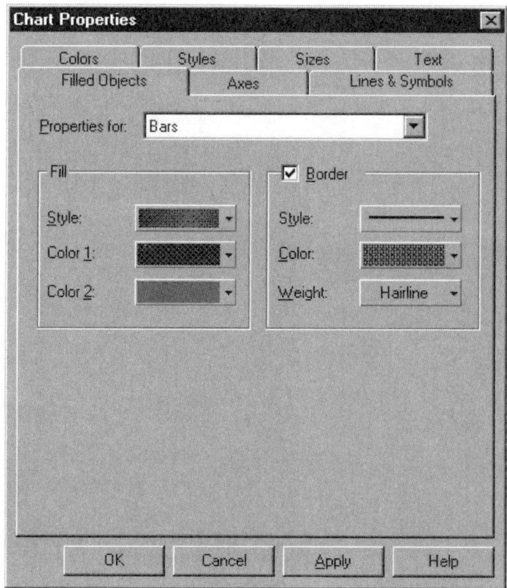

Properties can be specified for objects that have a fill and a border. These include bars, histograms, pie slices, boxes, surfaces, data region, legend frame, ribbons, and key frame. The applicable properties are displayed as you select each object from the drop-down list.

Fill specifications selected in this dialog box are applied to objects that are not affected by variable assignments. For example, if there is a variable assigned to the color legend, objects such as bars take their color according to the legend rather than the color assigned here.

To Change Chart Properties: Filled Objects

- Click the Filled Objects tab.
- Select a type of filled object from the drop-down list.
- Select the desired properties for the type.

Optionally, you can:

- Change the fill color or style.
- Turn the border on or off and change its style, color, and weight.

Chart Properties: Lines and Symbols

Figure 12-47
Chart Properties: Lines & Symbols tab

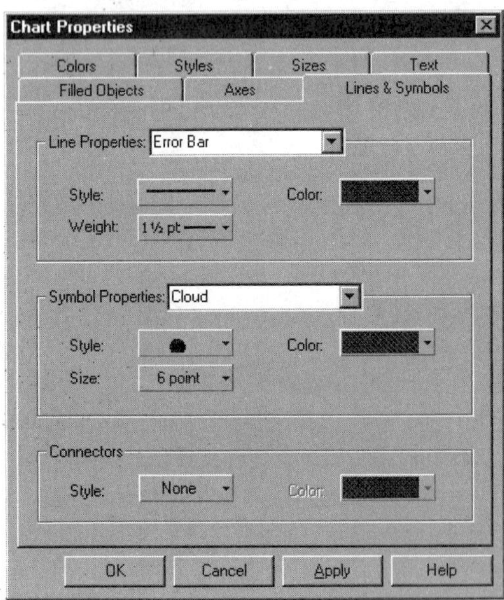

Properties for lines, symbols, and connectors can be specified for each ChartLook. Specifications that are selected in this dialog box are applied to objects that are not affected by variable assignments. For example, if there is a variable assigned to the style legend, symbols or lines take the style according to the legend rather than the style assigned here.

Line Properties. Lines include error bar, box median line, box whisker, smoother, regression, normal curve, drop line, and summary line element. For each type of line, you can choose the style, weight, and color.

Symbol Properties. Symbols include cloud, box outlier, box extreme, error bar (symbol in the middle), and dot summary element. For each type of symbol, you can choose style, size, and color.

Connectors. Connectors are used to associate a case number or a label with a symbol, bar, or other chart object. You can choose the style and color of connectors.

To Change Chart Properties: Lines and Symbols

- Click the Lines & Symbols tab.
- Select a type of line from the drop-down list.
- Select the desired line properties.
- Select a type of symbol from the drop-down list.
- Select the desired symbol properties.
- Specify the style and color of connectors, used with labels.

Optionally, you can specify properties for each type of line, symbol, and connector that appears in a chart.

Chart Properties: Axes

Figure 12-48
Chart Properties: Axes tab

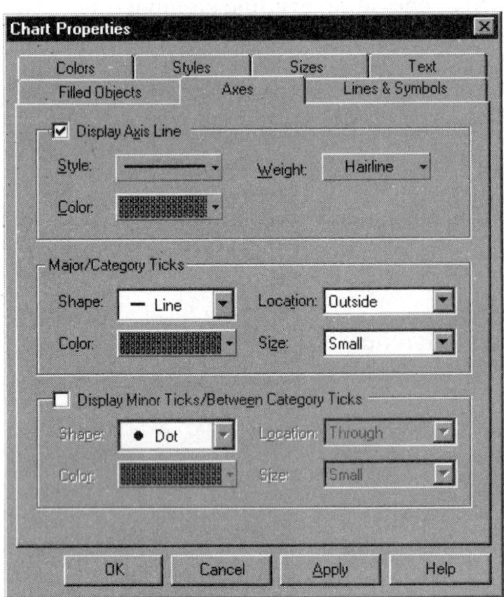

Properties on this tab apply to both scale and category axes.

Display Axis Line. The axis lines can be turned on or off. You can choose style, weight, and color.

Major/Category Ticks. For major ticks on a scale axis or category ticks, you can specify shape, color, location, and size.

Display Minor Ticks/Between Category Ticks. For minor ticks on a scale axes and between category ticks on category axes, you can specify shape, color, location, and size.

To Change Chart Properties: Axes

- Click the Axes tab.
- Specify properties for the axis line, major or category ticks, and minor or between category ticks.

  Optionally, you can change style, color, weight, shape, location, and size, as applicable.

Colors and Styles

Objects in charts can have colors and styles assigned by using the properties dialog boxes for each type of object or by selecting the object and using one of the tools.

Colors in Charts

Each chart has an attached color palette that is saved with the chart. The color palette can be used to color objects in the chart, including the fill of elements, lines, and text. Borders are colored using the Border Color tool. A filled object can have both color and style assigned. Color can be applied to chart elements, axes, text, the data region, or other chart objects.

Tool	Icon	Description
Fill Color		Changes color of filled object, line, or text
Border Color		Changes color of border

The Fill Color and Border Color tools each show a color that will be applied to any objects that are selected when you click the tool (tools show the color that will be applied; they do not show the color of the currently selected item in the chart).

Clicking the arrow attached to the Fill Color tool or the Border Color tool displays a palette of colors. The 48 colors at the top of the color palette are the standard program colors. Tool tips show either the names of colors or RGB values as the cursor passes over them. The 16 spaces at the bottom can be filled with custom colors for the current chart. Custom colors are defined by using the standard Windows color palette. If you define more than 16 custom colors, the seventeenth color replaces the first custom color, the eighteenth replaces the second, and so on.

Clicking a color in the palette changes the color of any selected items and changes the color swatch displayed in the tool. Clicking No Color makes the selected object transparent.

To Change the Fill Color in Selected Objects

- Activate the chart (double-click it).
- Select one or more objects in the chart.
- Click the arrow next to the Fill Color swatch. This opens the color palette.
- Click the color you want applied to the selected objects and to the Fill Color tool.

  or

- If the Fill Color tool already has the color you want, click the color swatch of the Fill Color tool.

  This changes the color in all of the selected objects to the current color of the Fill Color tool unless their color is controlled by the data.

To Change Border Color in Selected Objects

- Activate the chart (double-click it).
- Select one or more objects in the chart.
- Click the arrow next to the border color swatch. This opens the border color palette.
- Click the color you want applied to the border of selected objects and to the Border Color tool.

  or

- If the Border Color tool already has the color you want, click the border color swatch of the Border Color tool.

This changes the border color in all of the selected objects that have borders unless their style is controlled by the data.

Styles in Charts

The Fill Style tool shows the style that will be applied to selected objects when you click the tool (tools do not show the state of the currently selected item in the chart). The Symbol Style tool has a fixed design.

Tool	Icon	Description
Fill Style		Changes style of filled object
Symbol Style		Changes style of symbols

For Fill Styles, you can choose a style from the palette, or you can click More Styles and select patterns, gradients, or textures. These are selected by clicking one of the following effects:

Figure 12-49
Patterns effect

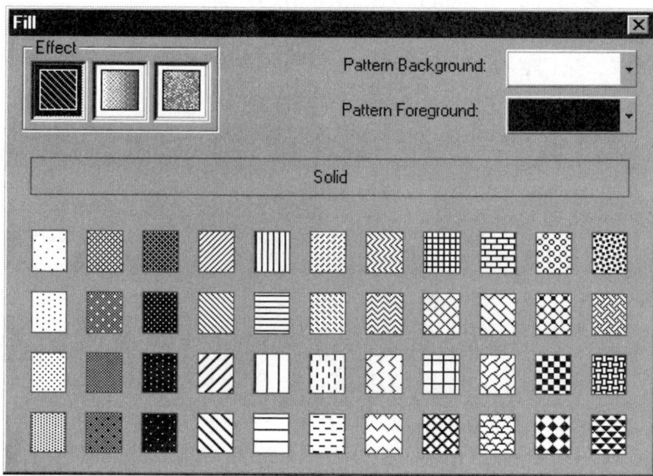

Patterns have foreground and background colors.

Figure 12-50
Gradients effect

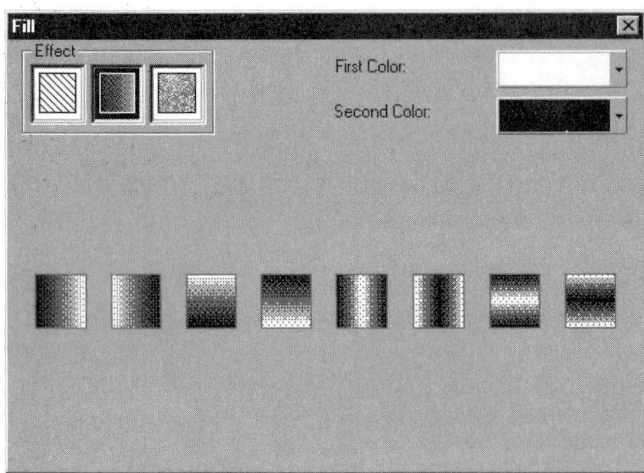

Gradients shade from one color to another. You can specify the colors.

Figure 12-51
Textures effect

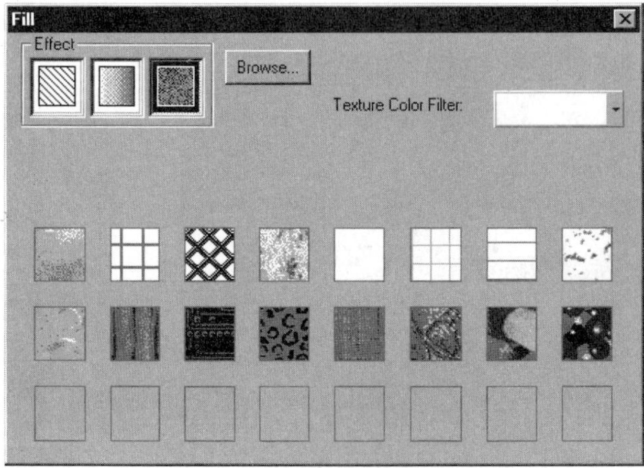

Textures can have a color filter. With a color filter, the texture is drawn in shades of the selected color. To display the texture with its original colors, the selected object should have no color.

Custom textures. By using the Browse button on Textures, you can insert any bitmap file as a texture. The bitmap should be square and sized to a number of pixels equal to a power of 2 (for example, 64 by 64 or 128 by 128). Otherwise, the program will clip the bitmap to the nearest lower power of 2.

To Change Fill Styles

- Activate the chart (double-click it).
- Click the arrow on the Fill Style tool.
- On the Style palette, select a style or click More Styles.

  When the Fill palette is displayed:

- Select the effect (pattern, gradient, or texture).
- Select the desired style.

  Optionally, you can:

  - Change the colors for patterns and gradients.
  - Change the colors for some of the textures.
  - Assign custom textures (click the Textures icon and then click Browse).

To Change Symbol Styles

- Activate the chart (double-click it).
- Select the symbols you want to change.
- Click the Symbol Style tool and select a style.

  This changes the style of all selected symbols unless the symbol style is controlled by variable assignment.

Line and Connector Styles

Line styles. The Line Style tool can be used to change the style of selected lines. Line styles can be changed for axes, borders, chart element lines, error bars, and grid lines. (A 3-D object does not have borders.) Styles include a solid line and various dotted or dashed patterns.

Connector styles. Connectors are drawn between a graph object and a label. The style of connectors can be changed.

Tool	Icon	Description
Line Style		Changes line style
Connector Style		Changes connector style

To Change Line Style

- Activate the chart (double-click it).
- Select one or more lines or objects with borders in the chart.
- Click the Line Style tool and select a line style.

  This changes the style in all of the selected objects unless their style is controlled by the data.

To Change Connector Styles

- Activate the chart (double-click it).
- Select one or more connectors in the chart.
- Click the Connector Style tool and select a style.

  This changes the style in all of the selected connectors.

Sizes of Objects in Charts

Sizes of symbols in scatterplots and boxplots can be changed. The weights of lines in the chart, borders, and other linear objects can be changed. (A 3-D object does not have borders.)

Tool	Icon	Description
Symbol Size		Changes symbol size
Line Weight		Changes line weight

To Change the Size of Symbols

- Activate the chart (double-click it).
- Select one or more symbols in the chart.
- Click the Symbol Size tool.

  This changes the size in all of the selected symbols unless their size is controlled by variable assignment.

To Change Line Weight

- Activate the chart (double-click it).
- Select one or more lines or objects with borders in the chart.
- Click the Line Weight tool in the toolbar.
- Select a line weight.

  This changes the style in all of the selected objects unless their size is controlled by variable assignment.

Modifying Text

You can change fonts and sizes in text by using a dialog box or the Text toolbar.

Text: Font

Figure 12-52
Text: Font tab

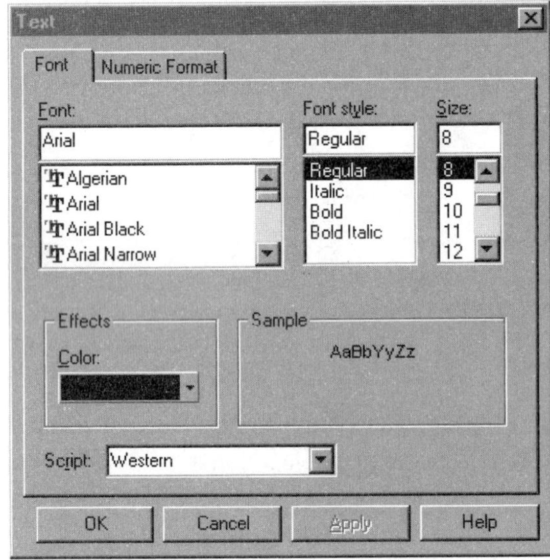

In the Text dialog box, you can change the appearance of a selected text object. You can choose a font, font style, point size, and color.

The Script drop-down list displays the available language scripts for the specified font. Select the one that is appropriate for your computer setup.

Text: Numeric Format

Figure 12-53
Text: Numeric Format tab

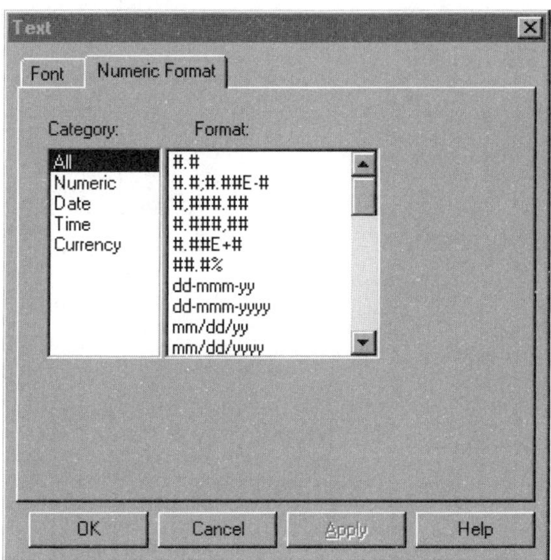

If the text is a number, the numeric format can be specified. The Category list allows you to group numeric formats.

To Format Text in a Chart with a Dialog Box

- Activate the chart (double-click it).
- Select a text object.
- From the menus choose:

  Format
  Text...

- Click a tab: Font or Numeric Format.

Optionally, you can:

- Select a different font, font style, size, color, or script.
- Change the numeric format.

To Format Text in a Chart with the Toolbar

▶ Activate the chart (double-click it).

▶ From the menus choose:

View
 Toolbar
  Text

▶ Select the text you want to format.

Optionally, you can:

- Change the font.
- Change the size.
- Change the font style (bold or italic).

Index